SOFTENG 2019

The Fifth International Conference on Advances and Trends in Software Engineering

March 24 - 28, 2019

Valencia, Spain

SOFTENG 2019 Editors

Luigi Lavazza, Università dell'Insubria - Varese, Italy

Printed from e-media with permission by:

Curran Associates, Inc.
57 Morehouse Lane
Red Hook, NY 12571

Some format issues inherent in the e-media version may also appear in this print version.

Printed by Curran Associates, Inc. (2019)

International Academy, Research, and Industry Association (IARIA)
412 Derby Way
Wilmington, DE 19810

Phone: (408) 893-6407
Fax: (408) 527-6351

petre@iaria.org

Additional copies of this publication are available from:

Curran Associates, Inc.
57 Morehouse Lane
Red Hook, NY 12571 USA
Phone: 845-758-0400
Fax: 845-758-2633
Email: curran@proceedings.com
Web: www.proceedings.com

Table of Contents

SOFTENG 2019

Forward

The Fifth International Conference on Advances and Trends in Software Engineering (SOFTENG 2019), held between March 24, 2019 and March 28, 2019 in Valencia, Spain, continued a series of events focusing on the challenging aspects for software development and deployment, across the whole life-cycle.

Software engineering exhibits challenging dimensions in the light of new applications, devices and services. Mobility, user-centric development, smart-devices, e-services, ambient environments, e-health and wearable/implantable devices pose specific challenges for specifying software requirements and developing reliable and safe software. Specific software interfaces, agile organization and software dependability require particular approaches for software security, maintainability, and sustainability.

We welcomed academic, research and industry contributions. The conference had the following tracks:

- Challenges for dedicated software, platforms, and tools
- Software testing and validation
- Software requirements
- Maintenance and life-cycle management

We take here the opportunity to warmly thank all the members of the SOFTENG 2019 technical program committee, as well as all the reviewers. The creation of such a high quality conference program would not have been possible without their involvement. We also kindly thank all the authors who dedicated much of their time and effort to contribute to SOFTENG 2019. We truly believe that, thanks to all these efforts, the final conference program consisted of top quality contributions.

We also thank the members of the SOFTENG 2019 organizing committee for their help in handling the logistics and for their work that made this professional meeting a success.

We hope that SOFTENG 2019 was a successful international forum for the exchange of ideas and results between academia and industry and to promote further progress in the field of software engineering. We also hope that Valencia, Spain provided a pleasant environment during the conference and everyone saved some time to enjoy the historic charm of the city.

SOFTENG 2019 Chairs

SOFTENG Steering Committee

Mira Kajko-Mattsson, Royal Institute of Technology, Sweden
Miroslaw Staron, University of Gothenburg, Sweden
Yoshihisa Udagawa, Tokyo Polytechnic University, Japan
Ulrike Hammerschall, University of Applied Sciences Munich, Germany

SOFTENG Industry/Research Advisory Committee
Philipp Helle, Airbus Group Innovations - Hamburg, Germany
Sigrid Eldh, Ericsson AB, Sweden
Tomas Schweigert, SQS Software Quality Systems AG, Germany
Michael Perscheid, Innovation Center Network, SAP, Germany
Janne Järvinen, F-Secure Corporation, Finland
Paolo Maresca, VERISIGN, Switzerland
Doo-Hwan Bae, Software Process Improvement Center - KAIST, South Korea

SOFTENG 2019 Special Tracks Chair
Raquel Lacuesta, University of Zaragoza, Spain

SOFTENG 2019
Committee

SOFTENG Steering Committee
Mira Kajko-Mattsson, Royal Institute of Technology, Sweden
Miroslaw Staron, University of Gothenburg, Sweden
Yoshihisa Udagawa, Tokyo Polytechnic University, Japan
Ulrike Hammerschall, University of Applied Sciences Munich, Germany

SOFTENG Industry/Research Advisory Committee
Philipp Helle, Airbus Group Innovations - Hamburg, Germany
Sigrid Eldh, Ericsson AB, Sweden
Tomas Schweigert, SQS Software Quality Systems AG, Germany
Michael Perscheid, Innovation Center Network, SAP, Germany
Janne Järvinen, F-Secure Corporation, Finland
Paolo Maresca, VERISIGN, Switzerland
Doo-Hwan Bae, Software Process Improvement Center - KAIST, South Korea

SOFTENG 2019 Special Tracks Chair
Raquel Lacuesta, University of Zaragoza, Spain

SOFTENG 2019 Technical Program Committee

Ibrahim Akman, Atilim University, Turkey
Issam Al-Azzoni, Al Ain University of Science and Technology, UAE
Rafael Alves Paes Oliveira, The Federal University of Technology - Paraná (UTFPR - Dois Vizinhos-PR), Brazil
Jocelyn Aubert, Luxembourg Institute of Science and Technology (LIST), Luxembourg
Doo-Hwan Bae, School of Computing - KAIST, South Korea
Alessandra Bagnato, SOFTEAM R&D Department, France
Marcello M. Bersani, Politecinco di Milano - DEIB, Italy
Anna Bobkowska, Gdansk University of Technology, Poland
Luigi Buglione, Engineering SpA, Italy
Azahara Camacho, Carbures Defense, Spain
Gerardo Canfora, University of Sannio, Italy
Pablo C. Cañizares, Universidad Complutense de Madrid, Spain
Rafael Capilla, Universidad Rey Juan Carlos, Madrid, Spain
Gemma Catolino, University of Salerno, Italy
Byoungju Choi, Ewha Womans University, South Korea
Morshed U. Chowdhury, Deakin University, Australia
Dario Di Nucci, Vrije Universiteit Brussel, Belgium
Amleto Di Salle, University of L'Aquila, Italy
Cesario Di Sarno, University of Naples "Parthenope", Italy

Sigrid Eldh, Ericsson AB, Sweden
Pål Ellingsen, Høgskulen på Vestlandet, Norway
Faten Fakhfakh, University of Sfax, Tunisia
João Pascoal Faria, University of Porto, Portugal
Fausto Fasano, University of Molise, Italy
Rita Francese, Università di Salerno, Italy
Barbara Gallina, Mälardalen University, Sweden
Matthias Galster, University of Canterbury, Christchurch, New Zealand
Alessia Garofalo, COSIRE Group, Aversa, Italy
Pascal Giessler, SYNDIKAT7 GmbH, Germany
Jiaping Gui, University of Southern California, USA
Ulrike Hammerschall, University of Applied Sciences Munich, Germany
Noriko Hanakawa, Hannan University, Japan
Qiang He, Swinburne University of Technology, Australia
Philipp Helle, Airbus Group Innovations, Hamburg, Germany
Samedi Heng, HEC Liège - Université de Liège, Belgium
Jang-Eui Hong, Chungbuk National University, South Korea
Fu-Hau Hsu, National Central University, Taiwan
Shinji Inoue, Kansai University, Japan
Anca Daniela Ionita, University Politehnica of Bucharest, Romania
Ludovico Iovino, Gran Sasso Science Institute, Italy
Takashi Ishio, Nara Institute of Science and Technology (NAIST), Japan
Janne Järvinen, F-Secure Corporation, Finland
Mira Kajko-Mattsson, Royal Institute of Technology, Sweden
Atsushi Kanai, Hosei University, Japan
Afrina Khatun, University of Dhaka, Bangladesh
Abdelmajid Khelil, Landshut University of Applied Sciences, Germany
Takashi Kitamura, National Institute of Advanced Industrial Science and Technology (AIST), Japan
Johann Krautlager, Airbus Helicopters Deutschland GmbH, Germany
Stephan Krusche, Technische Universität München, Germany
Herbert Kuchen, Westfälische Wilhelms-Universität Münster, Germany
Dieter Landes, University of Applied Sciences Coburg, Germany
Karl Leung, Hong Kong Institute of Vocational Education (Chai Wan), Hong Kong
Bruno Lima, University of Porto / INESC TEC, Portugal
Chu-Ti Lin, National Chiayi University, Taiwan
Panos Linos, Butler University, USA
Tongping Liu, University of Texas at San Antonio, USA
Francesca Lonetti, CNR-ISTI, Pisa, Italy
Damian M. Lyons, Fordham University, USA
Yingjun Lyu, University of Southern California, USA
Ivano Malavolta, Vrije Universiteit Amsterdam, Netherlands
Eda Marchetti, ISTI - CNR, Pisa Italy
Paolo Maresca, Verisign, Switzerland

Alessandro Margara, Politecnico di Milano, Italy
Sanjay Misra, Covenant University, Nigeria
Masahide Nakamura, Kobe (National) University, Japan
Mohammad Reza Nami, TUDelft University of Technology, The Netherlands
Krishna Narasimhan, Itemis AG, Germany
Risto Nevalainen, Finnish Software Measurement Association (FiSMA), Finland
Flavio Oquendo, IRISA - University of South Brittany, France
Fabrizio Pastore, University of Milano – Bicocca, Italy
Antonio Pecchia, Federico II University of Naples, Italy
Andréa Pereira Mendonça, Amazonas Federal Institute (IFAM), Brazil
Michael Perscheid, Innovation Center Network, SAP, Germany
Heidar Pirzadeh, SAP SE, Canada
Pasqualina Potena, RISE SICS Västerås, Sweden
Fumin Qi, Wuhan University, China
Zhengrui Qin, Northwest Missouri State University, USA
Oliviero Riganelli, University of Milano Bicocca, Italy
Michele Risi, University of Salerno, Italy
Alvaro Rubio-Largo, Universidade NOVA de Lisboa, Portugal
Gunter Saake, Otto-von-Guericke-University Magdeburg, Germany
Kazi Muheymin Sakib, University of Dhaka, Bangladesh
Rodrigo Salvador Monteiro, Universidade Federal Fluminense, Brazil
Pasquale Salza, USI Università della Svizzera italiana, Switzerland
Hiroyuki Sato, University of Tokyo, Japan
Daniel Schnetzer Fava, University of Oslo, Norway
Tomas Schweigert, SQS Software Quality Systems AG, Germany
Alberto Sillitti, Innopolis University, Russian Federation
Paulino Silva, ISCAP - IPP, Porto, Portugal
Rocky Slavin, University of Texas at San Antonio, USA
Maria Spichkova, RMIT University, Australia
Praveen Ranjan Srivastava, Indian Institute of Management (IIM), Rohtak, India
Miroslaw Staron, University of Gothenburg, Sweden
Bernard Stepien, University of Ottawa, Canada
Ting Su, Nanyang Technological University, Singapore
Tugkan Tuglular, Izmir Institute of Technology, Turkey
Yoshihisa Udagawa, Tokyo Polytechnic University, Japan
Carmine Vassallo, University of Zurich, Switzerland
Sylvain Vauttier, Ecole des Mines d'Alès, France
Miroslav Velev, Aries Design Automation, USA
Colin Venters, University of Huddersfield, UK
Laszlo Vidacs, Hungarian Academy of Sciences, Hungary
Andreas Vogelsang, Technical University of Berlin, Germany
Song Wang, University of Waterloo, Canada
Yan Wang, The Ohio State University, USA
Hironori Washizaki, Waseda University, Japan

Ralf Wimmer, Albert-Ludwigs-University & Concept Engineering GmbH, Freiburg im Breisgau, Germany
Krzysztof Wnuk, Blekinge Institute of Technology (BTH), Sweden
Xin Xia, Monash University, Australia
Guowei Yang, Texas State University, USA
Cemal Yilmaz, Sabanci University, Turkey
Mansooreh Zahedi, IT University of Copenhagen, Denmark
Yongjie Zheng, University of Missouri - Kansas City, USA
Peter Zimmerer, Siemens AG, Germany
Alejandro Zunino, ISISTAN-UNICEN-CONICET, Argentina

Copyright Information

For your reference, this is the text governing the copyright release for material published by IARIA.

The copyright release is a transfer of publication rights, which allows IARIA and its partners to drive the dissemination of the published material. This allows IARIA to give articles increased visibility via distribution, inclusion in libraries, and arrangements for submission to indexes.

I, the undersigned, declare that the article is original, and that I represent the authors of this article in the copyright release matters. If this work has been done as work-for-hire, I have obtained all necessary clearances to execute a copyright release. I hereby irrevocably transfer exclusive copyright for this material to IARIA. I give IARIA permission or reproduce the work in any media format such as, but not limited to, print, digital, or electronic. I give IARIA permission to distribute the materials without restriction to any institutions or individuals. I give IARIA permission to submit the work for inclusion in article repositories as IARIA sees fit.

I, the undersigned, declare that to the best of my knowledge, the article is does not contain libelous or otherwise unlawful contents or invading the right of privacy or infringing on a proprietary right.

Following the copyright release, any circulated version of the article must bear the copyright notice and any header and footer information that IARIA applies to the published article.

IARIA grants royalty-free permission to the authors to disseminate the work, under the above provisions, for any academic, commercial, or industrial use. IARIA grants royalty-free permission to any individuals or institutions to make the article available electronically, online, or in print.

IARIA acknowledges that rights to any algorithm, process, procedure, apparatus, or articles of manufacture remain with the authors and their employers.

I, the undersigned, understand that IARIA will not be liable, in contract, tort (including, without limitation, negligence), pre-contract or other representations (other than fraudulent misrepresentations) or otherwise in connection with the publication of my work.

Exception to the above is made for work-for-hire performed while employed by the government. In that case, copyright to the material remains with the said government. The rightful owners (authors and government entity) grant unlimited and unrestricted permission to IARIA, IARIA's contractors, and IARIA's partners to further distribute the work.

Survey on Trends in Big Data: Data Management, Integration and Cloud Computing Environment

Washington Henrique Carvalho Almeida[1], Luciano de Aguiar Monteiro[1], Anderson Cavalcanti de Lima[1], Raphael Rodrigues Hazin[1] and Fernando Escobar[2]
[1]Recife Center for Advanced Studies and Systems
Recife, Brazil
[2]PMI-DF
Brasília, Brazil
E-mail: {washington.hc.almeida, lucianoaguiarthe, andclima, raphaelhazin}@gmail.com
Email: fernando.escobar@pmidf.org

Abstract — **The evolution of the processing power of computers has increased the applicability of Big Data, reinforced by the advent of Internet of Things and Industry 4.0. This article conducts a literature review in order to address aspects of Big Data related to Data Management, Integration, Processing, and Cloud Computing Environment. This paper presents a perspective on the major conceptual foundations of this technology in cloud environments. Also, the survey presents trends and concerns related to this subject.**

Keywords- Big Data; Cloud; Architecture; Hadoop.

INTRODUCTION

This paper discusses trends in Big Data, challenges and opportunities. The motivation for this work is to identify trends through a survey in the most recent publications on the subject, as well as challenges and opportunities.

Recently, there has been increased interest in Big Data, mainly driven by a widespread number of research problems strongly related to real-life applications and systems, such as representation, modeling, processing, querying and mining massive, distributed, large-scale repositories. The term 'Big Data' identifies specific kinds of data sets, mainly of unstructured data, which populate the data layer of scientific computing applications [1].

Big Data can be understood as "datasets whose sizes are beyond the ability of typical database software tools to capture, store, manage, and analyze" [2]. Also, the term is generally used to describe the collection, processing, analysis and visualization associated with very large data sets. Although it is difficult to define Big Data, it can be described in terms of the data characteristics of Big Data (the 'what' of Big Data); the architectures and processing for Big Data (the 'how' of Big Data); and the applications of Big Data (the 'why' of Big Data) [3]. Figure 1 illustrates this approach.

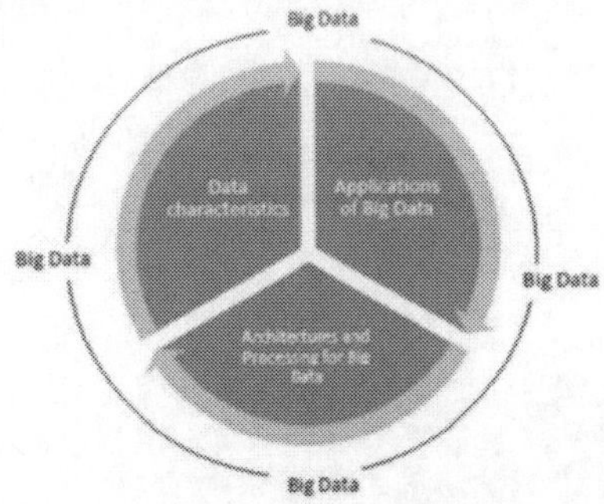

Figure 1. The components of a Big Data Definition [3].

'Big Data' is used mostly as an umbrella term to cover a range of data, technologies, and applications. This contrasts with previous data management approaches, which are typically based on data models that define the structure and operations on a database and specify elements, such as data structures and data operators [3].

The process of collecting and organizing raw data to discover patterns and draw conclusions about the information is called data analytics. It differs from data mining in three aspects – scope, purpose and focus of analysis. Data mining sorts through Big Data to identify patterns that are undiscovered and to identify hidden relationships, whereas data analysis focuses on the conclusion and process of deriving it based only on information already known by the researcher. Organizations can better understand the content of data and help them to identify the data, which will be useful for future scope in business [4].

The approach known as the 3V's (Volume, Velocity, Variety) is widely used, particularly in the practitioner and technical literature. Volume, Velocity and Variety are not by themselves regarded as sufficient to define Big Data and these terms also require definition. 'Volume', for example, is understood differently in different contexts. The 3Vs approach focuses on the characteristics of data and does not consider the wider Big Data environment [3][5].

Big Data is characterized by what is often referred to as a multi-V model. As depicted, Variety represents the data types, Velocity refers to the rate at which the data is produced and processed and Volume defines the amount of data. In addition, expanding the multi-V model, Veracity refers to how much the data can be trusted, given the reliability of its source, whereas Value corresponds to the monetary worth that a company can derive from employing Big Data computing [6]. Below, we summarize the definitions of the 5V's:

Variety - Data types

Velocity - Data production and processing speed

Volume - Data size

Veracity - Data reliability and trust

Value - Worth derived from exploiting Big Data

Figure 2 shows the information applied to travel and transportation companies, but it can be used to exemplify data complexity; it illustrates the multi-V model.

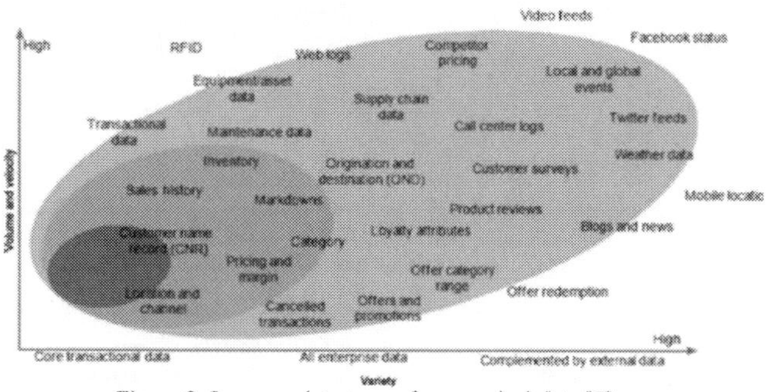

Figure 2. Large variety type of companies' data [7].

With Big Data, it is evident that many of the challenges of cloud analytics concern data management, integration, and processing [6]. The overview of the analytics workflow for Big Data is presented in Figure 3.

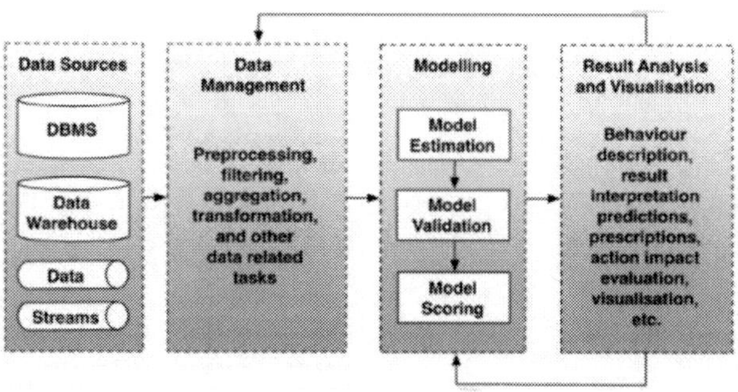

Figure 3. Overview of the analytics workflow for Big Data [6].

As shown in Figure 3, 'Data Sources' represents the Variety of sources and types. 'Data Management' describes the transformation process, because the large Volume can demand it; after that, on 'Modelling', the processed data is used to train a model and to estimate the parameters; finally, on 'Results Analysis and Visualization', the results are analyzed and evaluated, generating Value [6].

Regarding researches related to Big Data, in the first stage, they were primarily focused on the technology requirements that companies needed in order to correctly process the huge amount of data [8]. To extract knowledge from Big Data, various models, programs, software, hardware, and technologies have been designed and proposed. They tried to ensure more accurate and reliable results for Big Data applications. However, in such environment, it may be time-consuming and challenging to choose among numerous technologies [9].

The trends in Big Data are focused on the challenges for the popularization of its use in corporations, as well as in the predictive analysis. The future of the technology is being called Big Data 3.0.

The main contributors of Big Data 3.0 are the Internet of Things (IoT) and applications that generate data in the form of images, audio, and video. The IoT refers to a technology environment in which devices and sensors have unique identifiers with the ability to share data and collaborate over the Internet even without human intervention. With the rapid growth of the IoT, connected devices and sensors will surpass social media and e-commerce websites as the primary sources of Big Data [10].

Also, the fourth revolution, Industry 4.0, is mainly based on the IoT, Cyber-Physical-Systems (CPS), Internet of Services (IoS), Internet of People (IoP), and Internet of Energy (IoE) [11]. Big Data will integrate all technologies.

In this scenario, a big concern is related to human resources, especially data scientists. As the need to manipulate unstructured data, such as text, video, and images increases rapidly, the need for more competent data scientists grows. According to Kearney's survey [10] of 430 senior executives, despite the prediction that firms will need 33% more Big Data specialists over the next 5 years, roughly 66% of firms with advanced analytics capabilities were not able to obtain enough employees to deliver insights into their Big Data [10].

Challenges and opportunities will be addressed in this article and in the following sections: Section II introduces the data management. Section III presents integration and Section IV shows the processes adopted in solutions to Big Data. Also, Section V describes the cloud environment and Section VI lists the standards and solutions; finally, Section VII presents our conclusion.

II. DATA MANAGEMENT

Data management is one of the great challenges of this approach. Trends for the future are related to the volume of data growing exponentially bringing a series of advantages and, at the same time, handicaps.

In this aspect, data complexity is a fundamental problem related to how to formulate or quantitatively describe the essential characteristics of the complexity of Big Data. The study on complexity theory of Big Data will help understand essential characteristics and formation of complex patterns in Big Data, simplify its representation, get better knowledge abstraction, and guide the design of computing models and algorithms on Big Data. To do so, we will need to establish the theory and models of data distribution under multi-modal interrelationships. We will also need to sort out intrinsic connections between data complexity and spatio-temporal computational complexity [12].

Over time, key challenges were related to storage, transportation, and processing of high throughput data. This is different from Big Data challenges to which we have to add ambiguity, uncertainty and variety. Consequently, these requirements imply an additional step where data is cleaned, tagged, classified and formatted [2].

Also, social media and streaming sensors generate massive amounts of data that need to be processed. Few firms would be able to invest in data storage for all Big Data collected from their sources [10]. For example, in recent years, cloud computing has rapidly evolved from a vague concept at the beginning to a mature technology. Many big companies, including Google, Microsoft, Amazon, Facebook, Alibaba, Baidu, Tencent, and other Information Technology (IT) giants, are working on cloud computing technologies and cloud-based computing services. Big Data and Cloud Computing are seen as two sides of the same coin: Big Data is a killer application of Cloud Computing, whereas Cloud Computing provides the IT infrastructure to Big Data. The tightly coupled Big Data and Cloud Computing nexus are expected to change the ecosystem of the Internet, and even affect the pattern of the entire information industry [13].

Focusing on proper security aspects of Big Data, query processing and, in particular, on confidentiality of data during such a critical task are the major concern. Here, the main problem consists in defining models which protect cloud private data via the widely-accepted solutions: (i) encryption approaches and (ii) trust computing. Both aim at trading-off strong confidentiality and high efficiency of query processing over Big Data [14].

In this paper, we will cover the following Big Data main elements:

A. Data Quality

Data quality refers to the fitness of data with respect to a specific purpose of usage. Data quality is critical to confidence in decision making. As data are more unstructured and collected from a wider array of sources, the quality of data tends to decline. For firms adopting data analytics for their supply chain, data quality is paramount. If the data are not of high quality, managers will not use the data, let alone want to share the data with their partners. Streaming analytics use data generated by interconnected sensors and communication devices [10].

B. Data Security

Weak security creates user resistance to the adoption of Big Data. It also leads to financial loss and damage to a firm's reputation. Without installing proper security mechanisms, confidential information could be transmitted inadvertently to unintended parties. Also, cloud infrastructure has become an appealing target for cyber attackers [15]. Blockchain, an underlying technology behind the Bitcoin cryptocurrency, is a promising future technology for Big Data security management [10].

C. Data Storage

Service Oriented Architecture (SOA) and virtualization altered the whole paradigm of Information and Communication Technology (ICT) resources management from traditional computing to Cloud Computing. Storage, computing power, infrastructures, platforms, and software are provided as a service in the form of Pay-as-you-go on demand usage. Infrastructure as a Service (IaaS), Platform as a Service (PaaS), and Software as a Service (SaaS) are the three main service models of Cloud Computing. IoT Cloud Computing architecture plays a tremendous role in IoT data. IoT data and applications are stored in the cloud to make it accessible from anywhere with any web browser or client software [11][16].

These Bid Data's main elements are fundamental to the organized implementation of Big Data solutions and have been adopted; hence they were considered in this survey.

Information, privacy and security are the most concerning issues for Cloud Computing due to its open environment with very limited user-side control posing great challenges. Especially on cloud-based platforms, where there are two important aspects of Big Data security. One is how to protect data. The other is how to use Big Data analytic techniques to enhance security of the whole system. Current work on Big Data focuses on information processing, such as data mining and analysis [17].

Big Data are valuable because they are a treasured source of knowledge that turns to be useful for decision making and prediction purposes. Analytics are exploited to this end, but they expose the underlying knowledge discovery process to challenging research issues, due to the fact that analytics process huge volumes of (big) data; hence privacy of target data sets is not preserved [18].

Another relevant data management context for Big Data research is represented by the issue of effective and efficiently supporting analytics over Big Data, a collection of models, algorithms and techniques oriented to extract useful knowledge from cloud-based Big Data repositories for decision making and prediction purposes, e.g., by means of multidimensional data analysis paradigms [14].

III. INTEGRATION

Data integration is the cornerstone of Big Data, due to distributed and heterogeneous data sources and data types to provide data discover and predictive analysis. The big difference is that the software must go to the data rather than the traditional approach to data warehouse.

Concurrent with the success of the regional integration of computers and advances in fixed computers everywhere, smartphones have gained a significant contract rate capacity and resources, particularly movement and awareness related to a sensor's unique location-based services and multimedia data. The data generated through heterogeneous resources are unstructured and cannot be stored in traditional databases [19].

Alternatives appear, like the Data Vault, a persistent staging area, which advocates for less structured repositories. This trend reaches the extreme in the form of Data Lake as a repository where raw data is stored in waiting for an analytical resolution [20].

For analysis of Big Data, database integration and cleaning are much harder than the traditional mining approaches. Manipulation of large datasets possesses problems of computational speed and error recovery. In this survey, the issue of speed has been addressed by distributing the computation over several nodes each of which works in parallel on a subset of the complete dataset and maintains coherence for producing appropriate result [21].

Through effective integration and accurate analysis on multisource heterogeneous Big Data, better predictions of future trends of events can be achieved. It is possible for Big Data analysis to even promote sustainable developments of society and economy and further give birth to new industries related to data services [13].

To overcome the delays in storing Big Data on distributed cloud storage, public storage is used as a solution. However, using public storage will make the data vulnerable to transmission and storage. Therefore, there is a need for a security algorithms to provide tradeoffs during time delay, security strength, and storage risks with encryption techniques based on flexible key [22]. The data which is being stored onto the cloud is most likely to be infiltrated with. This data can be best protected using encryption [23].

IV. PROCESSING / ANALYTICS

Big Data analytics are used in many areas, such as machine learning, computer vision, Web statistics, medical applications, Deoxyribonucleic Acid (DNA) analysis, data classification and clustering [7].

Related to this, *data validation is a major concern and is applied to define* data validity, data completeness and data consistency, as well as to validate if data are trustworthy, accurate, and meaningful. It has been reported [24] that more than half of the time spent on Big Data projects goes towards data cleansing and preparation. This section discusses the validation process for Big Data. Data collection, data cleaning, data transformation, data loading and results report are the necessary data validation processes [24].

Further, in visual analytic applications for Big Data, it is often the case that one or more models are used to calculate or to transform data prior to visualizing the results [25]. Algorithmic intelligence has gained popularity along with the rise of Big Data and current advancements in technology and organizations are increasingly able to rely on such intelligence to analyze Big Data [26].

However, the adoption of Big Data technologies is complex. The deployment and setup of an implementation of Big Data solution are time-consuming, expensive, and resource-intensive. Companies need tools and methodologies to accelerate the deployment of Big Data analytics. For this reason, Cloud Computing is becoming a mainstream solution to provide large clusters on a pay-per-use basis [27].

V. CLOUD ENVIRONMENT

As stated, Big Data is intrinsically linked to Cloud Computing; hence, its expansion will require the adoption of cloud environments due to the various aspects presented in this work. Several privacy and security discussions are covered when talking about the cloud environment, but the big-time trend is the adoption of this kind of solution. Figure 4 shows the exponential growth in digital data during the current decade.

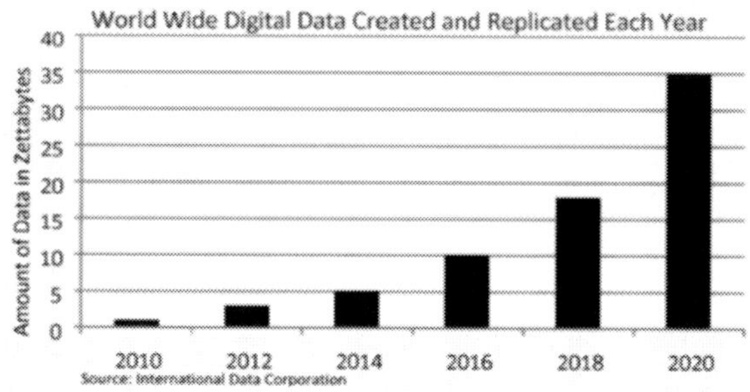

Figure 4. Exponential growth in digital data during current decade [7].

Cloud Computing provides an interesting model for analytics, where solutions can be hosted on the Cloud and consumed by customers in a pay-as-you-go fashion. For this delivery model to become reality; however, several technical issues must be addressed, such as data management, tuning of models, privacy, data quality and data currency [6].

Reinforcing the approach, cloud appears as hot topic to Big Data, which explains the importance of their 'relationship'. Table I presents a research [28] of more important topics in Big Data, where (A) represents the abstracts found, (K) for keywords, and (T) for title of the papers analyzed.

TABLE I. NUMBER OF PAPERS DEDICATED TO BIG DATA AND TO ONE OF HOT TOPICS [28]

Numbers of Papers Dimensions	with chains in A, K or T	with chains in K or T	with chains in T
Cloud	154	66	25
Analytics	136	49	36
Social	99	33	11
Mobility	78	15	5
Internet of things	37	15	4

In order to setup their Big Data on cloud environment, organizations would need to setup a master cloud to achieve the performance against the Big Data requests. All incoming client requests are submitted to the master cloud, which analyses the Big Data request size and detects the availability of suitable slave clouds (private/public), according to the priority set on the cloud table. Master cloud diverts incoming request intelligently to those slave clouds, which contain big size clusters so that it takes less time to fulfill their computational needs [29].

Related to security issues, Architectural Security includes various parameters like distributed nodes, shared data, data ownership, inter-node communication, etc. The security measures elaborated in are related to the architecture of Big Data. Mostly, the security and privacy concern of Big Data arises due to its distributed file system and large volumetric data. The capabilities of the architecture need to use the data generated for mapping [23]. Moreover, we can classify the security issues as a hierarchy of security weaknesses with challenges on the present Cloud Computing models, specifically deployment and service models [30].

There are many solutions for Big Data related to Cloud Computing. Depending on the level of volume, velocity, and variety, it is important to choose appropriate Big Data tools. Thanks to the cloud, the tendency is towards Big Data as a Service and Analytics as a Service. Thus, customer and provider's staff are much more involved in the loop [28].

VI. BIG DATA STANDARDS AND SOLUTIONS

Several solutions and standards were found in this research. In this section, we present fundamental elements that have become trends.

The pioneer in managing Big Data was Google. In order to be able to store up to petabytes, they moved away from Relational Database (RDBMSs) and created a distributed file system that could scale to thousands of machines [5][20].

Recently, Big Data platforms are supported by several processing analytical tools as well as dynamic visualization [31].

Highly Archived Distributed Object Oriented Programming (HADOOP) [24][31][32][33] was created by Cutting and Cafarella, in 2005, for supporting a distributed search Engine Project. It is an Open source Java Framework technology that helps to store, access, and gain large resources from Big Data in a distributed fashion at lower cost, high degree of fault tolerance and high scalability [34].

A key component of HADOOP is the Hadoop Distributed File System (HDFS), which is used to store all input and output data for applications [4][31].

HADOOP Architecture [15][35][36] should be implemented within the slave clouds registered in the existing stack. HADOOP is a map/reduce framework that works on HDFS, which provides high throughput access to application data and has the capability to store large data across thousands of servers. In the context of the HADOOP architecture, a job is split into smaller identical tasks that can be executed closer to the data node in two phases. In map phase each task is distributed and parallelized. After map phase, all intermediate results are combined into one result, which is called reduced phase [29].

MapReduce [2][5][31][37] is a framework for writing applications that can handle large volumes of structured and unstructured data in parallel on a cluster of thousands machines, reliable and fault tolerant. The distribution of data across multiple servers allows parallelized processing of multiple tasks, each bearing on separate pieces of files. The Map function performs a specific operation on each item. The Reduce transaction combines the elements according to a particular algorithm, and provides the result [38].

Data Nodes are responsible for storing the blocks of files as determined by the Name Node. Data file to be stored is first split into one or more blocks internally. Data Nodes serve the read/write requests from file system's client data. These are also responsible for creating, deleting and replicating blocks of file after being instructed by the Name Node [39].

Hive [31][32][40] is a data warehousing solution built on top of HADOOP. It provides SQL-like query language named HiveQL. The Apache Mahout free machine learning library's goal is to build scalable machine learning tools and data mining framework for use on analyzing Big Data on a distributed manner [41].

Apache Spark [9][31][42] is an open source distributed processing framework that was created at the UC Berkeley AMPLab. Spark is like HADOOP, but it is based on in-memory system to improve performance. It is a recognized analytics platform that ensures fast, easy-to-use and flexible computing. Spark handles complex analysis on large data sets. Indeed, Spark runs programs up to 100x faster than Hive and Apache Hadoop via MapReduce in memory system. Spark is based on the Apache Hive codebase. In order to improve system performance, Spark swaps out the physical execution engine of Hive. In addition, Spark offers APIs to support a fast application development in various languages, including Java, Python, and Scala. Spark [40][43][44] is able to work with all files storage systems that are supported by HADOOP [9].

Supported Database. All of these selected tools support different types of databases, including both relation databases and non-relational databases. The most popular supported relational databases include MySQL, DB2, Oracle, PostgreSQL, Vertica and Teradata. The commonly used non-relational databases include Hive and Hbase [9]. In addition, Datameer also supports Windows Azure Blob Storage and Amazon Redshift [24]. In order to remove the scalability limit of index searching and have a fast searching speed simultaneously, HBase, the Hadoop NoSQL database, is often exploited to store chunk index table in current Hadoop-based deduplication system [45].

Supported File Format. All of the listed tools have a wide range support for different types of data files formats. The commonly supported file formats include: CSV/TSV, TXT Files, Fixed Width Text, HTML, and Server Log File [24].

VII. CONCLUSION

This survey presents elements of Big Data in the Cloud Computing environment. In the search carried out, references were searched for the construction of a framework for better understanding Big Data trends.

The models proposed increasingly based on this concept were found in the most recent research on the subject. The main issues run into problems faced in the Cloud Computing environment, such as security and privacy.

The standards adopted have been found in many studies with the implementation of increasingly flexible solutions. Regardless of the technology used, this work presents the main features of Big Data and some barriers to the use of the resources.

A more detailed analysis of privacy problems can be made due to the exposure of the Bid Data in cloud, since only the use of the researched model does not guarantee the implementation of this architecture reliably. Some issues that we can also highlight is the investigation of new patterns that may arise, since technological changes have been increasingly fast and can be investigated and analyzed for the discovery of new techniques.

Trends identified in this paper include the growing contribution of the Internet of Things adoption, promoting exponential increasing in the volume of data analyzed as a data source for Big Data solutions. This trend also highlights the growth in the demand for qualified professionals for the data scientist profile. In the context of data management, we verified in the study as a trend the need for the definition of a data distribution model that allows a multi-modal interrelationship, with the adoption of less structured repositories.

In the processing and analysis of Big Data, it was also shown as a tendency the adoption algorithmic intelligence to create models to calculate and transform data in order to facilitate the visualization of the analysis results. In this sense, the use of distributed file systems to facilitate access and manipulation of the large volume of data analyzed by Big Data solutions was also a trend. Finally, a trend strongly identified in the study was the use of Cloud Computing environments for the deployment of Big Data solutions, allowing the use of large solutions in the form of clusters that promote significant gains in the treatment of the data maintained by the solution.

Many problems will undoubtedly arise, as for monitoring, deployment, elastic scheduling and runtime adaptation when the architecture of solutions based on Big Data will replace the data warehouse solutions and, in this context, their adoption can become complementary, since in this research a complete study on the post-migration reality was not closed.

References

[1] A. Cuzzocrea, D. Saccà, and J. D. Ullman, "Big Data: A Research Agenda," Proc. 17th Int. Database Eng. Appl. Symp. - IDEAS '13, pp. 198–203, 2013.

[2] C. Kacfah Emani, N. Cullot, and C. Nicolle, "Understandable Big Data: A survey," Comput. Sci. Rev., vol. 17, pp. 70–81, 2015.

[3] E. Dumbill, "Defining Big Data," Forbes, 2014.

[4] S. Garion, "Big Data Analytics Hadoop and Spark," pp. 1–55, 2016.

[5] U. Kazemi, "A Survey of Big Data : Challenges and Specifications," no. May, 2018.

[6] M. D. Assunção, R. N. Calheiros, S. Bianchi, M. A. S. Netto, and R. Buyya, "Big Data computing and clouds: Trends and future directions," J. Parallel Distrib. Comput., vol. 79–80, pp. 3–15, 2015.

[7] A. Ben Ayed, M. Ben Halima, and A. M. Alimi, "Big data analytics for logistics and transportation," 2015 4th IEEE Int. Conf. Adv. Logist. Transp. IEEE ICALT 2015, pp. 311–316, 2015.

[8] J. F. Aldana, "Big Data. New approaches of modelling and management," Comput. Stand. Interfaces, vol. 54, pp. 61–63, 2017.

[9] A. Oussous, F. Z. Benjelloun, A. Ait Lahcen, and S. Belfkih, "Big Data technologies: A survey," J. King Saud Univ. - Comput. Inf. Sci., 2017.

[10] I. Lee, "Big data: Dimensions, evolution, impacts, and challenges," Bus. Horiz., vol. 60, no. 3, pp. 293–303, 2017.

[11] R. M. Ward, R. Schmieder, G. Highnam, and D. Mittelman, "Big data challenges and opportunities in high-throughput sequencing," no. March, pp. 1–6, 2013.

[12] X. Jin, B. W. Wah, X. Cheng, and Y. Wang, "Significance and Challenges of Big Data Research," Big Data Res., vol. 2, no. 2, pp. 59–64, 2015.

[13] S. Yu, "The Role of Big Data Analysis in New Product Development," 2016.

[14] A. Cuzzocrea, "Warehousing and protecting big data: State-of-the-art-analysis, methodologies, future challenges," ACM Int. Conf. Proceeding Ser., vol. 22–23–Marc, pp. 1–7, 2016.

[15] T. Y. Win, H. Tianfield, and Q. Mair, "Big Data Based Security Analytics for Protecting Virtualized Infrastructures in Cloud Computing," IEEE Trans. Big Data, vol. 7790, no. c, p. 1, 2017.

[16] M. Dastbaz, H. Arabnia, and B. Ahgkar, "Technology for smart futures," Technol. Smart Futur., pp. 1–363, 2017.

[17] Q. Liu, A. Srinivasan, J. Hu, and G. Wang, "Preface: Security and privacy in big data clouds," Futur. Gener. Comput. Syst., vol. 72, pp. 206–207, 2017.

[18] A. Cuzzocrea, "Privacy and Security of Big Data : Current Challenges and Future Research Perspectives," pp. 45–47, 2014.

[19] I. Yaqoob et al., "Big data: From beginning to future," Int. J. Inf. Manage., vol. 36, no. 6, pp. 1231–1247, 2016.

[20] A. Abelló, "Big Data Design," Dol. '15 Proc. ACM Eighteenth Int. Work. Data Warehous. Ol., pp. 35–38, 2015.

[21] A. Saldhi, "Big Data Analysis Using Hadoop Cluster," 2014 IEEE Int. Conf. Comput. Intell. Comput. Res., pp. 0–3, 2014.

[22] P. Adluru, S. S. Datla, and X. Zhang, "Hadoop eco system for big data security and privacy," 2015 Long Isl. Syst. Appl. Technol., pp. 1–6, 2015.

[23] S. Bahulikar, "Security measures for the Big Data , Virtualization and the Cloud Infrastructure .," pp. 0–3, 2016.

[24] C. Xie, J. Gao, and C. Tao, "Big data validation case study," Proc. - 3rd IEEE Int. Conf. Big Data Comput. Serv. Appl. BigDataService 2017, pp. 281–286, 2017.

[25] A. Endert, S. Szymczak, D. Gunning, and J. Gersh, "Modeling in Big Data Environments," Proc. 2014 Work. Hum. Centered Big Data Res., p. 56:56--56:58, 2014.

[26] W. A. Günther, M. H. Rezazade Mehrizi, M. Huysman, and F. Feldberg, "Debating big data: A literature review on realizing value from big data," J. Strateg. Inf. Syst., 2017.

[27] M. Ciavotta, E. Gianniti, and D. Ardagna, "Capacity Allocation for Big Data Applications in the Cloud," Proc. 8th ACM/SPEC Int. Conf. Perform. Eng. Companion - ICPE '17 Companion, pp. 175–176, 2017.

[28] J. Akoka, I. Comyn-Wattiau, and N. Laoufi, "Research on Big Data – A systematic mapping study," Comput. Stand. Interfaces, vol. 54, no. April 2016, pp. 105–115, 2017.

[29] M. Adnan, M. Afzal, M. Aslam, R. Jan, and A. M. Martinez-Enriquez, "Minimizing big data problems using cloud computing based on Hadoop architecture," 2014 11th Annu. High Capacit. Opt. Networks Emerging/Enabling Technol. (Photonics Energy), pp. 99–103, 2014.

[30] G. J.-W. Communication and undefined 2017, "Cloud Security Issues and Privacy," Ciitresearch.Org, pp. 499–514.

[31] A. Oussous, F. Z. Benjelloun, A. Ait Lahcen, and S. Belfkih, "Big Data technologies: A survey," J. King Saud Univ. - Comput. Inf. Sci., vol. 30, no. 4, pp. 431–448, 2018.

[32] C. Dincer, G. Akpolat, and E. Zeydan, "Mobil Operatörler Tarafından Servis Edilen Büyük Veri Uygulamalarında Güvenlik Sorunları Security Issues of Big Data Applications Served by Mobile Operators," pp. 0–3, 2017.

[33] J. Eckroth, "Teaching Future Big Data Analysts : Curriculum and Experience Report," 2017.

[34] B. Saraladevi, N. Pazhaniraja, P. V. Paul, M. S. S. Basha, and P. Dhavachelvan, "Big data and Hadoop-A study in security perspective," Procedia Comput. Sci., vol. 50, pp. 596–601, 2015.

[35] A. O'Driscoll, J. Daugelaite, and R. D. Sleator, "'Big data', Hadoop and cloud computing in genomics," J. Biomed. Inform., vol. 46, no. 5, pp. 774–781, 2013.

[36] Y. Yetis, R. G. Sara, B. A. Erol, H. Kaplan, A. Akuzum, and M. Jamshidi, "Application of Big Data Analytics via Cloud Computing," 2016 World Autom. Congr., pp. 1–5, 2016.

[37] M. M. Rathore, A. Paul, and A. Ahmad, "Big Data Analytics of Geosocial Media for Planning and Real-Time Decisions," 2017.

[38] K. Abouelmehdi, A. Beni-Hssane, H. Khaloufi, and M. Saadi, "Big data emerging issues: Hadoop security and privacy," Int. Conf. Multimed. Comput. Syst. -Proceedings, pp. 731–736, 2017.

[39] K. Singh and R. Kaur, "Hadoop: Addressing challenges of Big Data," Souvenir 2014 IEEE Int. Adv. Comput. Conf. IACC 2014, pp. 686–689, 2014.

[40] zhihan Lv, H. Song, P. Basanta-Val, A. Steed, and M. Jo, "Next-Generation Big Data Analytics: State of the Art, Challenges, and Future Research Topics," IEEE Trans. Ind. Informatics, vol. 3203, 2017.

[41] J. P. Verma, B. Patel, and A. Patel, "Big data analysis: Recommendation system with hadoop framework," Proc. - 2015 IEEE Int. Conf. Comput. Intell. Commun. Technol. CICT 2015, pp. 92–97, 2015.

[42] K. S and I. Bodrušić, "A Big Data Solution for Troubleshooting Mobile Network Performance Problems," pp. 472–477, 2017.

[43] I. Sorić, D. Dinjar, and D. Orešćanin, "Efficient Social Network Analysis in Big Data Architectures," pp. 1397–1400, 2017.

[44] J. Eickholt, "Teaching Big Data and Cloud Computing with a Physical Cluster," Proc. 2017 ACM SIGCSE Tech. Symp. Comput. Sci. Educ., pp. 177–181, 2017.

[45] Q. Liu, Y. Fu, G. Ni, and R. Hou, "Hadoop Based Scalable Cluster Deduplication for Big Data," Proc. - 2016 IEEE 36th Int. Conf. Distrib. Comput. Syst. Work. ICDCSW 2016, pp. 98–105, 2016.

Microservices: A Review of the Costs and the Benefits

Ahmed Elfatatry
Information Technology Department
Alexandria University
Alexandria, Egypt
elfatatry@alexu.edu.eg

Abstract—**This work is concerned with analyzing the merits and the costs of Microservices. Following the hype associated with a new technology may result in more problems rather than solutions. The Microservices approach offers many benefits in terms of flexibility and scalability. However, rushing to use Microservices without balancing the situation may add unnecessary complexity and there is a possibility that the costs may outweigh the benefits. The key question is: are Microservices in their current form solving more problems than they create? In this paper, we analyze the benefits and the costs of switching to Microservices. The aim is to support the decision of whether to move to Microservices or not based on the evaluation of the advantages and the disadvantages. The main contribution of this work is the provision of a clear picture of the costs and benefits of the technology to help decide if and when a switch to Microservices is the correct choice.**

Keywords- Microservices; Flexibility, Scalability, Software Engineering.

I. INTRODUCTION

Software Engineering has a long history of proposing ways to deal with change. Flexibility is a desirable software attribute, especially in business systems [1]. The ability to change a system as a result of changing requirements with minimum cost has been at the heart of Software Engineering solutions [2] . Targeting low coupling, high cohesion, modularization, and separation of concerns are just a few examples.

The "service thinking" has been a shift in how software is created and delivered. The core of such thinking is that the focus should be on how to consume a functionality rather than the means by which the functionality is produced [3]. In software terms, it is the decoupling of the producer from the product. The Service Oriented Architecture (SOA) has been an early implementation of such concept.

Micorservices are software components where independence of development and deployment is a key concern [4]. The concept of loose coupling is fundamental to the idea of Microservices. Better flexibility can be achieved if a system is built using independent services.

In this work, we provide an analysis of the costs and the benefits of Microservices with respect to achieving flexibility. The aim is to support the decision of switching to Microservices.

This paper is structured as follows. Section 2 examines the concept of Microservices and highlights the benefits of applying such thinking. In Section 3, the Microservices model is compared with the monolithic model in the context of flexibility. Section 4 analyzes the inherent problems of Microservices. The challenges of and future of Microservices are discussed in Section 5. Finally, the conclusions are presented in Section 6.

II. PROBLEM STATEMENT

Microservices architecture is a relatively new architecture which originated in the industry. While there is a great interest in the academia, however, there is an obvious gap between the academia and the industry concerning the topic. Few experience reports by the industry are available, and less practical solutions from the academia [5]. Research efforts usually focus on a single aspect of Micorservices such as migration from legacy systems, architecture, security, database heterogeneity, or service patterns. Other research works highlight only benefits [6], or otherwise only disadvantages. There is a gap in the literature concerning studies that balance the costs versus the benefits.

III. WHAT ARE MICROSERVICES?

The Microservices approach is another way to think about how to build software applications. The approach advocates building the applications as suites of small, independently deployable services, each running its own process. There is no universally accepted definition of Microservices. The independence of Microservices is a key design issue. A service has to be independently deployable. The reason is that this issue has an impact on managing large scale deployment. Each service would be independently developed as a self-contained product with its own complete team. Microservices are built to serve a specific context. Services are built around business capabilities [7]. Related functionalities are combined into a single business capability, and each Microservice implements one such capability [7]. The development team would include a user interface person, a database person, and a business logic person. A team is usually responsible for the whole life cycle of a Microservice [8].

Having described what Microservices are, in the following we discuss the benefits of such approach.

- It is possible to release functionality faster. The reason is that it is not needed to wait until it is possible to release the whole system. Bringing changes into production rapidly is a priority for any business. The more an application is broken down into smaller components, the easier it is to deal with changes. Currently, this is not the case with most monolithic applications [9] [10].

- Braking a system into smaller components supports flexibility. The consumer of a specific functionality may choose from a number of providers that provide the same functionality with different non-functional attributes. The more the software is loosely coupled, the easier it is to engage with open source, provided that there is a license. If a company needs some functionality to be incorporated into the systems from open source components, it has to decompose the system into smaller loosely coupled components.
- Independent scaling. Only the parts of the application that need to be scaled up can be assigned the required resources. There is no need to upgrade the whole infrastructure only to serve selected parts of the system [11]. The result is efficient use of resources. Parts of the system that need more computing power can be assigned the needed resources without having to scale up the whole system [12].
- It is easier to focus on security wherever it is needed. More sensitive services could be put into more protective zones. Less sensitive services that require less protection can be assigned the appropriate resources.
- Each service can be built using the best and most appropriate tool for the task. It can be possible to move parts of the system to the cloud [13]. A company may decide to put some components on the cloud to be managed by specialized competencies. Whether or not the decision is to use multiple technologies in a system, there is a possibility to do it if needed [13].
- Redundancy. Usually, it is assumed that redundancy should be avoided. In a Microservice design, redundancy is a classic way of increasing resilience. Microservices can help implementing this concept more easily.

IV. MICROSERVICES VERSUS MONOLITHS

In a monolithic appication, modules cannot be executed independently. Any change in one module of a monolith requires rebooting the whole application. Scalability is usually a problem in monolithic applications. Often, the entire application does not need to be scaled up. Only a subset of the modules need to be scaled up. The usual strategy for handling such situation is to create new instances of the entire application.

Typically, when monolithic architectures are exposed to a growing load, it is difficult to locate which components of the system are actually affected, since the system runs within a single process. This means that although only a single component may be experiencing load, the whole monolith will need to be scaled up. This will be the only solution even if it is known which component is experiencing the load, as it is difficult to scale it in isolation

V. MICROSERVICES VERSUS SOA

Microservices are mainly focused on application architecture, but they may have some elements that can be taken to the enterprise level. This depends on the size of the enterprise. SOA is an enterprise level concept. SOA is on the enterprise scale while Microservices is on the application scale. In short, a Microservice is a component while SOA is an architecture.

In the traditional SOA, organizations would buy and deploy an Enterprise Service Bus (ESB) and then deploy their individual services on that ESB. But if more scalability is needed, then, the entire ESB has to be scaled up [13]. The Microservices advantage here is that individual services can be scaled up. As Martion Fowler points out, the difference is the shift from the intelligence that is built into the transport layer to having the end points more intelligent and the pipes being a little less intelligent [7].

VI. PROBLEMS OF MICROSERVICES

As stated in [11], the first disadvantage of Microservices is its name. The goal of Microservices is to decompose an application in order to facilitate development and deployment of agile applications. Building small services is not the goal of Microservices, but rather facilitating agile development.

Although individual services may be very simple, there is an increase in complexity as a result of having communications between different components. Distributed systems are more complex compared to monolithic systems. In addition, managing running services is more complex compared to monolithic services.

Partitioning a database across a number of different Microservices makes it difficult to implement some business transactions that can be implemented much easier in monolithic systems. Implementing a query that needs multiple joins can be a problem in some cases. Managing consistency between databases is a difficult task.

Every single time a computation is done outside the module boundary, the request has to travel through the network. This results in communication overhead. The Microservices approach will result in slower services.

From a mobile development perspective, a large number of calls to backend Microservices is very expensive in terms of battery usage. It is not possible to build a version of the application for mobile devices only because all calls have to eventually go to the backend servers.

The core idea of Microservices is having a large number of small services, each doing small part of the work. Here, the focus is not only on what such services are doing but on the communications between them. Every single communication between one service and another is a potential place for something that can go wrong. In addition to unit testing, testing a portion of communicating services all together is necessary to obtain a better image of how the system would behave in production.

Knowing what other services expect without hardcoding such requirements may not be an easy task. In contract testing, ingoing and outgoing attributes are checked for conformance with the expected attributes in each case. The development team of each Microservice has to check communication with other services for conformance of contracts.

Sharing code is harder. The objective of Microservices is to create truly independent services. However, if there is a need to share common utility code between services, then the only option is to replicate a functionally across a number of different services.

VII. CHALLENGES

While the concept of Microservices is simple, its implementation is not. The problem is building a system of Microservices. There are no specific rules for many issues: only tradeoffs. One of the underlying tenets of Microservices is that each service runs in its own isolated process. In such case, the question is: how do services find each other to connect? Hence, there is a need for a service discovery mechanism to avoid hard coding the addresses.

One challenge of Microservices is deciding when to include functions inside one service, and when to break them into separate services. The shift to Microservices requires changing the development methodology. The agile approach would be suitable for the Microservices way.

Monitoring the system is another challenge because each service may be running on a different computer or even on a different platform. There is a potential that something might go wrong. Having a mechanism for viewing which service is causing a bottle neck is essential for such systems.

Having dispersed services, and more opened ports leads to a greater attack surface. If each service has its own database, then there is more potential for database related attacks.

Although the Microservices approach offers substantial benefits, a Microservices architecture requires extra machinery, which can impose substantial costs. To enhance the economics of Microservices, it is useful to be integrated with the cloud [12].

Discovery, granularity, and security are among the challenges that faced prior technologies as well, such as Web services [14]. While security and granularity had some solutions, automatic discovery has never been solved.

VIII. CONCLUSION

The term Microservices implies something small, but this name can be misleading since not all services in a Microservices architecture need to be micro [7]. A service will become as big as it needs to be to provide a coherent, efficient, and reliable function. However, it is not about the size. It is about focus and logical cohesion. The main advantage is breaking the system into smaller chunks that can be managed individually.

Before switching to Microservices, a number of questions need to be answered depending on each individual case: why it is needed? Is it scalability? Is it flexibility? Which parts of the business have such needs? An additional issue concerns the readiness of the teams for the journey. If the answers are not clear enough and justified, then finding the correct answer should come first. Unless the goals are clear enough, benefits cannot be measured.

Writing Microservices based application involves many different issues compared to writing monolithic applications. However, transitioning from a monolith is even more difficult than building Microservices from scratch. Advocates for Microservices implicitly suggest that monoliths are outdated. While flexibility and scalability are weak points in monoliths, they may not be priority for all applications.

Everything comes with a cost, and so do Microservices. If the benefits of switching to Microservices do not outweigh the gains, then the decision is not rational. Whether to move the whole monolith to Microservices is a critical question and does not have a black or white answer. Chosen parts of the application can be migrated into Microservices. The Microservices design thinking can be applied to a monolith. Decomposition strategy, and interaction patterns have to be revisited. A monolithic system can still implement asynchronous communication.

REFERENCES

[1] S. Peng, L. Shen , H. Liu and F. Li, "User-Oriented Measurement of Software Flexibility," in *2009 WRI World Congress on Computer Science and Information Engineering*, vol. 7, IEEE, pp. 629-633, 2009,.

[2] M. Elkholy and A. Elfatatry, "Change Taxonomy: A Fine-Grained Classification of Software Change," *IT Professional*, vol. 20, no. 4, pp. 28-36, 2018.

[3] A. Elfatatry, "Dealing with Change: Components Versus Services," *Communications of the ACM*, vol. 50, no. 8, pp. 35-39, August 2007.

[4] P. Jamshidi, C. Pahl, N. Mendonca, and J. Lewis, "Microservices: The Journey So Far and Challenges Ahead," *IEEE Software*, vol. 35, no. 3, pp. 24-35, 2018.

[5] N. Alshuqayran , N. Ali, and R. Evans, "A Systematic Mapping Study in Microservice Architecture," pp. 44-51, 4-6 Nov. 2016.

[6] M. Fowler, "martinfowler.com," 2017. [Online]. Available: https://martinfowler.com/articles/microservices.html. [Accessed January 2109].

[7] J. Thönes, "Microservices," *IEEE Software*, vol. 32, no. 1, pp. 116, 2015.

[8] S. Newman, Building Microservices, CA: O'Reilly Media, Inc., pp. 9-12, 2015.

[9] C. Pautasso, O. Zimmermann, M. Amundsen, J. Lewis, and N. Josuttis, "Microservices in Practice, Part 2: Service Integration and Sustainability," *IEEE Software*, vol. 34, no. 2, pp. 97-104, 2017.

[10] A. Kwan, H.-A. Jacobsen, A. Chan, and S. Samoojh, "Microservices in the modern software world," pp. 297-299, 2016.

[11] S. Green, How To Build Microservices: Top 10 Hacks To Modeling, Integrating & Deploying Microservices, pp. 24-32, 2015.

[12] A. Singleton, "The Economics of Microservices," *IEEE Cloud Computing*, vol. 3, no. 5, pp. 16-20, 2016.

[13] L. S. David, "Practical Use of Microservices in Moving Workloads to the Cloud," *IEEE Cloud Computing*, vol. 3, no. 5, pp. 10-14, 2016.

[14] C. Zeng , Z. Lu , J. Wang , P. Hung, and J. Tian, "Variable Granularity Index on Massive Service Processes,", IEEE 20th International Conference on Web Services, Santa Clara, CA, USA pp. 18-25, 2013.

Microservice Development Based on Tool-Supported Domain Modeling

Michael Schneider, Benjamin Hippchen, Pascal Giessler, Chris Irrgang, Sebastian Abeck

Cooperation & Management (C&M), Institute for Telematics
Karlsruhe Institute of Technology
Karlsruhe, Germany
Email: {michael.schneider, benjamin.hippchen, pascal.giessler, abeck}@kit.edu
Email: chris.irrgang@student.kit.edu

Abstract—**Developing complex business-related software solutions with domain-driven microservices has become popular recently. Based on the concepts of domain-driven design, the business is expressed as a domain model. However, domain-driven design does not mention any modeling guidelines or tools for assisting the design process. In addition, modeling a complex domain can lead to a complex domain model that is difficult to read and implement. To tackle the complexity of the domain model, we introduce a concept for splitting the domain model into several diagrams, and we apply formalization based on the Unified Modeling Language. Furthermore, we illustrate how the created domain model is transferred step by step into code.**

Keywords–Domain-Driven Design; Modeling; Tool; Microservices; UML profile; Model to Code.

I. Introduction

Modeling the domain of a business unit is part of many design procedures and decisions in software development. For the development of microservices-based systems, Domain-Driven Design (DDD) is a suitable approach [1]. The concept of the domain model was clarified by Eric Evans in his book *Domain-Driven Design: Tackling Complexity in the Heart of Software* [2], and it was further refined by Vernon [3]. After DDD, everything goes for modeling the domain. This includes the activities or business processes, the information involved, and any restrictions that may appear. Therefore, the creation of a domain model helps not only to better build the software architecture through a mannequin-driven design but also to increase the understanding of the business area in which an application operates.

When one is modeling with DDD, there are no restrictions as to how to express the domain. However, DDD emphasizes that the domain implementation should represent the domain model. Without a systematic modeling approach, it is possible that the development of the domain model results in models that are not suitable for the implementation. Furthermore, our experiences have shown that modeling the domain without any tool support can lead to domain models that are different. One example of the differences relates to the used designations, such as notations, names, and elements. This makes collaboration on the models within a team challenging and makes the automatic code generation from the domain model impossible. A further step can entail automatically generating the code from the model. However, a certain degree of formalization of the model is required in order to generate code automatically. Formalization can ensure that the model and the code are synchronized. For example, the automatic generation of Java code when one uses a UML-compliant domain model could be possible [4]. To assist the modeling process of a formalized model, as well as automatic code generation, a tool should be used. Furthermore, interfaces of microservices, which often are RESTful APIs, can be derived [5] when one follows API guidelines [6]. In addition, in terms of a microservice architecture, it is important to maintain the domain model in order to maintain the microservices. Without a tool, this maintenance can be difficult. Therefore, applying a tool-supported domain model creation process can help to solve this problem. Furthermore, we discuss how to generate the code from the created domain models.

The paper is structured as follows. Section II presents related work and articles. Section III illustrates why there is the requirement of additional modeling elements. In addition, a suggestion for structuring the domain models is shown. Section IV discusses the UML profile enhancements. Section V explains the necessary steps for using the UML profile with the tool; moreover, this section illustrates the usage of the tool. Section VI discusses the conversion of the model into the code. Finally, Section VII gives a summary of the paper and surmises what the prospects are for future research.

II. Related Work

Our results presented in this paper are related to or were inspired by the work of several other authors. First of all in this section, we introduce DDD as our main software development approach for modeling patterns in greater detail. Its concepts are the basis for our research. After this section, a first step for formalizing DDD's domain modeling is evaluated. Furthermore, we explain how our systematic approach is based on model-to-code approaches, such as the Model-Driven Architecture (MDA).

A. Domain Modeling with Domain-Driven Design

DDD is a software development approach introduced by Evans [2] that emphasizes the design phase in modeling activities. Model activities aim at gathering information about a given customer's domain–the so-called domain knowledge. The domain knowledge is stated in a domain model, the central artifact of DDD. In line with the principles of Evans, only business logic is relevant to the domain model. Other information, such as technical aspects of applications is neglected. DDD provides several stereotypes of domain objects; a domain object represents a business object from the real world. Classifying the domain objects is important for both the domain model and the implementation of the application. The stereotype is stated in the domain model at the modeling element. Two of the most important stereotypes are "entities" and "value objects". Entities are real-world objects with an identity; this identity enables to find the specific instance of this real-world object. This identity never changes for these kinds of domain objects. Value objects describe also real-world objects, but an identity is not necessary in this case. A more detailed look at these stereotypes has been provided by Vernon [3]. Derived from this stereotype, the implementation is adapted accordingly.

DDD offers a substantial number of useful patterns that help to understand the domain and manifest it into a model. Nevertheless, one major problem of DDD is the missing modeling guideline, such as a specified modeling language. Actually, Evans emphasizes the use of any kind of representation for domain models as long as it supports the understanding of the customer's domain. When one examines the domain models in [2], they mostly remind one of UML class diagrams, but Evans has never stated that UML acts as modeling syntax. In Section IV, we build on a DDD-based UML profile to tackle the missing modeling guidelines.

B. *Formalization of Domain-Driven Design's Domain Model*

While DDD does provide useful patterns to model the domain, the application for the representation within the model is challenging. The look and feel of domain models differ from development team to development team. Especially when one develops applications in a microservice architecture, it is necessary that development teams have a common understanding of how to model a given customer's domain. Thus, applying these patterns would be more efficient with the help of a formalized modeling language.

To tackle these problems, [7] has provided a first Unified Modeling Language (UML) profile for DDD. Based on the domain models used by Evans in [2], the authors have created an overview of which UML elements are used, and they have derived their domain-driven MSA modeling (DDMM); MSA stands for "microservice architecture." More or less, Evans has used UML modeling elements which has led to the decision that a UML profile would close the lacking modeling guidelines.

The UML profile provided by [7] presents an inspiring first step for closing the modeling language gap for DDD. Nevertheless, we can see further room for improving the UML profile. When one considers a complex domain, modeling it in a domain model can lead automatically to a complex model. Thus, we have introduced a concept called "relation view" that decreases the complexity of the domain model by splitting the model apart. Further, we have provided a concrete example for a modeling tool that is able to apply UML profiles.

C. *Model-to-Code Transformation*

The classic approach for model-to-code transformation is directly associated with an Object Management Group's (OMG) Model-Driven Architecture (MDA) [8]. MDA is a software development approach that emphasizes the use of models. Different types of models have different purposes in the software development phases. Furthermore, depending on the model's type, the depth of details is more fine-grained or coarse-grained. The idea behind MDA is to focus on the modeling aspects, while software development for providing (domain) knowledge rich models. As a next step, the source code can be generated automatically based on the knowledge within these models. Previous research has claimed a great number of advantages for MDA-based software development [9], but the establishment in software development companies has proven that this approach has its own problems to apply. The main problem is that the automated generation of source code is not well realized. Often source code has to be adjusted to either work or fit to the problem modeled in the model. Due to this knowledge about automated model-to-code transformations, we elected a systematic (not automated) approach to transform a model into the source code. We provided a fix structure (for example, packages) for the microservice's source code.

III. Structuring and Modeling of the Domain

Domain-driven design differs between several types of objects that we translate into a systematic modeling approach. A domain may contain several domain objects located in distinct bounded contexts. Modeling each domain object into only one diagram may lead to a complex and incomprehensible diagram. Therefore, we separate the domain model into different diagrams: for instance, the relation view for modeling the structural domain aspects.

A. *Systematic Domain Structure*

When modeling the domain, several diagrams are created. Figure 1 shows a simplified version of a so-called "relation view", a tactical diagram concerning the to-do list domain. The to-do list domain is concerned with managing to-do lists as well as the to-dos themselves. The considered domain is simple and easy to understand, but the handling of the relation view can be shown well. Especially for modeling larger and complex domains we see a benefit for using the relation view diagram. Developers can work simultaneously on the different relation view diagrams. Tactical modeling focuses on a partial aspect of the domain within a bounded context, while strategical modeling concerns the higher-level structure of the domain model. A bounded context defines the scope of validity of the model and the code [10]. For each bounded context, we modeled the relation view as depicted in Figure 1.

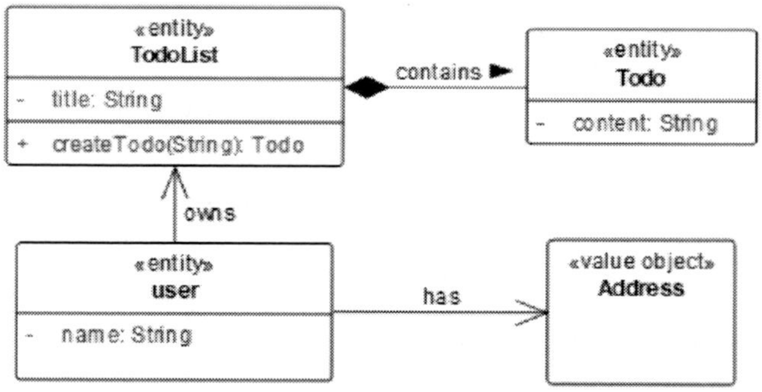

Figure 1. Extract of a relation view

The model is similar to a UML class diagram [2][7], but, in addition, the excerpt contains additional identifiers. These

```
TodoListManagement
└─Domain Model
   ├─TodoList (Context Map)
   ├─«subdomain> IAM
   └─«subdomain» TodoList
      └─«bounded context» TodoManagement
         ├─TodoManagement (Orchestration
         │ View)
         ├─TodoManagement (Relation View)
         ├─«entity» Todo
         ├─«entity» TodoList
         ├─«entity» User
         └─«value object» Address
```

Figure 2. Domain structure

identifiers represent several elements that are required for modeling DDD, such as entities, value objects, and different kinds of relationships. Additionally, attributes and methods express the domain logic. For example, the method *createTodo(String):Todo* is responsible for creating a "to-do" that belongs to the to-do list.

The DDD elements need to be formalized in order to support tool-assisted modeling. In addition, the diagrams need to be stored in a structured way. Structuring the domain leads to several advantages, such as an easier communication across the team - thus, each team member knows exactly where the necessary diagrams are located. Therefore, we have provided a suggestion for structuring the different diagrams of the domain in order to increase retrievability and the value of the diagrams for the teams.

Each domain is structured in its own repository, comparable to folders and paths. Figure 2 illustrates the structure of the domain "TodoListManagement" of the *TodoListManagement* application. The repository contains strategical and tactical modeling diagrams. In this work, we only focus on the tactical diagrams, and we only briefly mention how the strategical modeling diagrams are placed in this structure. Each folder contains a domain model. The domain model is structured as follows. On the top level, the context map of the domain is shown. The context map is a concept of DDD [2] that contains bounded contexts related to a domain. In a microservice architecture, each bounded context is a candidate for a microservice that could be reused by other applications [11]. Using the context map diagram, the tool-support allows the easy access and navigation of the related diagrams simply by allowing one to click on the modeled bounded contexts.

Following the context map, all subdomains are located on the top level path. Figure 2 depicts two subdomains: identity and access management (IAM) as well as the TodoList, whereby the subdomain "TodoList" is unfolded. Each subdomain contains their related bounded contexts. In the example of the *TodoListManagement* the bounded context is called *TodoManagement*. Each bounded context contains diagrams concerning this bounded context (see Figure 2). The first diagram is a strategical diagram — the context orchestration that concerns the orchestration. In addition to the context orchestration, the tactical diagrams follow. Each bounded context consists of at least one relation view. The relation view is the tactical diagram that contains the domain elements and their relationships. In addition to the structural elements, the behavior of the domain behavior is modeled as well in different diagrams. For the dynamic components, ordinary sequence and activity diagrams can be used, which are, therefore, not considered further in the following analysis. The diagram elements corresponding to the relation view, such as entities, value objects, or relations, are located directly below the diagrams. These elements can be reused for all diagrams concerning the related bounded context.

IV. UML Profile

In this section, the formalization of the model is discussed. Possible options are UML profiles or metamodels, but each has their own advantages and disadvantages. The creation of a UML profile is preferable to an extension of the metamodel due to the low added value. Therefore, we used a UML profile for our modeling purposes (see [7]) and added the relation view.

A. UML Profile of the Relation View

The *relation view* describes the inner structure of a bounded context, essentially corresponding to a class diagram and representing the tactical part of DDD. A first approach for dividing the model into several views has already been mentioned by other scholars [1]. Many domains are complex and contain many domain objects. The relation view reduces the complexity for modeling the domain and should be used for complex domains. Only the domain objects corresponding to the current bounded context are considered in the relation view. Therefore, the relation view describes a manageable section of the domain. Each bounded context has at least one relation view, which can consist of entities, value objects, domain services, and their relationships. Therefore, the relation view defines the domain terms and correlates them into a relationship. The elements and relations used in the relation view are also already largely defined in UML. Established DDD concepts, such as entities and value objects, are supported with the UML profile. Due to the large intersection, only minor adjustments compared to UML are necessary since mainly new stereotypes have to be introduced and the behavior of existing elements, such as packages, components, and classes can be maintained. Thus, the power provided by heavyweight modeling using metamodels would hardly be used. The most important UML additions for the relation view are based on [7] and discussed in the following.

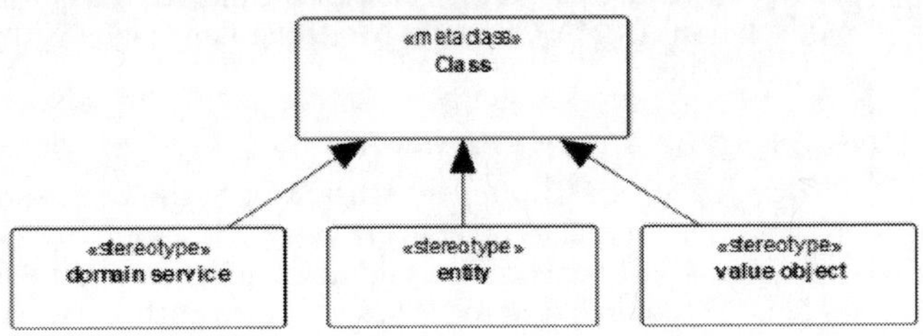

Figure 3. Profile of the relation view

1) Entity: An entity is one of the most important elements of the relation view. The entities represent the corresponding objects from the domain, are defined as UML classes, and include attributes and methods. They encapsulate all functionality associated with or emanating from this entity. Entities can be provided via the API. As Figure 3 illustrates, we added the stereotype "entity" to the UML class element. For example, the domain object "todo" (see Figure 1) is an entity; therefore, the modeling element for an entity (declared with the stereotype "entity") was added to the diagram.

2) Value Object: A value object behaves similarly to an entity but does not have an identity. Another difference between entities and value objects is that a value object is not immutable, and, therefore, a new object must be created when changes are made. This means that only the attributes are considered in object comparisons, which makes a comparison between two different objects with the same attribute values true. For example, an address consisting of first name, surname, street, and the city used by several people (in this example, "users") - could become a value object. In a different domain, the address could be an entity as well. Value objects are identified with the stereotype "value object."

3) Domain Service: Domain services are used when the responsibility of a process is incumbent upon several entities or value objects. A domain service does not maintain any state in order to guarantee consistent and predictable behavior. The stereotype "domain service" identifies a domain service.

4) Relationships between Domain Objects: The relation view does not contain any additional self-defined stereotypes for relationships. Instead, the most important relationships from the UML class diagrams are used. This includes the generalization, the composition, the aggregation, and the binary association. Relationships between the domain elements are usually defined by means of a verb and the reading direction. In addition, multiplicities and directions are assigned in the same manner as in a UML class diagram.

V. USED TOOL AND EXAMPLE

This section presents Enterprise Architect (EA) [12], which is the tool we are have used for modeling the domain. Furthermore, this section explains how the UML profile is applied in the tool.

A. Enterprise Architect

EA is a software modeling tool that is based on OMG UML [13]. By default, Enterprise Architect provides support for user-defined extensions, including the use of UML profiles. Enterprise Architect already provides some useful profiles for popular modeling languages, such as Business Process Model and Notation (BPMN), Systems Modeling Language (SysML), or ArchiMate.

B. Enterprise Architect Profiles (MDG)

Besides the UML profile discussed in Section IV, further profiles are required. In order to create a UML profile for DDD with optimal user experience, additional diagram and toolbox profiles are required next to the previous (see Section IV) UML profiles. These diagram and toolbox profiles are specified in EA. The diagram profiles allow the easy creation of custom diagram types that are suitable for the DDD modeling problem. Figure 4 depicts an excerpt of the definition of the custom

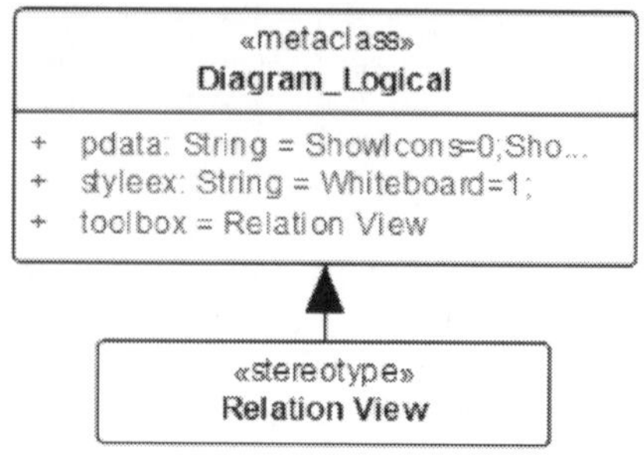

Figure 4. Excerpt of the EA DDD profile

diagram profile for the relation view. The custom diagrams illustrated in Figure 4 extend the standard UML diagram metaclasses and predefine the appearance and feature visibility of the diagram elements. These diagrams can be accessed via toolboxes. Therefore, in addition to the profiles, a toolbox profile is specified. The toolbox profile links an arbitrary diagram type to a custom-built toolbox. Opening a diagram type automatically displays the corresponding toolbox. This toolbox contains the configured elements and connectors. For example, the toolbox of the relation view contains elements, such as "Entity", "Value Object", and "Domain Service". Figure 5 illustrates our defined toolbox for the relation view. Thus,

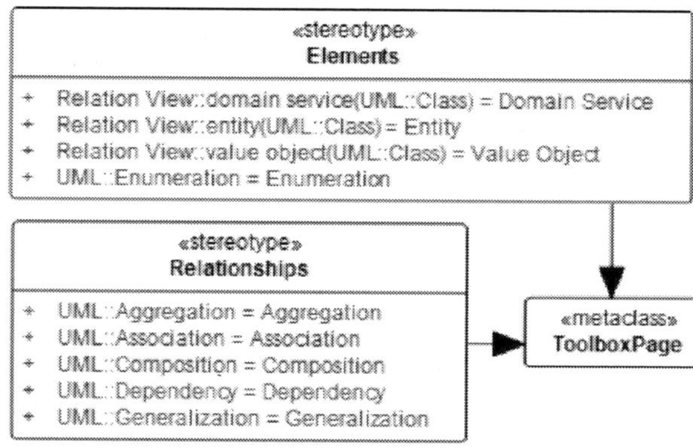

Figure 5. Toolbox profile for relation view

the user has only the necessary self-defined and predefined standard modeling elements available; this, in turn, simplifies the modeling process and reduces modeling inconsistencies.

C. Modeling with EA

In order to model the different diagram types, the corresponding DDD profile is loaded. For example, the relation view is modeled by using the previously defined relation view toolboxes. This simplifies the modeling process because EA offers many modeling elements. The result of the toolbox defined in Section V-B is illustrated in Figure 6. The toolbox contains all the previously discussed elements as well as the relationships. For modeling purposes, the elements are simply dragged out of the toolbox into the diagram. In Section III, several domain objects are illustrated in Figure 1 – "TodoList," "Todo," "User,"

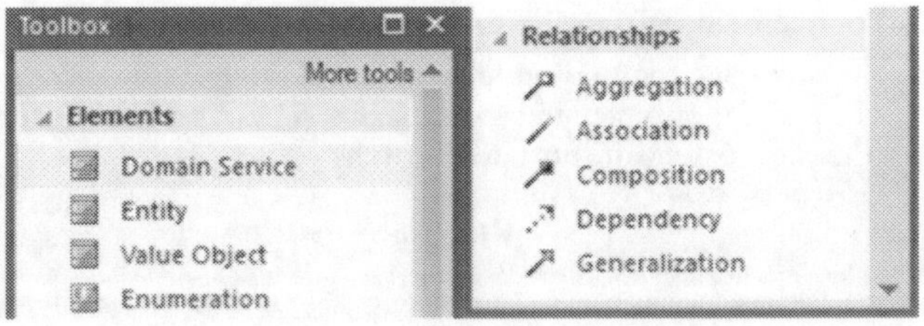

Figure 6. Resulting EA toolbox for the relation view

and "Address" – as well as several relationships. The diagram itself was created by using EA and the corresponding DDD profile.

VI. MODEL-TO-CODE AND CODE-MODEL EQUALITY

The tool-supported domain modeling based on an extended UML profile enables the possibility of generating code directly from the model. Enterprise Architect and other tools automatically generate classes, attributes, and methods (including parameters) from the model. Using this generation process ensures that the model and code are equal at the point of the code creation process. During implementation, there is a high chance that the developers will notice that the modeled methods, attributes, and classes are not enough or that they require changes. Therefore, the code should be adjusted according to the needs. Adding new classes, methods, and attributes to the implementation does not automatically adjust the model. If the model is not adjusted afterwards, the model is no longer useful as a convenient reference. This model state is not desired; therefore, an interface between the tool and the code is required that can automatically adjust the model when code changes happen. EA allows importing source code that can be used to automatically create a model. The imported source code creates a new model, but it does not adjust the model used to generate the code.

A. Step-Wise Model-To-Code Transformation

For the implementation of the todo list domain, we used Java as a programming language and the framework Spring [14], which simplifies the developing of enterprise applications. The relation view that we created was transferred step by step into code. Figure 7 shows the different steps for implementing the domain model. To simplify the implementation process, we implemented an entity-base class that provides useful DDD functionality and can reduce the boilerplate code of the microservice implementation. As depicted in Figure 8 line 2, this base class is inherited and provides useful classes, configurations, and methods (for example, an ID and corresponding equals- and hashCode methods,) and it simplifies the microservice-based development with Spring Boot. The annotation *@Entity* in line 1 enables the mapping to a database by an ORM framework and is used for domain objects that are entities. In addition, the annotation *@ValueObject* is used for value objects.

In the next step, the infrastructural annotations were added. As shown in line 7 of Figure 8, domain database annotations define the relationships and cardinalities between the domain objects for the database. These database-specific annotations are sufficient in this simple case since the domain can be

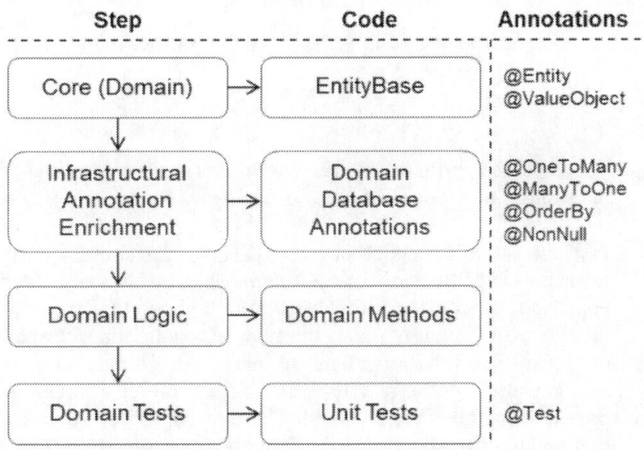

Figure 7. Implementation steps and code annotations

mapped to the database as it is–a structural adjustment of the class by database restrictions did not take place accordingly. The annotations were added to relating domain objects, for example, *TodoList* and *Todo*. After this step, the methods that contained the domain logic were implemented. It should be noted that the class does not contain any "getters" and, especially, no "setter" methods because business methods are not covered with simple setter methods [3]. Getters are only used if they are really necessary for fulfilling business capabilities and cannot be queried indirectly by the use of business methods.

```
1  @Entity
2  public class TodoList extends EntityBase {
3
4   @Column(nullable = false)
5   private String title;
6
7   @OneToMany(cascade = CascadeType.ALL,
8    mappedBy = "todoList",
9    orphanRemoval = true)
10  private List<Todo> todos;
```

Figure 8. Excerpt of the TodoList implementation

Once the implementation of the domain model were completed, the implementation was tested. At the domain level, unit tests were used for the testing purpose that focused on the formal correctness of the domain at a technical level and ensured the correct behavior of the domain implementation. For aggregate elements, the root element methods were called in order to test the domain logic within the aggregate.

B. REST-based Web API

According to [15] and with consideration for the Richardson maturity model (RMM) [16], several questions have to be answered to provide a REST-based Web API: 1) Which domain objects should be exposed? 2) Which information from these selected domain objects should be exposed? 3) Which methods of the domain should be provided?

TABLE I. END POINTS OF THE TO-DO LIST EXAMPLE

Entity	Collection	Resource ID
TodoList	/todo-lists	/{id}
Todo	/todo-lists/{id}/todos	/{number}

Once these questions have been clarified, an initial specification of the Web API can be derived. For the specification, the domain objects will be mapped onto so-called "resources" that act as data transfer objects (DTOs) that contain (partial) information of the respective domain objects. By using such an approach, we introduce an abstraction layer so that the domain objects can develop independently of each other without a necessary Web API change. A Web API change can result in a negative side-effect for existing service customers if the provided methods are changed. The domain object methods are mapped to corresponding HTTP methods to reflect on the operation semantically (create, read, write, update, delete, execute). The positive impact of a good Web API is uncontroversial especially when offering the underlying service to a wide range of possible service customers. That is why several companies apply dedicated review cycles and also create guidelines on how to build Web APIs with quality in mind [17][18]. There is also an aggregation of well-known best practices that should be kept in mind during the design process [6][19][20]. For the purpose of formalization and further processing, dedicated specific languages, such as OpenAPI can be used, which, in turn, come with corresponding tool support. For instance, dedicated client libraries can be automatically generated to simplify the integration.

In our case, we derived two end points for our to-do list example, as illustrated in Table I. Using the tool *SwaggerUI*, we could visualize and interact with the Web API with no written code from client side. The end points of the to-do list example are displayed in Table I. Requests to the entity *Todo* are always passed over to-do lists because the entity *TodoList* is the aggregate root.

VII. Conclusion and Limitation

We focused on the tactical modeling of a domain based on UML profiles in order to formalize the modeling process. Our approach has allowed us to divide the domain model into multiple models; this has allowed us to develop different models simultaneously, which reduces the complexity of the modeling process. In order to model the diagrams, we used EA as modeling tool; this enables an automatic translation of the model into code. For entities and value objects, we implemented base classes that provide useful functionality for these domain concepts. However, at this point we transferred the model into code manually. For an automatic code generation, additional work is required. Currently, we are only able to automatically generate the classes, methods, and attributes. Further research is required, because the annotations and mappings could be automatically added by the modeling tool as well. The annotations remove boilerplate code from the implementation, but the tool needs to automatically provide the annotation when code is generated. For example, the annotations *@Entity, @ValueObject* need to be automatically generated. In addition, relationships and database annotations need to be considered as well. In future work, we need to add the mappings that are required to automatically create the complete code from the toolset we presented.

Since we focused on tactical models only, strategical modeling and the implementation aspects should be investigated to a greater extend in further research.

References

[1] B. Hippchen, P. Giessler, R. Steinegger, M. Schneider, and S. Abeck, "Designing Microservice-Based Applications by Using a Domain-Driven Design Approach," in International Journal on Advances in Software, Vol. 10, No. 3&4, Pages 432 - 445, 2017.

[2] E. Evans, Domain-Driven Design: Tackling Complexity in the Heart of Software. Addison-Wesley Professional, 2004.

[3] V. Vernon, Ed., Implementing Domain-Driven Design. Addison-Wesley, 2013, ISBN: 978-0321834577.

[4] M. Usman and A. Nadeem, "Automatic generation of Java code from UML diagrams using UJECTOR," International Journal of Software Engineering and Its Applications, vol. 3, no. 2, 2009, pp. 21–37.

[5] P. Giessler, "Domain Driven Design of Resource-oriented Microservices," Ph.D. dissertation, Karlsruhe Institute of Technology, Germany, 2018.

[6] P. Giessler, M. Gebhart, D. Sarancin, R. Steinegger, and S. Abeck, "Best Practices for the Design of RESTful Web Services," in International Conferences of Software Advances (ICSEA), 2015, pp. 392–397.

[7] F. Rademacher, S. Sachweh, and A. Zündorf, "Towards a UML Profile for Domain-Driven Design of Microservice Architectures," in International Conference on Software Engineering and Formal Methods. Springer, 2017, pp. 230–245.

[8] A. G. Kleppe, J. Warmer, W. Bast, and M. Explained, The model driven architecture: practice and promise. Addison-Wesley Longman Publishing Co., Inc., Boston, MA, 2003.

[9] K. Czarnecki and S. Helsen, "Classification of model transformation approaches," in Proceedings of the 2nd OOPSLA Workshop on Generative Techniques in the Context of the Model Driven Architecture, vol. 45, no. 3. USA, 2003, pp. 1–17.

[10] E. Evans, Domain-Driven Design Reference: Definitions and Pattern Summaries. Dog Ear Publishing, 2014.

[11] S. Newman, Building Microservices: Designing Fine-grained Systems. " O'Reilly Media, Inc.", 2015.

[12] Sparx Systems, "Enterprise Architect - Model Driven UML Tool," URL: https://www.sparxsystems.eu/start/home/ [retrieved: 2019.03.15].

[13] O. OMG, "Unified Modeling Language (OMG UML)," Superstructure, 2007.

[14] Pivotal Software, "Spring Framework," URL: https://spring.io/projects/spring-framework/ [retrieved: 2019.03.15].

[15] R. T. Fielding, "REST: architectural styles and the design of network-based software architectures," Doctoral dissertation, University of California, Irvine, 2000, URL: http://www.ics.uci.edu/~fielding/pubs/dissertation/top.htm [retrieved: 2019.01.31].

[16] J. Webber, S. Parastatidis, and I. Robinson, REST in Practice: Hypermedia and Systems Architecture, 1st ed. O'Reilly Media, Inc., 2010.

[17] A. Macvean, M. Maly, and J. Daughtry, "API Design Reviews at Scale," in Proceedings of the 2016 CHI Conference Extended Abstracts on Human Factors in Computing Systems. ACM, 2016, pp. 849–858.

[18] Zalando, "Zalando RESTful API and Event Scheme Guidelines," 2017, URL: https://zalando.github.io/restful-api-guidelines/ [retrieved: 2019.01.31]. [Online]. Available: https://zalando.github.io/restful-api-guidelines/

[19] M. Masse, REST API Design Rulebook: Designing Consistent RESTful Web Service Interfaces. " O'Reilly Media, Inc.", 2011.

[20] P. Giessler, M. Gebhart, R. Steinegger, and S. Abeck, "Best Practices for the Design of RESTful Web Services," International Journal On Advances in Internet Technology, vol. 9, no. 3 and 4, 2016.

Towards a Modelling Language for Managing the Requirements of ISO/IEC 27001 Standard

Daniel Ganji
Centre for Secure, Intelligent and Usable Systems (CSIUS)
University of Brighton
Brighton, UK
d.ganji2@brighton.ac.uk

Haralambos Mouratidis
Centre for Secure, Intelligent and Usable Systems (CSIUS)
University of Brighton
Brighton, UK
h.mouratidis@brighton.ac.uk

Saeed Malekshahi Gheytassi
Centre for Secure, Intelligent and Usable Systems (CSIUS)
University of Brighton
Brighton, UK
m.s.malekshahi@brighton.ac.uk

***Abstract*—Security standards help organisations to continually review and refine the information security procedures to remain safe and secure, however, organisations face difficulties and are concerned about understanding the requirements of the standards. The research to date from the industry and academia tended to focus on the overall description of the standard and such expositions are unsatisfactory because little is being contributed to the practicality of the Information Security Management System (ISMS) structure. The generalisability of much-published research on the standard is insufficient for organisations aiming to implement the standard. An objective of this paper is to offer a direction towards a new modelling language to assist organisations to better understand the requirements of the International Organization for Standardization (ISO) and the International Electrotechnical Commission (IEC) 27001 standard. The methodological approach took in developing our proposed research was found by systematically investigating the current gap in the literature and to explore the underlying needs of organisations to adopt the ISMS. This paper contributes a set of original components and concepts to holistically capture, model, and manage the requirements of the standard. Our modelling language enables information security practitioners and interested parties in organisations to develop an ISMS and promote their corporate compliance with a well-established standard.**

Keywords–information security management system; requirements engineering; ISO/IEC 27001; PDCA; ISMS.

I. Introduction

In the new global economy, organisations face tougher pressure in securing the information of their clients. Some of these pressures are through mandatory rules and regulations, such as complying with the European Union General Data Protection Regulation (EU GDPR), the interested parties' requirements, or their own requirements to safeguard their trade secret from their competitors. Increasingly, regulations demand software engineers to analyse, design and implement responsible systems to comply with laws and regulations [1]. It is an important task for organisations to meet their information security requirements and take appropriate actions to satisfy their expectations.

The number of information security breaches is getting bigger and invaders are getting smarter in ways to exploit security vulnerabilities [2] [3]. Conventional and outdated management of security systems does not answer the needs of the current structure. Improving security in an organisation is not just about expenditure on new technologies but correctly addressing the basics of information security and risk-related elements such as threat and vulnerability management, log management, backup and system hardening [4]. To date, there has been no solid evidence to absolute security and protection, however, there are available frameworks and approaches such as the International Organization for Standardization (ISO) and the International Electrotechnical Commission (IEC) 27001 standard to promote the best practices in managing information security. Organisations need to prepare towards sophisticated approaches considering security techniques under one interconnected application known as Information Security Management System (ISMS) to preserve the confidentiality, integrity, and availability of information assets.

ISO/IEC 27001 is an international standard and applicable to all organisations, regardless of their type, size, or nature [5]. It constitutes a certifiable standard and is widely used with steady growth in a number of adoptions [6]. The standard is composed of processes, policies, and resources that can be used to systematise the security demands of an organisation. The ISO/IEC 27000 family of standards helps organisations to implement a robust approach to managing information security and building resilience. By providing compliance to a globally known standard, certification significantly reduces the need for repeated client audits.

Understanding and applying the requirements of any standard into an organisation is not always a straightforward process. From the review of the literature, it appears that opportunities exist to evaluate the implementation and effectiveness of the standard in organisations, but academic researchers as described in Section III have not taken the challenge. Our research proposes a model-driven approach to enable organisations to adopt the requirements of the standard using requirements engineering concepts.

The remainder of the paper is thus set out as follows: Current challenges are described in Section II, and the related work in Section III. In Section IV, we present the mapping methodology and mapping requirements for our proposed framework. Our modelling language and its concepts are described in Section V. Finally, our conclusions and future work will be set out in Section VI.

II. Current Challenges

IT Governance, a provider of IT compliance solutions to organisations released an annual survey [7] centred around the experience and implementation challenges of the ISO/IEC 27001 for organisations in 2016. The investigation of 250 information security professionals from 53 countries who participated in the survey were mostly certified or working towards certification (80%). 71% of respondents received either regular or occasional requests to provide the ISO/IEC 27001 certification from clients or when proposing for new business. By providing compliance to a globally known standard, certification significantly reduces the need for repeated client audits. The survey also found that a third of all respondents were concerned about understanding the requirements of the standard and 28% considered the creation and managing the standard documentation a challenging task. Other substantial challenging tasks were conducting the information security risk assessment and identifying the required controls for 22% and 14% of the respondents respectively.

Organisations understand that it is in their interest to follow some type of internationally recognised reference framework to create environments for ISMS rather than doing it ad hoc [8]. From the commercial aspect, it is rather difficult and costly task to identify the resource required to plan, implement, measure information security management system.

From an academic perspective, ISMS has mostly drawn from the views of practitioners [9] and the investigation of the literature indicates that ISMS has not been particularly attractive in academia with a lack of research and approaches are egregious. Management systems on information security have received very limited observation and research from the academic community despite the high interest from organisations in particular for IT, operational and compliance audits [10]. There is a relative paucity of scientific literature focusing specifically on the requirements of the standard; most of these studies have been on the previous version of the standard prior to 2013. In response to the real-world and academic challenges, this research contributes a model-based approach to organisations to identify and manage the requirements of the standard.

III. Related Work

Mayer proposed Information System Security Risk Management (ISSRM) [11] [12], which provided a reference conceptual model for security risk management. The author proposed a model-based approach for ISSRM, applicable since the early phases of IS development. The work focused on the modelling support to such an approach, by proposing a domain model for ISSRM. The work defined a reference conceptual model for security risk management and enhancement of the domain model with the different metrics used in a risk management method. Further, the authors developed a proposal of the Secure Tropos language and a process to use the extension in the frame of risk management.

Beckers et al. proposed PAttern-based method for establishing a Cloud specific informaTion Security management system (PACTS) [13] [14]. An approach for creating an ISMS methodology compliance to the ISO/IEC 27001 standard cloud environment with a specific interest in legal compliance and privacy. The overview of the methodology was leadership commitment, asset identification, threats analysis, risk assessment, security policies and reasoning, ISMS specification, identify relevant laws and regulations, the definition of compliance controls, instantiating privacy patterns, privacy threats analysis.

Beckers et al. proposed ISMS-CORAS [15] [16], an extension of the COROS method to support the establishment of the ISO/IEC 27001 compliant ISMS. Authors proposed a methodology following the CORAS method. CORAS is a risk management methodology based on the ISO 31000 standard.

Susanto et al. proposed Integrated Solution Framework (I-SolFramework) [17] [18] to assesses the readiness level of an organisation towards the implementation of the ISO/IEC 27001. The framework offered e-assessment and e-monitoring to analyse and perform an assessment of the readiness level of the standard implementation. E-assessment measures the standard parameters based on the framework, which is consist of six components. It helps to validate the ISMS parameters through an analytical interface such as histogram, charts and graphs, provided by a framework.

The investigation of the related work indicates that far too little attention has been paid to address all or most requirements of the standard. Limited studies were found to support most requirements of the standard. Restricted to no evidence of some requirements were detected in the literature, such as monitoring and evaluation of the information security performance, internal audit, management review to consider the effectiveness of the management system, nonconformity and corrective action to identify and eliminate the root of nonconformities, and continual improvement to improve the effectiveness of the ISMS. Majority of the literature such as PACTS, I-SolFramework, ISMS-CORAS mainly support the planning stage of the standard, which is the pre-implementation of the standard, therefore, the post-implementation is missing from the current literature.

IV. Methodology

The ISO/IEC 27001 standard is a set of requirements for establishing, implementing, deploying, monitoring, reviewing, maintaining, updating and improving an ISMS with regard to an organisation's overall risks and opportunities. The former version of the standard was based on a process approach is known as Plan-Do-Check-Act (PDCA) model which each is defined below:

- Plan: Establish the ISMS policy, objectives, processes and procedures relevant to managing risk and improving information security.
- Do: Implement and operate the ISMS policy, controls, process and procedures.
- Check: Assess and measure process performance against ISMS policy.
- Act: Maintain and improve the ISMS by taking corrective actions where nonconformity occurs.

An organisation must identify and implement the standard requirements in order to claim conformity with the standard. It needs to be able to distinguish these requirements from other recommendations where there is a certain freedom of choice. The standard document consists of many clauses and sub-clauses in the form of normative phrases. There is no specific method in the interpretation of the ISO/IEC 27000 family of standards, however, an approach developed by the

ISO to extract and interpret the clauses of the standard is available. The interpretation rules are based on the provisions of the ISO/IEC Directives, Part three, Rules for the structure and drafting of international standards, Annex H.

The requirements set out in the standard are generic and exclusions of any of the requirements specified in clause four to ten are not allowed when an organisation claims conformity to this international standard. Compliance with ISO/IEC 27001 can be formally assessed and certified by an external accredited certification body. A detailed descriptions of all requirements used as part of this paper are summarised in Table I.

V. Proposed Modelling Language

The requirements of the standard were described in the previous section. Part of the aim of this paper is to introduce a mapping between the requirements of the standard and concepts taken from the requirements engineering to assist with the implementation of the ISMS, the result of the mapping is illustrated in Fig. 1. The top part of the figure shows the requirements of the ISMS and the layers of the PDCA covering the requirement. The bottom part of the figure represents the concepts proposed in our modelling language indicating the area of relevancy with the requirements of the standard.

In this section, we present our modelling language which enables the expression of the relationships and concepts in correspondence with the ISO/IEC 27001 standard. The rest of this section focuses on presenting the various building blocks of the proposed language. First, an overview of the language components will be explained. Next, each concept will be discussed in details. The concepts attributes and relationships proposed in the modelling language are demonstrated in the meta-model, provided in Fig. 2.

The four components used in the modelling process include:

- Information security requirements elicitation: The first component captures the overall organisational structure in relation to information security.
- Information security analysis: The second component analyses the organisational standing in relation to information security.
- Management system requirements elicitation: The third component develops management system posture with the organisational structure.
- Management system analysis: The fourth component identifies and analyses the processes of the management system.

A. *Information Security Requirements Elicitation*

This component discusses each concept required to model the organisational structure including Actor, Constraint, Goal, Asset, and Dependency. A description of each concept and its properties are discussed below.

Actor: A concept of actor represents a person or entity that has intentionality and strategic goal relevant to the scope of the ISMS. An actor could have a direct or indirect effect, be affected by or perceive themselves to be affected by a decision or activity within the scope of the ISMS. This concept has four properties including Id, Description, Type, and Competency.

An actor is also known as a user or stakeholder, however, this interpretation may isolate the full characteristics of an actor, hence, types of actors were introduced to capture the interest of an actor within the organisation. The two types of actor are external or internal. An external actor is a person or entity from the external environment of the organisation who pays for a service or expects the level of principles in relation to the external context of the organisation as a whole, and not necessarily from the ISMS. This could be an independent person(s) like a client or an entity like a national or international authority such as governmental agencies and regulatory bodies. An internal actor is a person or entity from the internal environment of the organisation who benefits

TABLE I. REQUIREMENTS OF ISO/IEC 27001:2013 STANDARD

Requirement	Description
Organisational context	Define the external and internal parameters and issues affecting the outcome of ISMS.
Interested parties	Identify the interested parties and their information security requirements relevant to the ISMS.
Determining the scope	Identify the logical or physical boundaries and applicability of the ISMS.
ISMS	Establish, implement, and continually improve an ISMS under the requirements of the standard.
Leadership	Top management to demonstrate leadership and commitment with respect to the ISMS that are compatible with the strategic direction of the organisation.
Policy	Establish directions and making references to IS objectives and appropriate to the purpose and context of the organisation.
Roles	Top management to assign and communicate the responsibilities and authorities relevant to information security for reporting performance of the ISMS within the organisation.
Risk and opportunities	Systematically determine the potential risks and opportunities that may be involved in a projected activity or undertaking.
Information security objectives	Define measurable information security objectives.
Resources	Identify the resources needs to manage the ISMS.
Competence	Identify the necessary ability of a persons knowledge and skills doing work under its control that affects information security performance.
Awareness	Persons working under the organisation's control to be aware of the information security policy and their contribution to the effectiveness of the ISMS.
Communication	Apply internal and external communication process relevant to the ISMS.
Documented information	Create, update, and control documented information required by the standard and necessary for the effectiveness of the ISMS.
Operational planning	Plan, implement and control the process needed to meet information security requirements including risk and opportunities, and information security objectives.
IS risk assessment	Perform security risk assessment.
IS risk treatment	Implement information security risk treatment.
Monitoring & measurement	Evaluate the information security performance and its effectiveness.
Internal audit	Conduct regular internal audits and systematically evaluate the effectiveness of the implemented and maintained ISMS.
Management review	Top management to review the organisation ISMS at planned intervals to ensure its continuing suitability, adequacy and effectiveness.
Nonconformity & corrective action	React and evaluate nonconformity occurrences, review and deal with appropriate corrective actions.
Continual improvement	Recurring activity to continually improve the suitability, adequacy and effectiveness of the ISMS.

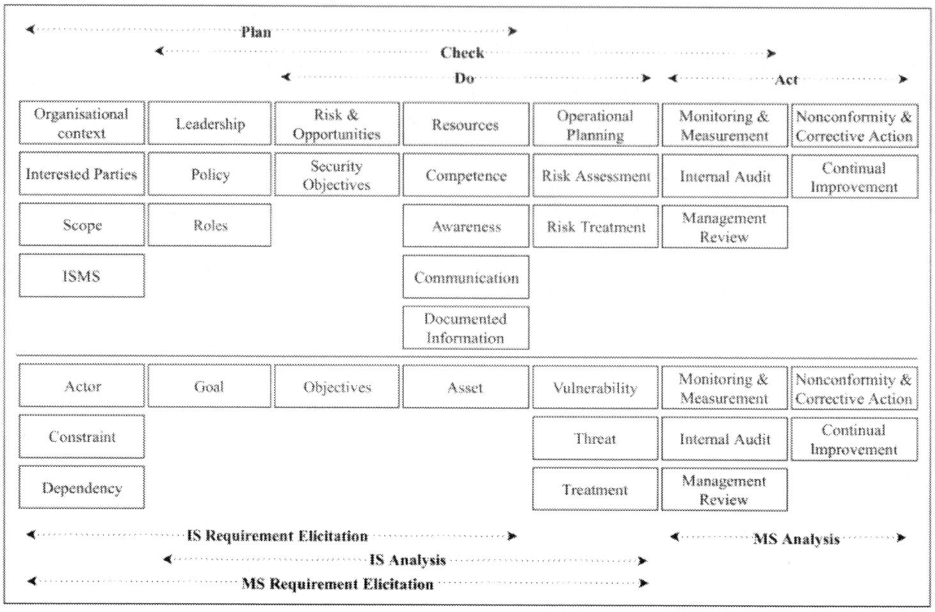

Figure 1. Language mapping to the requirements of the ISO/IEC 27001 standard

from the success of the ISMS or contribute to the success of the ISMS. This could be an employee, a contractor who works under the supervision of the organisation, or a group of interested parties such as shareholders or owners who may only have a financial interest in the organisation.

The last property of an actor is the competency level, which indicates the ability to apply knowledge to intended goals within the scope of the ISMS. An actor must have the necessary competence for doing work under his/her control that affects its information security performances.

Constraint: A concept of constraint represents the restrictions that an actor may have within the scope of the ISMS. A constraint could limit the operation of goals or access to assets. Constraint represents boundaries that do not permit specific action to be taken or prevent a certain goal from being achieved. Constraints are often beyond the control of an organisation, these are conditions or expectations that actors wish to introduce and impose to the organisation. A constraint concept has three properties including Id, Description, and Type.

Consideration to all constraints are an important part of an ISMS, however, not all constraints are equal in their nature and an application of a constraint could be designated based on relevance and priority. Some constraints may have specific instructions on how they should be satisfied whilst some others may be more flexible and could be satisfied by a number of means, therefore, it allows the organisation to prioritise and effectively plan its resources. In the light of above, two types of constraints were introduced, obligatory or advisory. An obligatory constraint means the organisation has no control or negotiation capability over the implementation or dismissing such a constraint. An obligatory constraint could be introduced by any types of an actor but it is likely to be instructed by external actors such as governmental and regulatory bodies or as part of a contractual obligation with another entity. An advisory constraint means the organisation has some flexibility or negotiation capability to apply alternative means to satisfy a constraint. An advisory constraint could be introduced by both the internal and external types of actors.

Asset: A concept of asset refers to organisational assets and anything that has value for the organisation. An asset includes tangible or intangible items and not only refers to the monetary value of an item. An asset concept has four properties including Id, Description, Classification, and Ownership.

Information assets should be classified in terms of legal requirements, value, criticality and sensitivity to unauthorised disclosure or modification. Classification property categorises assets into three types of public, confidential, restricted. An organisation is responsible to define or extend the number of categories in accordance with the information classification scheme and suitable to their needs.

The last property is asset ownership. Each asset owner should be identified, this is an actor who owns an asset and could be different from an actor who uses the asset in the organisation. The owner is not necessarily a person but it could be a number of people or an entity such as a department in the organisation that owns an asset or group of assets.

Goal: This concept refers to the actor's strategic interest [19] or duty. Each actor could have a number of goals within the scope of the ISMS. A goal could be initiated by an internal actor such as an employee to being able to do their job such as accessing customer's account or from an external actor such as clients to access their services provided by the organisation. This concept has two properties including Id and Description.

A Goal could be divided into smaller goals known as sub-goals. Goals are an important part of a management system and they could lead the management system to success or failure if not identified and addressed correctly.

Dependency: A concept of dependency derived from the Secure-Tropos methodology [19], which express the relationship between an actor with a goal depending on another actor, goal or asset to accomplish its goal. The former actor called the depender and the latter is called dependee. The types of the

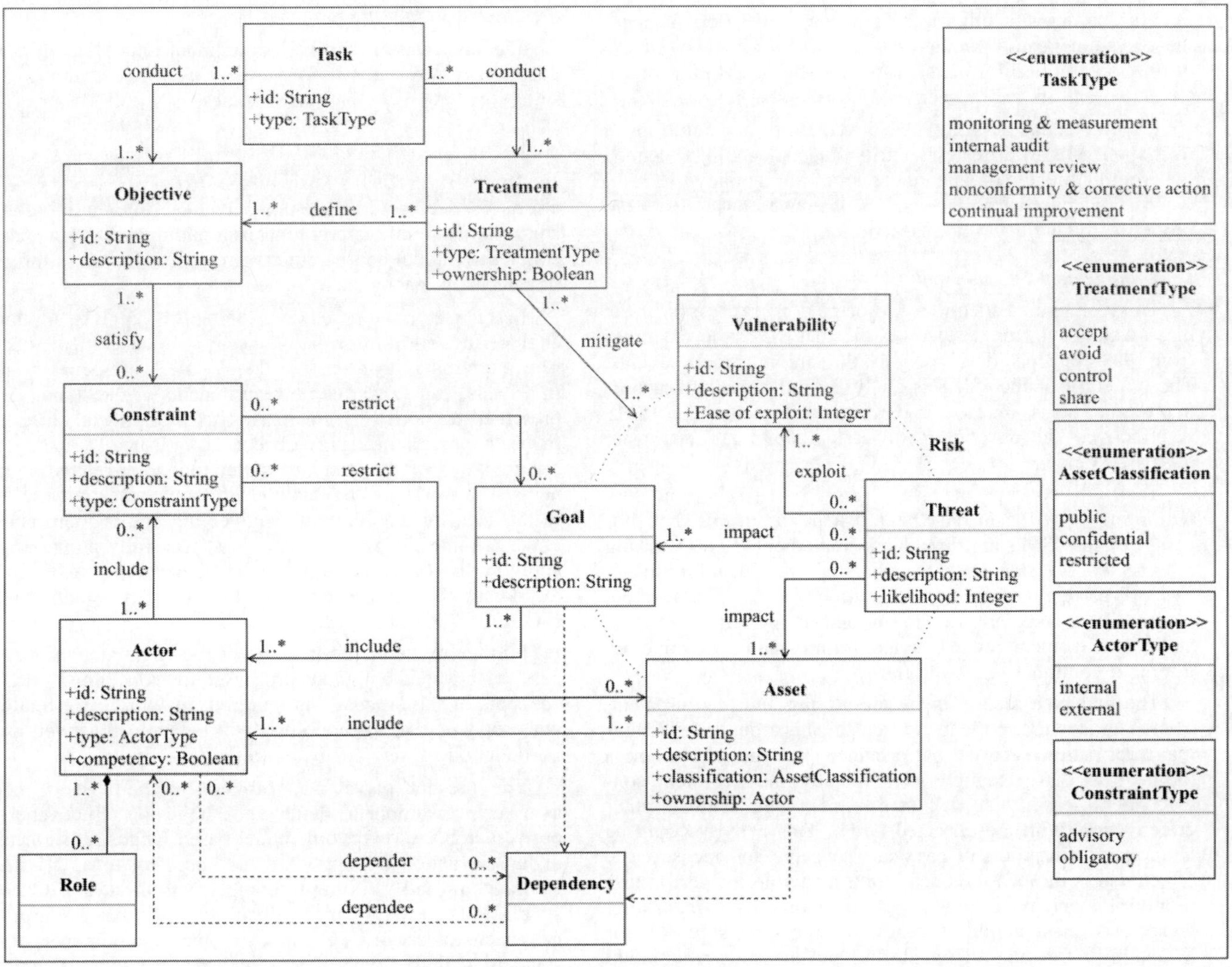

Figure 2. Proposed meta-model

dependency describe the nature of an object between dependee and depender is refereed as dependum. A dependency concept has no properties.

B. Information Security Analysis

This component exercises the concepts required to model the analysis of the organisation in relation to information security. The analysis is performed around a risk management methodology which enables to better understand the impacts of the information security risks on the organisational goals and assets by introducing concepts such as Vulnerability, Threat, and Treatment. A description of each concept and its properties are discussed below.

Vulnerability: A concept of vulnerability refers to a weakness of a goal, asset, or treatment which can be exploited by one or more threats. A threat that does not have a corresponding vulnerability may not result in risk. A vulnerability concept has three properties including Id, Description, and Ease of exploit. Ease of exploit determines a chance of vulnerability to happen and will be the subject of a successful attack.

Threat: A concept of threat refers to the potential cause of an unwanted incident, which may result in harm to a goal or asset. A threat has the potential to harm assets such as information, process, and systems and therefore organisation. A threat concept has three properties including Id, Description, and Likelihood. Threats may be of natural or human origin and could be accidental or deliberate. Both accidental and deliberate threat sources should be identified and assess their likelihood. Likelihood or probability indicates the severity of the cause of a threat.

Treatment: This concept refers to mitigate a risk arising from the impact of threats to assets or goals by exploiting a vulnerability. A treatment concept has three properties including Id, Type, and Ownership approval. A treatment type may involve one or more mitigating approach including accept, avoid, transfer, and reduce. Ownership approval indicates that a mitigating approach is approved by the responsible risk owner. The risk owners' approval for the information security risk treatment plan and acceptance of the residual information security risks is a mandatory requirement of the standard.

C. Management System Requirements Elicitation

This component utilises the concept to develop management system posture along with the organisational structure in relation to the information security. The description of the Objective and its two properties are discussed below.

Objective: It refers to the achievement of a specific result from the ISMS. Information security objective could be defined by targeting the aim of a treatment control or a policy to satisfy a constraint raised from actors. An objective concept has two properties including Id and Description.

D. Management System Analysis:

This component identifies the mandatory processes of the management system that involves the analysis of the outcomes from the concepts developed in the previous components. The structure of the ISMS is analysed and measured against the requirements of the standard to ensure that the ISMS is effective. The description of Task and its properties are discussed below.

Task: A concept of task refers to general mandatory requirements of the management system to ensures that processes of the ISMS are developed, implemented and working as expected. A task concept has two properties including Id and Type. Type refers to specific constitutions of the management system. Task types are monitoring and measurement, internal audit, management review, nonconformity and corrective action, and continual improvement.

The first type of task is the monitoring and measurement, a mandatory requirement for an organisation to evaluates the information security performance and the effectiveness of the ISMS. An example is to monitor the treatment controls identified in the risk management and evaluate their effectiveness with the expected target. This activity could be automated using tools or physically observe and measure the effectiveness of such treatment control. A role for performing monitoring and measurement and an interval for measuring and effectiveness should be identified. A person responsible for evaluating the results of monitoring and measurement should be identified.

The second type is the internal audit, a mandatory requirement of the management system to ensures that the organisation conforms to the requirements of the standard and own requirements for its ISMS. Internal audit should be carried out at a planned interval. The organisation should develop an audit programme, including the frequency, methods, and responsibilities for delivering the audit. Suitable auditors should be identified and the results of the internal audit to be reported to the relevant management.

The third type is the management review, a mandatory requirement for the top management to review and assess the outcome of the management system at an interval period. The management review should consider the status of the previous management reviews, feedback from actors, results of the internal audit, and monitoring and measurements. The outcome of the management review should include decisions related to continual improvement and any need for changes to the ISMS should be noted.

The fourth type is the non-conformity and corrective action, it is a task to model the cause of the non-conformities and identify the root causes. It is a mandatory requirement for an organisation to implement necessary corrective actions against the cause of the non-conformities.

The last type of task is the continual improvement, a task that requires an organisation developing ISMS to improve the suitability, adequacy and effectiveness of the ISMS.

VI. Conclusion

The work proposed in this paper extends existing research efforts in security requirements engineering, building upon concepts from software engineering and deliver a language to coherently model and capture the requirements of an information security management system.

In this paper, we focus on bridging the gap in requirements engineering with information security management system. The intention is to align the development of secure systems in organisations towards the requirements of the standard. We presented a model-driven approach to employ a number of requirements engineering concepts to holistically manage the requirements of the standard under four inter-related components. The work goes beyond the aim of the research in relation to the security requirements engineering and it contributes in understanding the key concepts in successfully preparing and applying the ISMS and how it can be developed as a process to address the specific needs of the normative standards like ISO/IEC 27001 standard.

Further research to enhance all four components and expand a series of complete processes to work along with the concepts of the language is required. In future investigations, our proposed risk methodology will be evolved as well as the introduction of new attributes to the task concept.

The present paper was limited by the absence of an assessment example to better understand the effectiveness of our research, however, our model-based language is currently under evaluation by applying our approach to a UK health insurance provider aiming to comply with the ISO/IEC 27001 standard. The preliminary feedback suggests that our approach has been successful in capturing the requirements of the standard and the experimentation from the top management has shown positive results in understanding the importance of the ISMS for the establishment. This has given confidence to the organisation that the implementation of the ISMS through a structured process would enhance operational excellence and reduce liabilities.

References

[1] T. D. Breaux and A. I. Anton, "Analyzing regulatory rules for privacy and security requirements," IEEE Transactions on Software Engineering, vol. 34, no. 1, 2008, pp. 5–20.

[2] E. Targett, "6 months, 945 data breaches, 4.5 billion records," 2018. [Online]. Available: https://www.cbronline.com/news/global-data-breaches-2018

[3] Breach Level Index, "Data breach database," 2018. [Online]. Available: https://breachlevelindex.com/data-breach-database

[4] S. Moore, "Gartner Says Worldwide Information Security Spending Will Grow 7 Percent to Reach $86.4 Billion in 2017," 2017. [Online]. Available: https://www.gartner.com/newsroom/id/3784965

[5] ISO, "ISO/IEC 27001 Information security management." [Online]. Available: https://www.iso.org/isoiec-27001-information-security.html

[6] ISO, "The ISO survey of management system standard certifications 2017," International Organisation for Standardisation, Tech. Rep., 2017.

[7] IT Governance, "ISO 27001 global report," IT Governance, Tech. Rep., 2016.

[8] B. Von Solms, "Information Security governance: COBIT or ISO 17799 or both?" Computers and Security, vol. 24, no. 2, 2005, pp. 99–104.

[9] E. Coles-Kemp, "The anatomy of an information security management system," Ph.D. dissertation, King's College London, 2008.

[10] E. W. Bernroider and M. Ivanov, "IT project management control and the Control Objectives for IT and related Technology (CobiT) framework," International Journal of Project Management, vol. 29, no. 3, 2011, pp. 325–336.

[11] N. Mayer, "Model-based management of information system security risk," Ph.D. dissertation, University of Namur, 2008.

[12] N. Mayer, "A cluster approach to security improvement according to ISO/IEC 27001," in 17th European Systems & Software Process Improvement and Innovation Conference (EUROSPI'10), Grenoble, France, 2010.

[13] K. Beckers, I. Cote, S. Faßbender, M. Heisel, and S. Hofbauer, "A pattern-based method for establishing a cloud-specific information security management system," Requirements Engineering, vol. 18, no. 4, 2013, pp. 343–395.

[14] K. Beckers, M. Heisel, I. Côté, L. Goeke, and S. Güler, "Structured pattern-based security requirements elicitation for clouds," Proceedings - 2013 International Conference on Availability, Reliability and Security, ARES 2013, 2013, pp. 465–474.

[15] K. Beckers, M. Heisel, B. Solhaug, and K. Stolen, "ISMS-CORAS : a structured method for establishing an ISO 27001 compliant information security management system," Sintef, Tech. Rep., 2013.

[16] K. Beckers, "Supporting iso 27001 establishment with CORAS," Pattern and Security Requirements: Engineering-Based Establishment of Security Standards, 2015, pp. 1–474.

[17] H. Susanto, M. N. Almunawar, and Y. C. Tuan, "Information security challenge and breaches : novelty approach on measuring ISO 27001 readiness level," International Journal of Engineering and Technology, vol. 2, no. 1, 2012, pp. 67–75.

[18] H. Susanto, M. N. Almunawar, Y. C. Tuan, and M. S. Aksoy, "I-Solframework: an integrated solution framework six layers assessment on ultimedia information security architecture policy compliance," International Journal of Electrical & Computer Sciences IJECS-IJENS, vol. 12, no. 01, 2012, pp. 20–28.

[19] H. Mouratidis and P. Giorgini, "Secure Tropos: a Security-Oriented Extension of the Tropos Methodology," International Journal of Software Engineering and Knowledge Engineering, vol. 17, no. 02, 2007, pp. 285–309.

Improving Software Quality and Reliability Through Analysing Sets of System Test Defects

Vincent Sinclair
Bell Labs Software and Systems Reliability
Dublin, Ireland
e-mail: vincent.sinclair@nokia-bell-labs.com

Abstract — **Telecommunications networks support many critical services, leading users to demand very high levels of quality and reliability from these networks. The quality and reliability of these services is mainly dependent on the network's software. At the same time, competition is driving the demand for new software features in short delivery cycles. There are many challenges to delivering high quality, highly reliable software in these short cycles. Overcoming these challenges requires fast feedback to the development processes to minimize the number of escaped defects. This fast feedback can be achieved through the systematic analysis of system test defects. This method contrasts with the typical practice of analysing customer found defects. This improved method analyses each system test defect as it is fixed and stores this data. A set of defect data is then analysed to identify the most common defect type and where they are injected. This enables teams to focus improvement efforts on their largest source of defects. By automating this method, teams can continually fine tune their development processes to minimise the number of escaped defects. This results in a steady improvement over time in the quality and reliability of the software.**

Keywords - software reliability; software quality; availability; defect analysis; continuous improvement.

I. Introduction

Today's communications networks enable critical services, such as e-health, video doctors, mobile banking and remote security. Given the importance of such services, customers are demanding high reliability from their network providers to ensure these services are available anywhere and at any time. Future networks will support driverless cars and robotic surgery, requiring even higher levels of reliability. The quality and reliability of these services is highly dependent on the quality and reliability of the underlying communications software. This software is very complex and hence intrinsically prone to failure [1]. The challenge for communications network suppliers is to deliver these complex software systems with high quality and high reliability, while at the same time delivering new functionality in short delivery cycles.

This paper describes a new method for the analysis of software defects to enable teams to quickly learn from escaped defects. Section II describes the challenges. Sections III and IV describe the solution and its automation. Section V outlines the proposed future evolution of the system.

II. Key Challenges

Network software suppliers face several challenges to delivering high quality, high reliability software. Large development organizations typically work in complex, multi-site, multi-time zone and multi-language teams. This environment raises many challenges to close communication and collaboration, a key enabler of high quality and high reliability software. Large teams usually have a very wide range of knowledge and skill levels, from highly experienced engineers to junior engineers. This results in teams with dissimilar defect patterns and hence different improvement priorities. Each team needs to drive its own improvement priorities. A common top down approach across different teams is not as effective. The development processes, tools, organisational structures, as well as roles and responsibilities regularly change, disrupting development activities.

The software solution is typically a combination of application, platform, third party and open source software, leading to very complex software interactions. This can lead to unforeseen quality and reliability challenges. Time pressures on an already stretched team leaves very limited time to implement improvements. Driven by end users, network operators are demanding faster deliveries of new features and functionality. This leaves less time for testing out defects at system or solution level testing.

The above challenges to large-scale development lead to defects escaping to system test and customers. Our challenge is how to quickly learn from these escaped defects. Review of current defect analysis methods shows that they tend to focus on technical aspects of the individual defects. The resulting actions focus on preventing the same defect from escaping in future through the addition of test cases. Previous studies on root cause analysis tend to focus on identifying the types of defect but not on where they should have been detected [4]. By collecting and analysing characteristic data on system test defects, we can identify the most common defect type and where they could have been detected. From this, we can identify the optimum improvement action(s) to give the largest reduction in escaped defects.

III. Solution

We will outline current analysis methods, compare these with our method and describe the key advantages of our improved method. Particular focus is put on the ability of the improved method to provide fast feedback to development.

A. *Current method*

The typical approach to root cause analysis of software defects is to focus on customer found defects. This results in relatively slow feedback to development. The analysis tends to focus on individual defects, with the resulting improvement focusing on the technical cause of the defect. Where the analysis looks at processes, it tends to focus on the superficial cause of the defect rather than the fundamental cause(s) of the defect and how the defect escaped [2][5].

B. *Learning cycle*

Key to addressing the wide variety of challenges listed in section two is a learning cycle which provides fast feedback to the development teams through analysing system test defects. The approach must ensure that developers identify and record the fundamental cause of each defect at the organisational and process level. The system can then identify the most common defect type through analysing sets of defect data, highlighting which improvement will give the biggest reduction in escaped defects. The system must also measure the percentage of actual defect reduction to ensure the improvements implemented have been effective. Using this approach, teams can continually learn from their escaped defects. This learning cycle is outlined in Figure 1.

C. *Improved method*

The innovation is the real time classification and analysis of sets of system test defects. This method is built on the idea that sets of defects have small but definite patterns or signatures [3]. The steps in the method are:

- Classify each system test defect at the time the defect is fixed, when all of the information about the defect is fresh in the mind of the developer. The developer selects from drop down menus the type of defect and the development phase where it should have been detected. This data is recorded in the defect management tool and is mandatory to move the defect to the next phase of the defect life cycle.
- Select a specific set of defects for analysis. This could be at a team level, a component/sub-system level or at the level of a complete product.
- Extract the data from the defect management tool.
- Apply decision tree techniques to determine the most common defect type and in what phase of development they should have been detected.
- Based on the most common defect type and where they should be detected, quality experts perform a deep dive analysis to identify the fundamental changes that will reduce this specific defect type.
- Measure the impact of the improvement action(s) to quantify the reduction in the specific defect type.

D. *Advantages of the method*

Analysing system test defects provides much faster feedback to the development teams, compared to analysing customer found defects. Characterising each defect at the time it is fixed by a developer is easy and quick, as the developers have all the defect details fresh in their mind. Classifying the defect in the management system facilitates easy and accurate data labelling. Using drop down menus to classify each defect guides the developer towards the real root cause. Using drop down menus to classify the defects also provides data standardisation, facilitating easy and accurate clustering. By applying clustering techniques within a set of defects, teams can identify the most common type of defect within the set and the source of these defects. Empirical experience shows that a set of fifty defects provides sufficient data to identify the most common type of defect. A deep dive analysis on the most common defect type will identify fundamental changes to the organisation that will systematically prevent a whole class of defects escaping from development. These are typically fundamental improvements in communications and collaboration, changes in roles and responsibilities as well as improvements in processes, tools, templates and checklists. Each team can analyse their own defects to help them identify improvements relevant to their team. This devolves accountability for quality down to team level. Teams can also focus on improvements in specific areas of the software to strengthen weaker components. Automation enables the method to be applied regularly, with sustained defect reduction over time.

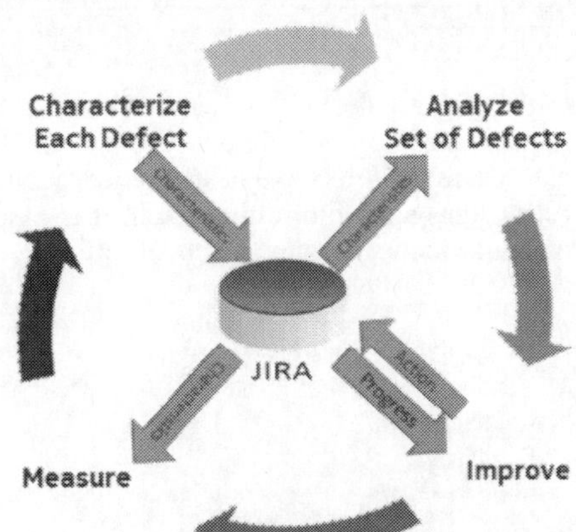

Figure 1. Learning Cycle.

E. *Testing the method*

Over a period of nine months, the improved method was tested with one product unit of seventy people, distributed across three continents and spanning systems engineering to system validation. The data processing and visualization were performed manually. The analysis identified the need for improvements in the areas of requirements gathering and communication, including detailed customer use cases, interface interoperability, corner cases, error cases and failure modes. For design, it identified improvements needed during design reviews, including communications tools and improved checklists to assure critical points were not missed. For the coding phase, it identified improvements in unit test, including additional rainy day/negative testing. At system validation, it identified the need for increased robustness testing as well as quality assurance of third-party software.

The parameter for evaluating the method is the number of escaped defects. Over the nine-month pilot period, these fundamental improvements resulted in a greater than 50% reduction in defects escaping to customers.

IV. AUTOMATING THE METHOD

A critical aspect related to the deployment of this method is the automation of the process, integrating the data collection, analysis and presentation of results into an organization's existing tool set.

A. Advantages

Automation of the method makes it fast and easy for teams to regularly analyse their own defects at any time. They can, for example, analyse the defects from the past four weeks to identify the most common defect type occurring today. This fast feedback enables teams to regularly fine tune their development and testing processes.

B. Web application

A cloud-based Web application was developed, which connects to the company's defect management systems. The application allows users to select a specific set of defects, extracts the defect classification data, performs data pre-processing and data analytics and finally visualises the results.

A typical defect pattern is shown in Figure 2. For this set of defects, the most common defect type is coding error. The next most common defect types are requirement gaps and high-level design gaps. From this graph, it is evident where the team should focus their improvement efforts.

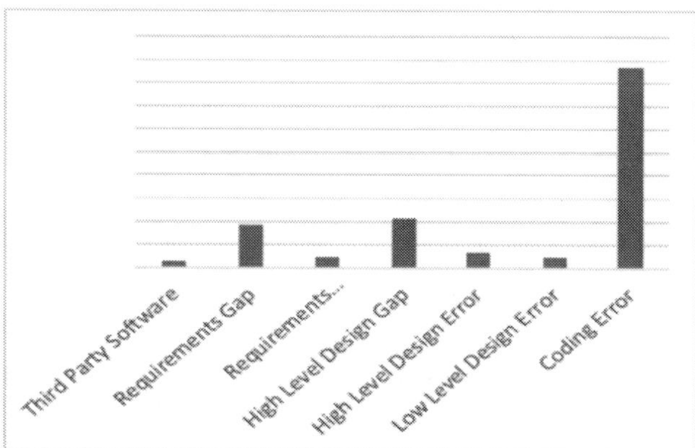

Figure 2. Defect Types – Set of 200 defects.

C. Scaling the adoption of the method

The application has been made available to all teams through the Nokia corporate cloud, enabling a wide variety of teams to test the usability of the application. This will also encourage an even stronger culture of learning from sets of defects to identify the most common defect type and trigger actions to prevent similar defects in future. Automation will also encourage a mindset of regular improvements to continually fine tune the development activity.

V. EXTENDING THE APPLICATION

A number of additional capabilities are planned for future releases.

Based on multiple factors, a weighting engine will quantify the impact of each defect. For example, a defect which causes a network outage or affects live traffic has more impact than a defect that does not affect live traffic. These weighted values will be used to rank the improvement priorities. A recommendations engine will use data analytics and machine learning techniques to automatically select the optimum improvement actions from a knowledge base of known effective solutions for specific defect type/phase combinations. This knowledge base will evolve over time based on the evaluation of the effectiveness of specific improvement actions. The system will include automated tracking of defect trends over time to measure the impact of specific improvement actions.

VI. CONCLUSION

This method has been shown to be effective in reducing escaped defects, resulting in improved software quality and reliability. A key enabler to widespread deployment of the improved method is the Web application, which enables teams to regularly analyse their own escaped software defects. Future releases will build on the current system to add further machine learning and artificial intelligence techniques to automatically recommend the most effective improvement actions. Machine learning techniques will also be used to optimise over time the knowledge base of known solutions for specific defect types. Results will be presented in a future paper.

REFERENCES

[1] R. I. Cook, "'How complex systems fail," Cognitive Technologies Laboratory, University of Chicago IL [Online]. Available:https://www.researchgate.net/publication/228797158_How_complex_systems_fail. [Accessed: Jan. 30, 2019].

[2] A. C. Edmondson, "'Strategies for learning from failure," Harv.Bus.Rev., vol. 89, no. 4, pp. 48-55, April 2011.

[3] M. Syed, "'Black Box Thinking: Why Most People Never Learn from Their Mistakes--But Some Do", November 2015.

[4] Timo O.A. Lehtinen, "What Are Problem Causes of Software Projects?, International Symposium on Empirical Software Engineering and Measurement, September 2011.

[5] Harsh Lal, "Root cause analysis of software bugs using machine learning techniques", International Conference on Cloud Computing, Data Science and Engineering, January 2017.

An Approach to Testing Software on Networked Transport Robots

Ichiro Satoh

National Institute of Informatics
2-1-2 Hitotsubashi Chiyoda-ku Tokyo 101-8430 Japan
Email: ichiro@nii.ac.jp

Abstract—**Networked transport robots have been widely used to carry products in manufacturing and warehousing spaces. Such robots communicate with servers in the spaces and other robots through wireless local-area networks. Therefore, software running on such robots is executed with the services that the robots are connected to through networks, including multicast protocols. To test such software, we need to execute it within the network domains of the locations that the robots may move and connect to because the correctness of the software depends on the services. To solve this problem, we present a framework for emulating the physical mobility of transport robots by using the logical mobility of software designed to run on computers. It enables such software to run within target network domains so that the software can locally access servers and receive multicast packets limited to the domains.**

Keywords–Software testing; Wireless communication; Protocol; Mobile agent.

I. INTRODUCTION

Many manufacturers and warehousers have been using automated vehicles, called *transport robots*, to undertake repetitive transport tasks inside their facilities. Modern transport robots for warehousing and manufacturing spaces have become smart and exchange information on dynamic demands and environmental changes in their target spaces with stationary servers and other robots. They then should adapt themselves according to the received information. Thus, robotics software plays a key role as it is the medium through which their autonomy and adaptation are embodied. One problem is that the complexity of their software is far greater than conventional transport robots. For example, these robots are networked with stationary servers to exchange information with other robots via wireless networking, e.g., Wi-Fi. Furthermore, networking for transport robots in large warehousing and manufacturing spaces results in another serious problem in testing software for transport robots in the sense that these robots frequently connect or disconnect to multiple network domains, which may be smaller than target warehousing and manufacturing spaces, while they move in such spaces.

In addition, not only the hardware of such transport robots but also their software tend to be complicated. In fact, software plays a key role in robotics as it is the medium by which machines are made smart and adaptive. Software testing is a popular methodology for finding information on the quality of a software product or service by executing software intent on finding its own problems, e.g., bugs, errors, or other defects. Test-driven development is an evolutionary approach to development that combines test-first development in which you write a test before you write just enough production code to fulfill that test and refactoring.

The development and testing software for such robots is more difficult than that for conventional systems. This is because, typically, software for robots need to make robots reactive, concurrent, embedded, real-time, and data intensive. Most transport robots tend to communicate with stationary servers. Therefore, they are networked in order to exchange a variety of information with stationary servers and other robots via wireless networking. As a result, when a transport robot moves between locations, it may lose connectivity to a network domain provided on the previous location and then gain connectivity at another network domain provided on the current location. The software for running the robot can no longer connect to the servers provided in only the former domain, only those in the latter domain. To verify the correctness of software for networked transport robots, developers need to test software with all servers in the areas that their robots may visit through the robots' itineraries. However, it is difficult for developers to actually move real robots between locations in facilities that are used for business.

The purpose of this paper is to present a framework for testing software designed to run on transport robots. The framework is based on an early approach presented in one of our past papers [11], in which the approach supported testing software to be running on mobile computers by using the movement of emulators used for mobile computers. Since a manufacturing company asked us to develop a method to test software designed to run on transport robots, we extended the past approach with the ability to test moving robots to solve the company's problems. One reason is that mobile computers, which the past approach focused on, do not move between locations under their own control, but transport robots themselves move between locations. The past approach also assumed that the coverage areas of wireless networks to which mobile computers connected did not overlap, but in small spaces for warehousing and manufacturing, network domains supported through wireless networks may not be separated. The approach was aimed at testing client-side software running on mobile computers but server-side software often runs on transport robots. Therefore, although the framework presented in this paper is constructed on the basis of the basic concept of the past approach, it is extended with several abilities to test software running on transport robots.

We do not intend the framework to be general. The framework is aimed at testing networked software, which should be application-level in the sense that it does not directly access low-level hardware. Conversely, any lower-level software, e.g., OS and device drivers, including software for directly monitoring and controlling sensors and actuators is not within the scope of the framework. The framework proposed in this paper is an extension of our two early frameworks [11][13]. The first enables software designed to run on portable computers to directly connect to network domains in the sense that the software could send and receive packets reachable within the domains, but it does not support the movement of robots. The second was designed for testing software running on robots but lacks any mechanisms for emulating networking, e.g., changing Internet Protocol (IP) addresses, when robots move between two coverage areas of IP-enabled wireless networks.

The remainder of this paper is organized as follows. In Section 2 we discuss an example scenario. Section 3 presents the design and implementation of the proposed framework. Section 4 shows demonstrates the usage of the framework through an example and discuss software testing with the framework. Section 5 surveys related work and Section 6 provides a summary.

II. Example Scenario

As mentioned in the previous section, our framework was inspired by practical problems discussed in our research collaboration with a manufacturing company. The company's factory is shared by the company itself and its subsidiary companies. They use modern transport robots to carry products between the areas managed and operated by them, where each of the areas provides its own wireless local-area network for communicating with transport robots running within it and local services provided only in the network. Transport robots move from area to area in the factory along their itineraries as shown in Fig. 1, where the coverage area of each wireless network access point is smaller than the target manufacturing spaces. Each network area has one or more local servers available. A service discovery mechanism in each area periodically multicasts User Datagram Protocol (UDP) packets within the network domain of the areas to avoid congestion due to the multicasting of packets.

- When a robot arrives at a new area in the factory, it can receive multicasted UDP packets issued from a service discovery mechanism, e.g., Universal Plug and Play (UPnP), in the current area and learn the network address of the mechanism's directory server.
- The robot connects to the server and then informs its own addresses to the server.
- When the robot leaves the area, it can no longer connect to the servers that it connected to in the area and it also cannot receive any UDP packets issued from the area's service discovery mechanism.

Networked software running on transport robots can be classified into two kinds, i.e., client-side and server-side software, independently of the transmission protocol, e.g., Transmission Control Protocol (TCP) and UDP. To test client-side software for the discovery mechanism on a transport robot, the software needs to be executed within each of the network domains of the areas that the target robot may visit because multicasted UDP packets for the mechanism can be reached within the individual domains. When a transport robot discovers available services within its current network domain one the server-side, its software also needs to be executed to multicast UDP packets so that discover other robots or stationary servers within each of the network domains of the areas that the target robot may visit.

Some readers may think that even when the target software runs outside the areas, it can receive multicasted UDP packets via a tunneling technique. That is, we forward these packets from a target area to a computer that runs the software. However, there are firewalls in networks for reasons of security, and the cost of forwarding often affects time constraints in protocols, e.g., timeouts.

III. Design and Implementation

Developers are required to test their target software within each of the areas that their target robots may visit. However, it is difficult for developers to actually move or carry robots between areas and connect them to networks in a running factory. Our proposed testing framework is used to deploy and execute software that is designed to run on transport robots that change their current networks as they move. This framework has two key ideas. The first is to provide a target software with software-level-emulated execution environment in which the software should run. The second is to provide the software with an emulation of the physical mobility of a robot by using the software's logical mobility, which has been designed to run on robots over various networks. Physical mobility entails the movement and reconnection of mobile computing devices between sub-networks, while logical mobility involves software that migrates between hosts on sub-networks. The above emulator enables the target software to be execute within the emulation of a target robot and to directly connect to the external environment, such as the resources and servers provided in the networks that a robot connects to.

- The first is to use host-level virtual machines, e.g., VMWare and Hyper-V, and migrate the target software and operating systems from a virtual machine host to another host by using a technique, called *live migration*. The technique enables virtual machines to migrate to other machines to emulate the disconnection/reconnection of transport robots to networks within which multicast packets for plug-and-play protocols are transmitted to servers, stationary embedded computers, and other mobile or stationary robots.
- The second is to introduce an emulator for testing software with plug-and-play protocols running on language-level virtual machines, e.g., a Java virtual machine called *JVM*. The emulator can carry the target software between hosts by using a mobile agent technology. This is useful for testing application-level or middleware-level software.

The current implementation is based on the latter because the former needs high-speed networked storage systems, e.g., a Storage Area Network (SAN), which are expensive and used in data-centers rather than warehousing and manufacturing spaces. Our target software is also Java-based software to communicate with stationary servers through TCP, UDP, or upper layer protocols. Each emulator provides the target software with not only the internal environment of its own target robot but also the external environment, such as the resources and servers provided in the networks that the robot connects to. Our final goal is to emulate the reconnection of networked robots to networks managed by multicast-based management protocols by using virtual machine migration. In this paper we explain our approach on the basis of the second, i.e., mobile agent-based emulator, because the first and second are common and

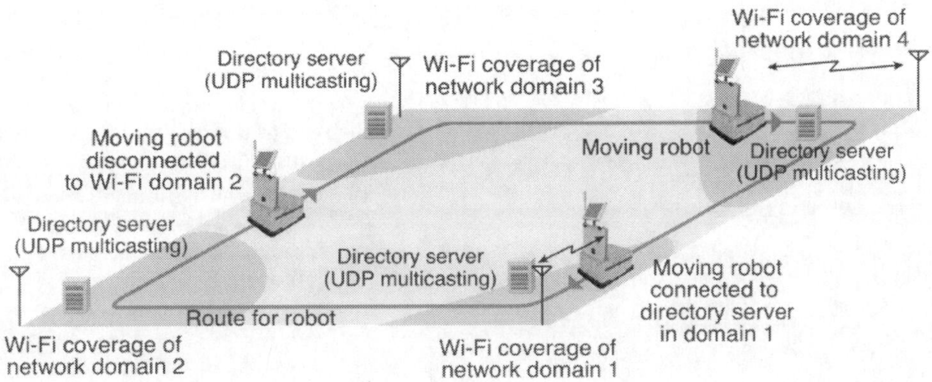

Figure 1. Transport robot with WiFi in a factory

it is simpler to implement the second than the first. Physical mobility entails the reconnection of a robot to a network, while logical mobility involves a mobile agent-based emulator of a robot.

- Like virtual machines, this framework emulates its target robot.
- Depending on the reconnection of its target robot, the mobile agent-based emulator can carry software that should run on the computer on behalf of the robot to networks that the robot may be moved into and connected to.
- The emulator allows us to test and debug software with computational resources provided through its current network as if the software were being executed on the target robot when dynamically attached to the network.
- Software successfully tested in the emulator can still be run in the same way without being modified or recompiled.

Each mobile agent is just a logical entity and must thus be executed on a computer. Therefore, this framework assumes that each of the sub-networks to which a device may be moved and attached to has more than one special stationary host, called an *access point host*, which offers a runtime system for executing and migrating mobile agent-based emulators. Each access point host is a runtime environment for allowing applications running in a visiting emulator to connect to local servers in its network. That is, the physical movement of a mobile computing device from one network and attachment to another is simulated by the logical mobility of a mobile agent-based emulator that carries the target applications from an access-point computer in the source network to another access-point computer in the destination network. As a result, each emulator is a mobile agent, and can thus basically not only carry the codes but also the states of the applications to the destination, so the carried applications can basically continue their processes after arriving at another host as if they had been moved with the target device.

The emulator delegates instruction-level emulation of target robots to JVM. In fact, each emulator permits its inner software to have access to the standard classes commonly supported by the JVM as long as the target robot offers them. The upper of Fig. 2 shows the physical mobility of robots and the lower of Fig. 2 shows the logical mobility of emulators.

In addition, each emulator offers its inner software as typical resources of the target robots. It can maintain a database to store files. Each file can be stored in the database as a pair consisting of a file/directory path name pattern and a content and provides its target software with basic primitives for file operation, e.g., file creation, reading, writing, and deletion. The framework provides the target software with two states in the lifecycle of the software running on the target robot, *networked running state* and *isolated running state:*. The former enables the target software to run within the target network domains, can link up with servers on the network through TCP and UDP and can send/receive UDP multicast packets. This state emulates that the robot is within the coverage area of one of the network domains provided through wireless networks. The latter runs the software but prohibits the software from communicating with any servers on the network. This state emulates a situation in which a robot is out any coverage areas of the network domains.

The framework provides an original runtime system for emulators by extending our existing mobile agent platform [12]. When an emulator with its target software is transferred over a network, the runtime system transforms the state and code of the agent, including its software, into a bitstream defined by Java's JAR file format, which can support digital signatures for authentication and transmit the bitstream to the destination host. Mobile agent-based implementation of the framework assumes that the target software is constructed as a set of Java bytecode, although its virtual machine-based implementation can support other software. Each emulator allows its target software to access most network resources from the host, e.g., the `java.net` package.

As mentioned in the first section, in an earlier version of this framework the target software must be client-side when communicating through TCP. The current implementation of this framework dynamically inserts a packet forwarding mechanism like Mobile IP [9] into the `java.net` package by using a bytecode level modification technique [1] when classes for TCP servers, e.g., `ServerSocket` and `InetAddress`, of `java.net`, are invoked from the target software. When wireless network domains overlap, robots may have more than one IP address. Our modified classes for IP addresses, e.g.,

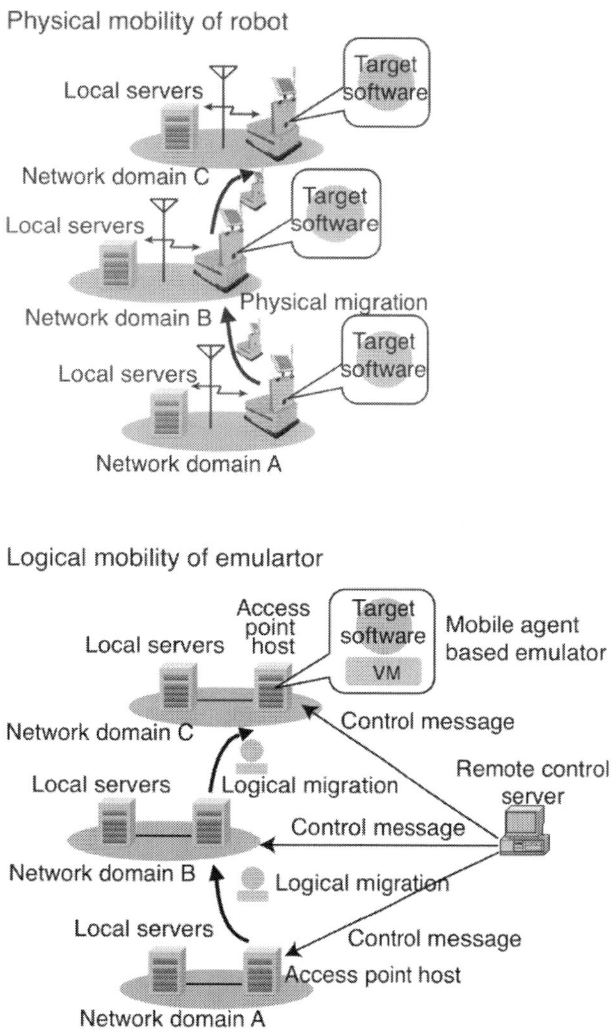

Figure 2. Physical mobility of robot (left) and logical mobility of emulator (right)

InetAddress, can return an IP address explicitly specified from developers.

IV. Experience

To illustrate the utility of the framework, in this section we present our experience with testing two typical kinds of software for networked transport robots.

A. *Testing software for transport robots*

In developing modern transport robots, we need to test transport robots with WiFi interfaces, which tend to be used in factories or warehouses (Fig. 3). We had five requirements:

- Each networked transport robot has an embedded computer (Intel Core i5, 2-GHz) with Linux and a WiFi interface.
- The factory has eight areas, where each area has its own wireless local area network provided through WiFi and provides directory servers available within the coverage space of the WiFi.
- Each robot discovers directory servers by receiving advertisement messages with their network addresses periodically issued from them through a UDP multicast-based original service discovery protocol available within the WiFi area of its current location.
- Each robot periodically updates its location to other robots or stationary servers within its current area through a TCP/IP-based original service discovery protocol.
- The coverage areas of the WiFi access points may overlap, and there are some spaces beyond the coverage areas of the WiFi access points.

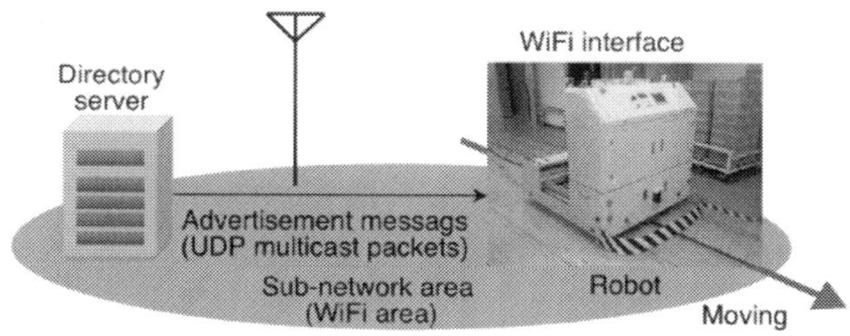

Figure 3. Communication between transport robot and directory server through WiFi

We tested two protocol stacks for the service discovery protocol through UDP multicast and session protocols between robots and directory servers by using the proposed framework. These protocols were constructed in Java so that we could directly use a mobile agent-based emulator based on JVM. To test the protocol stacks running on the client-side, i.e., robots, we customized a mobile agent-based emulator for the target robots. The emulator provided virtual I/O to control the movement of a robot for its target software, but it carried the software to a host within the target areas and enabled the software to receive UDP multicast packets, which were reachable within the area, and directly connected to the servers.

The developer could instruct the emulator to migrate to access-point hosts on the sub-networks of other areas. Also, since the emulator could define its own itinerary in the areas, it could precisely trace the movement of each robot. It could carry the target software, including the protocol stacks, to access-point hosts in the areas. It could continue to run the software in the local area network and permitted the software to directly receive UDP multicast packets, which servers only transmitted within the domains of the local area networks. We measured the processing overhead of the emulator, but the performance of software running in an emulator on an access-point host was not inferior to that of the same software running on the target robot, as long as the processing capability of the host was equivalent to that of the robot.

B. *Discussion*

While it was impossible to measure the framework's benefits quantitatively, it could eliminate the task of the developer having to carry and connect his/her target robot to local-area networks to verify whether software designed to run on the robot can successfully coordinate with servers or other robots. Let us now compare the framework with the other two existing approaches.

a) Comparison with field testing approach: This approach involves the developer carrying computers running the emulator of a target robot and testing the target software in the emulator within the local-area network at the current location. The developer can stay in front of his/her computer and directly view and operate the graphical user interface of a map viewer application on the computer. Like our framework, this approach permits the target software to receive packets that the location information servers multicast within the current local-area network because the software is running within the domain of the local-area. However, the developer carries the computer between places simply to check whether or not the software runs properly. This task is extremely cumbersome for the developer. Our framework, however, can replace the physical mobility of the developer with the logical mobility of an emulator of the robot and it thus enables the software to run and link up with servers within the local-area network.

b) Comparison with network-enabled emulator approach: A few emulators enable software to run on a local computer and link up with location information servers on target networks that their target devices may connect to through networks. Such existing emulators cannot send and receive packets beyond security mechanisms, e.g., firewalls. The cost of the approach is also inevitable in the sense that it often makes heavy traffics in networks, because packets transmitted only within the local-area networks at the location of a target robot tend to be much. The approach resulted in increased latency and network traffic in communication between the target application and servers, unlike ours, because the application in an emulator had to remotely communicate with the servers via routers and gateways, whereas the target robot could be directly connected to the servers. This is a serious problem in testing applications in gathering a large volume of data from servers, and vice versa.

V. Related Work

There have been many commercial and academic frameworks for simulating the target robots in virtual environments and for testing software for the robots in the environments. As far as we know, there is no paper on enabling software to be tested with networked environments that target robots may connect to.

Nevertheless, we discuss several existing approaches to testing software for robots. SITAF [14] is a framework for testing robot components by simulating environment. It generates test cases on the basis of specifications given by the developer. This test generation combined with simulation allows tests to be repeated. It also discards the need oto reuse tests, since they are generated. Biggs [3] presented testing software by using a repeatable regression testing method for software components that interact with hardware, but his approach focused only on individual components rather than whole robots. Among them, Chung et al. [5] showed experiments on applying International Organization for Standardization (ISO) for software testing (ISO 9126) to components for academic robotics. Laval et al. [7] proposed an approach to enabling the testing of not only isolated components but also whole robots. Their approach assumed standalone robots, so they did not support software for networked robots. Paikan et al. [8] proposed a generic framework for test driven development of robotic systems. It enabled functionalities to be tested but did not support any networking. Chen et al. [4] and Petters et al. [10] inserted an extra step in hybrid tests between simulation and tests based on three levels: component-level tests, online-level test with humans, and offline test (based on logs). Son et al. [15] proposed another three levels of tests: unit testing, state testing and API testing. However, their approaches did not support networked software running on robots. Laval et al. [7] proposed a safe-by-construction architecture based on a formal method instead of any testing approaches.

Reconnection and disconnection resulting from the movement of robots are similar to that when carrying portable computers, e.g., notebook PCs, tablets, and smartphones. There have been several attempts at testing software designed to run on portable computers. [2][6][16]. A typical problem in physical mobility is that the environment of a mobile entity can vary dynamically as the entity moves from one network to another.

VI. Conclusion

In this paper, we presented a framework for testing software running on networked transport robots, e.g., transport robots. The goal of the framework is to enable us to test networked software that reconnects and disconnects to the networks of the robots' destinations according the movement of the robots. It can emulate the physical mobility of target robots and enables software to directly connect to the networks of destinations in addition to the internal execution environment of the robots. Since our emulators were provided as mobile agents, which can travel between computers under their own control, they could carry and test software designed to run on their target robots in the same way as if they had been moved with the robots on which they were executed, and connected to services within their current local area networks. Our early experience with the prototype implementation of this framework strongly suggested that the framework could greatly reduce the time needed to develop and test software for networked industrial computers.

References

[1] Apache Software Foundation: "Byte Code Engineering Library," `http://jakarta.apache.org/bcel/`, October 2001.

[2] K. Beck: "Test Driven Development: By Example," Addison Wesley, November 2003.

[3] G. Biggs: "Applying regression testing to software for robot hardware interaction," In Proceedings of IEEE International Conference on Robotics and Automation (ICRA'2010), pp. 4621-4626, May 2010.

[4] I. Y. Chen, B. A. MacDonald, and B. C. Wunsche: "A flexible mixed reality simulation framework for software development in robotics," Journal of Software Engineering for Robotics, No.2, Vol.1, pp. 40-54, September 2011.

[5] Y. K. Chung and S. M. Hwang: "Software testing for intelligent robots," In Proceedings of International Conference on Control, Automation and Systems, pp. 2344-2349, October 2007.

[6] D. Gelperin and B. Hetzel: "The Growth of Software Testing," Communications of the ACM, Vol. 31, No. 6, pp. 687-695, June 1988.

[7] J. Laval, L. Fabresse, and N. Bouraqadi: "A methodology for testing mobile autonomous robots," IEEE/RSJ International Conference on Intelligent Robots and Systems (IROS'2013), pp. 1842-1847, November 2013.

[8] A. Paikan, S. Traversaro, F. Nori, and L. Natale: "A Generic Testing Framework for Test Driven Development of Robotic Systems," International Workshop on Modelling and Simulation for Autonomous Systems (MESAS 2015), pp. 216-225, Lecture Notes in Computer Science, vol. 9055. Springer, April 2015.

[9] C. Perkins, "IP Mobility Support", Internet Request For Comments RFC 2002, October 1996.

[10] S. Petters, D. Thomas, M. Friedmann, and O. Von Stryk: "Multilevel testing of control software for teams of autonomous mobile robots," Simulation, Modeling, and Programming for Autonomous Robots, pp. 183-194, November 2008.

[11] I. Satoh: "A Testing Framework for Mobile Computing Software," IEEE Transaction on Software Engineering, Vol.29, No.12, pp. 1112-1121, December 2003.

[12] I. Satoh: "Mobile Agents," Handbook of Ambient Intelligence and Smart Environments, pp. 771-791, Springer, October 2010.

[13] I. Satoh: "Testing software for networked industrial systems," Proceedings of 39th Conference of IEEE Industrial Electronics Society (IECON'2013), IEEE Industrial Electronics Society, October 2013.

[14] H. Seong and J. Seok: "SITAF: simulation-based interface testing automation framework for robot software component," In Florian Kongoli, editor, Automation. InTech, July 2012.

[15] J. Son, T. Kuc, J. Park, and H. Kim: "Simulation based functional and performance evaluation of robot components and modules," In proceedings of International Conference on Information Science and Applications (ICISA'2011), pp. 1-7, May 2011.

[16] J. A. Whittaker: "What is Software Testing? And Why Is It So Hard?," IEEE Software, pp. 70-79, January 2000.

Challenges of Cost Estimation for Software Testing

Bernard Stepien, Liam Peyton
School of Engineering and Computer Science
University of Ottawa
Ottawa, Canada
Email: {bstepien | lpeyton}@uottawa.ca

Abstract—**Cost estimation for software testing is a complex process due to a great variety of testing strategies and factors to consider. In current practice, some of these are often overlooked. The subject has been well researched all the way back to the early stages of software development but always within the specific context of a single application. As a result, managers and researchers have created application-dependent solutions to the problem rather than general solutions. As a first step towards development of a general solution, we provide a summary of cost estimation for software testing using a taxonomy of testing strategies and factors.**

Keywords: software testing; cost estimation; taxomomy.

I. INTRODUCTION

Cost estimation for software testing is a complex process due to the difficulty in determining precisely the factors affecting costs. One of the most difficult tasks consists in separating adequately software development costs from software testing costs especially since they are inter-related. This is especially true when both tasks are performed by the same person, which is often the case.

Historically, cost estimation for software testing used macroeconomic models based on empirical studies and produced only approximate cost estimations. Unfortunately, one interesting characteristic of those models is that they only estimate the combined software development and testing cost without a clear indication on the cost share allocated specifically for testing. Boehm started it all with the Constructive Cost Model (COMOCO) [7] at a time when software development models themselves, such as structured programming, were being addressed. The concept of testing at that time was limited and based mostly on test plans for manual testing that would be approved by upper management without any quantitative evaluation of costs or benefits. They were based on a strong belief that there could be only a finite set of bugs in a piece of software and that most of the bugs could be caught in the early stages of testing. Later research based on automated test case generation proved the opposite mostly for state based software with unpredictable traversal of state transitions.

More recently, Holzmann [4] pointed out that no single system of metrics exists to measure costs or to measure benefits of testing. A major effort on understanding cost estimation for testing was achieved by the National Institute of Standards and Technology in an extensive report [3]. Hu et al. [2] came up with economic projection models to quantify testing results. Ellims et al. [8] studied the economics of unit testing and compared it to code reviews, which were a prevailing substitute to testing at the time. Tables showing the relative benefits of software testing and models for cost estimation were produced by Tawileh et al. in [5].

Application specific solutions came in the early '80s with the development of a test specification language for the telecommunication industry that was based on formal description techniques that was later extended by the European Telecommunications Standards Institute as Testing and Test Control Notation version 3 (TTCN-3) [11]. TTCN-3 is now used in many different domains in addition to telecommunications. It is particularly efficient when applied to testing applications that use parallelism intensively. Others addressed the testing of web application and started comparing the performance of the solutions in this domain [13].

Another interesting aspect of testing is the variety of metrics for testing without any clear preference or even understanding of their values. They include fault density, requirement compliance, test coverage and mean time to failure. As well, some, like in [3], differentiate between technical metrics and economic metrics. Also, the basic unit of measurement is traditionally the number of lines of code. This applies for both the actual piece of software being tested and the test software in case of test automation. For example, in one industry we worked in, there was a de facto standard that one would develop only 7 lines of codes per day including testing for a given project that comprised 3 million lines of code. In all the literature cited above, we have never found a concept of measuring the complexity of a piece of software that would make two different pieces of software with an equal number of lines radically different from a costing point of view both for development and testing. This results in biased comparisons and questionable precision of decisions.

Interesting is the fact that recent literature, Keshta in [9], attempts to summarize the research on software costing over a 30 years period but again without talking about testing.

The awareness of the difficulty of estimation for software testing costs is expressed by Wagner et al in [6]. They propose an approach that structures the factors of costs for an optimization of fault detection techniques. They also distinguish between minor and major faults and propose a priority system for handling them. In any case, the application of solution blurs the picture further due to the fact that faults detected and corrected in previous steps no longer exist in the subsequent stages. Ideally, one should start from scratch every time a new technique is applied. This is both unrealistic and no manager would approve a budget around such an approach. Finally, most studies are empirical rather than following a rigorous model as in [14].

II. THE REALITY OF TESTING STRATEGIES

Personal experience in industry has shown there is a great variety of testing strategies. A good collection of strategies, including the fundamental black box and white box testing strategy, can be found in [1] but with no associated costing theories other than the financial consequences of unsatisfied customers. Brill et al [12] decomposes the software development life cycle and proposes enhancements. A similar taxonomy can be found in [15].

A. *Testing and test personnel configurations*

1) Testing as a way to learn a software

Testing is performed by novices to learn how a piece of software functions. The tester is thus a temporary position towards the more glamorous position of software developer. One may discover that this approach increases testing costs, however, this is also a kind of training session for the same persons once they become developers, thus potentially reducing development costs afterwards, as shown on Figure 1. This is a typical case of tradeoff between the two complementary activities.

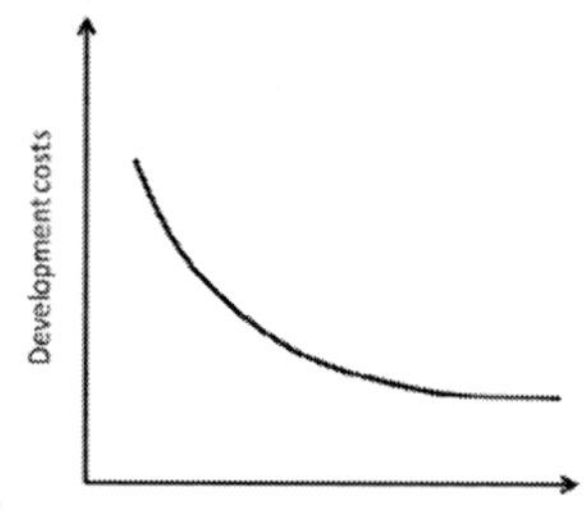

Figure 1. Relationship between development and testing costs

2) Developer is also tester

Testing is performed by the software developer. This approach has proven to be less efficient because the behavior of the developers involved has a tendency to be highly predictable. This results in always testing the same paths that they know and making all kinds of assumptions about their system. Whereas, an external tester, would try event sequences that the developer did not anticipate and uncover more bugs.

3) Independent team of testers approach

Testing is performed by an independent team devoted only to testing that develops test suites from the same requirements that the developers use. This approach has proven to be more efficient because it reveals the most unsuspected bugs. Testers are independent from developers and thus are not influenced by development activities and thus test unsuspected combinations of inputs. Also, from an economics perspective, testers were cheaper than developers since their activity was considered simpler than software development. However, this is not always true for testers who use sophisticated testing techniques, based on formal descriptions, with dedicated test specification languages, which require specialized knowledge and training.

4) Automated testing and test specification languages

When Object Oriented (OO) languages became common, software development languages were used as test specification languages to reduce testing costs mostly based on savings for personnel training costs and testing tools.

5) Reducing the number of programming languages

In the '80s, there was a proliferation of programming and test specification languages that required high training costs and recruitment difficulties that drove personnel costs up. This resulted in decisions to reduce considerably the number of programming languages for software development used in an organization especially in the light of the new object oriented approaches.

6) The software user is the tester

It is increasingly the fashion for widely publicly used software to use the end users as unsuspecting testers. By this, we mean the typical approach that consists upon a crash of the software when used by a user to ask the user if they want to report the problem. It is very economical for the software vendor but poses fundamental security problems since nobody knows nor controls the amount of user data that is sent to the software vendor. However, in a way, some of the testing cost is transferred to the end-user.

B. *The use of Testing tools and frameworks*

Some tools are application oriented while others are more general. However, the reality is that tools are often costly but reduce the cost of personnel because tools increase productivity as shown on Figure 2. Increased productivity results in a shallower total cost curve comprising cost of the tool and training the testers.

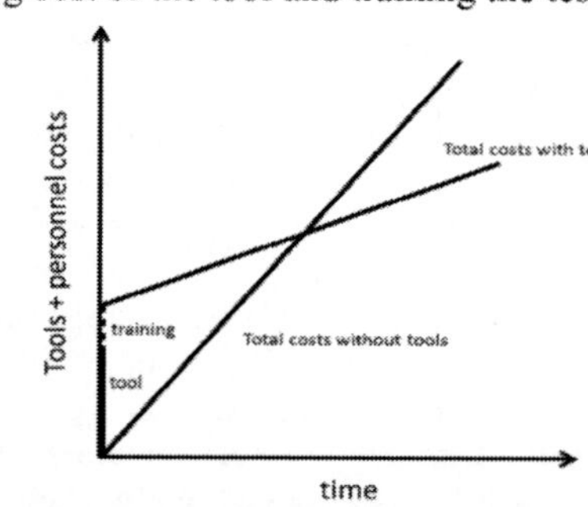

Figure 2. Testing cost savings when using tools

1) Manual testing

At the beginning, all tests were performed manually. This proved to be both expensive and difficult to reproduce especially in the case of personnel turn over. Thus, the concept of test automation using test software was introduced. These tests were either using General Programming Languages (GPL) or dedicated testing languages and later frameworks of all kinds.

2) Unit testing

Unit testing uses an open source framework (e.g. JUnit) that provides for ways of specifying the test as assertions on results from methods or functions. Unit testing consists mostly in testing applications functions or methods, one at a time and independently from each other. It verifies that given certain inputs, it correctly returns some specific output. It is an extension of traditional OO software testing languages and thus can be easily integrated in the software development process. Unit tests are developed first before software development itself. Initially all tests fail but as development progresses, tests pass. A special Graphical User Interface (GUI) that reports the failures or successes is provided by the framework, thus saving some test software reports development costs.

3) Application specificity of testing tools

Application specific tools are widely used for web application testing. Frameworks, such as Selenium, among others [13] feature the principle of record and replay based on the belief that the same input will always produce a unique result. In other words, there are no alternative software behavior considerations. This is mostly not the case and also test software is hard to maintain.

4) Automated test case generation

Test case generation derived from models, like finite state machines, can be very efficient if not running into state explosion problems. In this case, heuristics are used to choose a subset of test cases that would provide enough test coverage. Also, models allow testing the requirements themselves even before they are attempted to be implemented especially if they are specified in an executable language.

III. TAXONOMY OF TESTING COSTS

A. Categories of testing costs

There are many categories of testing cost:

- Tangible costs like the cost of manpower and equipment including testing tools to perform testing.
- Tangible costs of training personnel to a given testing technology.
- Intangible cost like traveling costs to the customer premises
- Intangible cost like loss of business due to lack of customer satisfaction.

However, it has been observed in industry that the cost of testing tools is considered as highly tangible while manpower to perform the tests is not in the sense that testing tools can be used only for a class of applications while manpower can be reassigned to other tasks or even projects, thus, not subject to a seemingly tangible loss.

B. Areas of difficulty in testing

1) Application making intensive use of parallelism

Applications making intensive use of parallel activities cannot be tested using unit testing alone because parallel test components need to be well coordinated. This is the case of most frameworks that are derivatives of unit testing. Also parallel testing is considered as very complex and most testers avoid it altogether. Testing tools, such as TTCN-3 are particularly efficient at testing parallel applications because of native features that enable to control several instances of parallel components easily and efficiently and provide methods to explore test logs efficiently. These cover applications based on Service Oriented Applications (SOA) and more recently Business Process Management (BPM). Both making extensive use of web applications as a front end that can be easily tested using TTCN-3.

2) Computation testing

Computation testing consists in testing software that depends solely on computation activities that upon an input are expected to return a predictable output. These are best tested using unit testing. This is particularly the case when the software is autonomous, i.e., it does not interact with other software components. It is, in a way, the benchmark in testing methodologies.

3) State testing

State testing consists in putting a system into different states and observing correctness of the transition to another state. A state can be represented by specific output values of a set of variables that the software manipulates. In this case, we do not only test the final value of the output but also any of the intermediary states to obtain it. This is often referred to as grey or white testing depending on the granularity.

C. Heterogeneous testing costing data

In theory, comparing testing approaches, strategies and supporting tools should be achieved on a specific application or groups of applications. The reality is that no one actually does that because having the same software developed several times using different approaches is highly counter-intuitive and no one would actually budget such a strategy. The solution that comes closes to that concept is found in [10] where an attempt to verify this theory is applied to past software development projects. This model also includes a technology factor. Consequently, comparisons are performed between different and heterogeneous applications on radically different domains and thus, results are not totally comparable. However, this has been achieved in a specific domain of GUI testing in [13] and in the transportation and financial sectors in [3].

D. Industrial behavior on testing

Most software is developed around a set budget. The same applies to testing with the difference that when budgets are overrun, it is the development budget that is allowed to do so while the testing budget is capped. Thus, we could say that testing is budget centric rather than application centric. Here, the most typical behavior consists in hiring testers without any performance consideration. The cases we have observed in industry include purchasing expensive testing tools and their related personnel training. Here, the costs are very tangible and require approval from upper management but these situations always resulted in the upper management requiring proof that there are benefits to do so. Again, decisions were guided by intuition and not by precise economic models.

As well, personnel turnover increases the cost of testing tools training costs because as people moved on, their expertise disappears with them. New personnel have to be re-trained. This has the result of reducing the benefits of dedicated testing tools as can be shown on Figure 3. Here the break-even point has moved up both in cost and time.

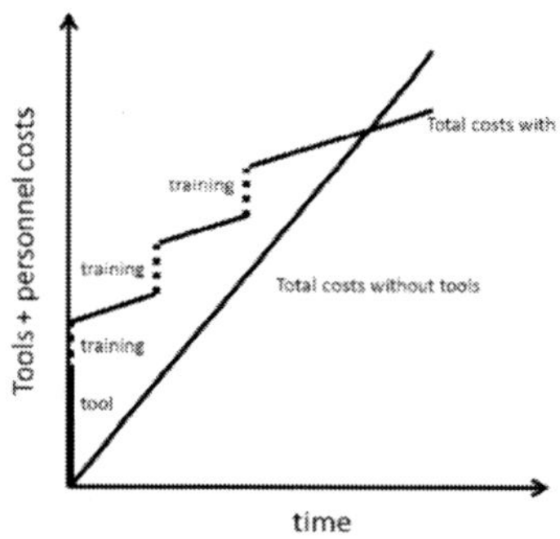

Figure 3. Incidence of personnel turnover on training costs

However, this is a false problem since most of the problem lies in the organization of testing tool usage. The most efficient way has been to create a pool of testing tool experts that train and mentor the testers along the testing life cycle. This is no different than the issues with the turnover of software developers that requires new developers to learn the software developed by their predecessors.

One case is particularly interesting: testing critical systems that require certification of tests. Here, changing test approaches regardless of the lack of efficiency of existing automated testing software is a major problem. Effectively, besides the cost of redeveloping test software using the new approaches, the certification process has to be redone from the start.

IV. CONCLUSION

Despite its long history, cost estimation of testing is mostly an ad hoc activity and still needs to explore new avenues. The great number of factors of cost makes it difficult to come up with an optimal solution to the problem. Also, a key factor, complexity of software, is missing completely from the literature. The available literature shows that tackling the problem is difficult and no final solution has been found as yet.

ACKNOWLEDGMENT

The authors would like to thank NSERC for funding this research.

REFERENCES

[1] G. J. Myers, C. Sandler and T. Badgett, The Art of Sotftware Testing, 3rd Edition,Wiley Pubishing, 2011, ISDN 978-1-118-03196-4
[2] Q. Hu, R. T. Plant and D. B. Hertz, "Software Cost Estimation Using Economic Production Models", Journal of Management Information Systems 15, no. 1, 1998. pp. 143-163.
[3] M. P. Gallaher and B. M. Kropp. "Economic impacts of inadequate infrastructure for software testing", Technical report 7007.011, RTI International, National Institute of Standards and Technology, 2002.
[4] G. J. Holzmann, "Economics of software verification", Proceedings of the 2001 ACM SIGPLAN-SIGSOFT workshop on Program analysis for software tools and engineering (PASTE 01), pp. 80-89. ACM, 2001.
[5] A. Tawileh, S. McIntosh, B. Work and W. Ivins, "The Dynamics of Software Testing", proceedings of the 26th international Conference of the System Dynamics Society, 2007.
[6] S. Wagner. "Towards software quality economics for defect-detection techniques", 3rd Workshop on Software Quality, 29th Annual IEEE/NASA, pp. 265-274, 2005. pp. 1-6.
[7] B. Boehm. Software engineering economics. Englewood Cliffs, NJ:Prentice-Hall, 1981. ISBN 0-13-822122-7
[8] M. Ellims, J. Bridges, and D. C. Ince, "The economics of unit testing", Empirical Software Engineering 11, no. 1,2006: pp 5-31.
[9] I. M. Keshta, "Software Cost Estimation Approaches: A Survey." Journal of Software Engineering and Applications 10, no. 10, 2017.
[10] K. Pillai and V. S. S. Nair. "A model for software development effort and cost estimation." IEEE Transactions on Software Engineering 8 (1997): pp 485-497.
[11] ETSI ES 201 873-1, The Testing and Test Control Notation version 3 Part 1: TTCN-3 Core Language, May 2017. Accessed March 2018 at http://www.etsi.org/deliver/etsi_es/201800_201899/20187301/04.09.01_60/es_20187301v040901p.pdf
[12] C. Brill and A. Olmsted, "Security and Software Engineering: Analyzing Effort and Cost", SOFTENG 2017, pp110-114. Accessed December 6, 2018 at https://www.thinkmind.org/download_full.php?instance=SOFTENG+2017.
[13] P. Sabev and A. Kanchev, "A Comparative Study of GUI automated Tools for Software Testing", SOFTENG 2017, pp7-16. Accessed December 6, 2018 at https://www.thinkmind.org/download_full.php?instance=SOFTENG+2017.
[14] L. P. Kafle, "An Empirical Study On Software Test Effort Estimation", International Journal of Soft Computing and Artificial Intelligence, ISSN: 2321-404X, vol. 2, issue 2, Nov. 2014.
[15] K. R. Jayakumar and A. Abran, "A Survey of Software Test Estimation Techniques", Journal of Software Engineering and Applications 6, no. 10, 2013. pp. 47-52.

What T-shirt Are You Wearing?

Towards the Collective Team Grokking of Product Requirements

Rob Fuller
Electrical and Computer Engineering
The University of British Columbia
Vancouver, Canada
email: rfuller@ece.ubc.ca

***Abstract*—This paper describes requirements engineering research that examines how cross-functional product teams, as a collective, create and nurture a shared mental model that accurately represents the external product domain and its realities and provides the context for understanding the requirements. In the conduct of this study, organisational factors have been identified that support or inhibit teams from achieving this deep collective understanding.**

Keywords—empathy-driven development; collective sensemaking; design science; requirements validation; product team organisation.

I. INTRODUCTION

In the late 1990s, a "model revolution" [1] began to emerge that took a new view on change, risk, and uncertainty. These 'agile' models typically embraced the possibility that requirements could change throughout the development effort in contrast to many earlier Software Development LifeCycles (SDLCs) that strived to lock down requirements in the specification and planning stages.

These new models had a greater focus on the software development team, usually cross-functional, as a critical success factor in delivering software. These teams often have the necessary collection of functional expertise and capacity in each functional area to be essentially self-sufficient. Many software development companies have gone even further, empowering their cross-functional teams to truly own the product. This approach is now quite common, no longer adopted only by industry thought-leaders. It is these organisations and teams that are the main focus of this research.

The rest of this paper is structured as follows. In Section II, we outline the general problem and in Section III, the general research question and importance. Section IV identifies the focus of the research, who is being sampled in the study. Section V is a summary of the literature review followed by Section VI, where we discuss the research methodology. Section VII briefly describes the status of the research to-date and in Section VIII, emerging observations, which is the main topic of this paper. Finally, Section IX offers thoughts on future direction.

II. THE PROBLEM

While agile models improve many of the issues that were breaking down during the crisis period, they still generally cling to the notion that there is a customer, an authoritative voice that the development team can interact with iteratively to clarify requirements and validate results. However, as software development became more product development intended for a market, a new and critical challenge emerged for software teams and that is how to gain a deep understanding of the world for which their product is intended. Certainly, techniques to 'hear' from the market are helpful but, as Polyani [2] noted, market participants have tacit knowledge -- people can know more than they can tell and they know more than can be easily observed. This is evidenced by an all-too-common experience when it is discovered that the so-called requirement does not reflect an actual need but rather simply an articulation of what someone wants -- "I know that is what I said I wanted but that does not seem to be what I need." -- they know more than they can tell.

It is important that the entire team gains this deep understanding because team members (individually, in sub-teams, and in all functional roles) make decisions almost continually based on their understanding of the *context* of the requirements, and much of that context understanding is also tacit.

Thus, it behooves product development teams to strive for a deep, collective understanding of the context of their product, that other world for which their product is intended, a shared mental model of the supra-domain, since many design and implementation decisions are unconsciously made within the team's understanding of the domain context. The success of the team, of their product, and often of the software company itself rests upon how well they do this. Teams do this with varying degrees of success. Some achieve reasonable success seemingly instinctively, while many struggle ineffectively. Software development leaders are often able to observe this phenomenon but have no theories that help explain why.

While labels are being used to describe what some they think this deep understanding (grokking) of that external world is (e.g., "empathy-driven development"), there does not appear to be any clear definition of what it is, but rather simply labels of what some think may be happening.

III. RESEARCH QUESTION AND IMPORTANCE

The purpose of this qualitative study is to develop a substantive theory that answers the following research question:

"what are the factors that support or impede multi-disciplinary software product teams, empowered to own their product, to collectively achieve a deep understanding of the environment for which their product is intended?"

This theory will help industry practitioners explain why certain prevailing techniques and empirical approaches for understanding software solution needs are often inadequate, why some succeed while others do not. These insights will offer guidance for more effective software development approaches.

In addition to assisting practitioners in industry, this interpretive theory aspires to illuminate areas of potential further research. For example, how are technically-oriented people (primarily millennials) working in teams (typically cross-functional) and following a rational process to create software solutions able to develop, nurture, and incorporate 'squishier' skills into a process that strives to be as rational and deterministic as possible? Or, how does that which cannot be easily observed nor expressed be equally understood and preserved within a team? Or, how does empathic appreciation of the context of a software solution translate across individuals, organisations, business domains, cultures?

IV. Focus of the Research

As the saying goes, "a fish does not know it is in water", thus the intended users often cannot clearly communicate the context in which they operate because they are trapped in that context. Thus, it is necessary for the team to somehow become one of the people targetted to use a software solution, and to truly learn from that immersion. It is very difficult to be an outsider and obtain an insider's perspective and knowledge. It is especially difficult for a team to do this collectively. And it does not easily fit into established software engineering practices nor is it well-supported by software engineers' training.

Thus, the focus of this research is practicing software product teams in action, specifically teams empowered to own their product. It also examines the empirical adaptations these teams make to established software engineering and design practices that represent an empathic-based development approach towards evolving an increasingly accurate understanding of the context in which their users operate, the supra-domain - the business needs, technology, culture, and politics. It also examines important organisational factors that either allow or inhibit a team's ability to collectively grok the domain.

V. Literature Review

Literature was reviewed in 3 areas - requirements engineering (specifically elicitation), design science, and collective sensemaking.

This inquiry may be seen as primarily placed within software requirements engineering, specifically requirements elicitation (attempting to obtain and understand the true needs). We looked at all the accepted papers for the IEEE International Requirements Engineering Conference over the past 10 years, plus many related papers published in other publications. There are increasingly more views being expressed about the shortcomings of prevailing approaches to requirements elicitation which tend to focus on techniques and methods rather than deepening practitioner and team understanding. We believe this is evidence that some software product development efforts still operate in the 'process-driven' paradigm and are experiencing what Kuhn [1] described as the incommensurability across paradigms. While acknowledging that the 'techniques and methods' approach is entirely appropriate in certain domains, our focus is on problem domains that don't lend themselves well to clear specifications. Controversy aside, the intent of requirements elicitation is to understand the true software needs and, therefore, this inquiry will contribute to the requirements engineering discipline.

In the design science space, we found a considerable scholarship regarding empathy-driven design, e.g., (Koppen and Meinel [3], van Rijn et al. [4], Postma et al. [5], Woodcock et al. [6], Dong et al. [7], Kourprie and Visser [8], Kolko [9]). However, this research falls short of addressing our inquiry question in three critical respects: 1) the focus is on the design activity as part of an essentially sequential product development process rather than design as part of an on-going continuous product development effort, 2) rather than considering the whole development team, they tend to focus on the design individual or just the design team, and, 3) when it does consider the design team, it tends not to be viewed as a unit to consider regarding its empathic ability. There are design science models described by Wieringa [10] that acknowledge the challenge that empathy-driven requirements understanding attempts to address (using very different vocabulary) but stops short of suggesting how those challenges are, or could be, addressed. We believe this inquiry could enrich those models and generally contribute to the design science field.

In the collective sensemaking field, the collective (team) is usually considered only insofar as its relationship to the organisation, not to its understanding of a specific domain outside of the organisation. Some researchers, notably Daniel Russell [11] look at sensemaking from Human-Computer Interaction (HCI) perspective and, although his view positions sensemaking in a collective context (the information world), he describes a style of engagement of sensemaking that is essentially personal, not collective. The Cynefin framework (Kurtz and Snowden [12]) is a sensemaking framework that is particularly useful for collective sensemaking in that it is designed to allow shared understandings to emerge which could be insightful with respect to how teams ingest, socialise, and collectively store insights. As with other collective sensemaking models, it has resonance in early problem-solving stages and for formal and finite periods of time. Other researchers (Klein et al. [13], Naumer et al. [14], Kolko [15]) elaborate further by bringing data-framing into the picture and defining design synthesis as a process of sense-making, trying to make sense of chaos. The data-framing activity of sensemaking lends itself to being part of a long-term collective effort to understand and therefore may have some relevance to this inquiry.

VI. Method of the Research

As the primary interest is on substantive theory generation, rather than extending or verifying existing theories, we are taking an interpretive epistemological stance, employing a Grounded Theory approach, as developed by Glaser and Strauss [16], and using the Constructivist Grounded Theory methodology described by Charmaz [17]. Grounded Theory is highly applicable in research such as this because it is explicitly emergent and can generate theory relating to a specific research situation. This is an area that is a relatively new, where there has been limited research, and where field data will come from observations and interviews, conditions for which Grounded Theory is particularly well suited.

Grounded Theory has been used successfully as a research method to study Agile software development teams: Adolph et al. [18], Dagenais et al. [19], Coleman and O'Connor [20], Martin [21], Hoda [22].

The research uses theoretical sampling (Charmaz [17]) where the analysis of the data collected prior informs the selection of and inquiry with the next participants. Individual participants and corporate sites selected are ones involved with software product development (teams developing software for market) and that claim to have cross-functional product development teams. The primary data collection methods are observations of team meetings and team interactions, enriched by semi-structured interviews with open-ended questions that can allow real issues to emerge.

Participants are carefully recruited through our professional network and via direct outreach to select software product organisations. Where permitted, we hold interviews in the participant's workplace to allow for environmental context to enrich the interview data. Also, where we have approval from the organisations involved, we locate ourselves as unobtrusively as possible in the workplace to allow for more casual direct observation as an additional data source which may direct further data collection and analysis. The individual interviews conducted are recorded whenever permitted. Our many years of leadership with the types of people that are participants affords us considerable comfort, understanding, and rapid rapport.

Iterative data collection and analysis (formulation, testing, and redevelopment of propositions) allows participant sampling and questions to purposefully evolve as patterns emerge in the data until we reach a theory. We use the NVivo software tool to analyse the unstructured qualitative data collected. Data collection will stop once the analysis indicates the achievement of theoretical saturation, the point at which gathering more data reveals no new properties nor yields any further theoretical insights about the emerging grounded theory (Charmaz [17]). This ensures a degree of consistency in the analysis.

Our professional experience allows for a certain considered positionality and we recognise that this shapes our objectivity and subjectivity of many aspects of perspective in this study. While acknowledging the challenges, we consider this experience, and the bias it creates, to be an asset to this research. As Eisner [23] suggests, the expert ability to "see what counts" -- the sensitivity to tacit elements of the data, meanings and connotations -- will guide the research, supported fully by the collected data, towards questions that matter.

Quality in research of this nature is generally assessed in terms of validity and generalizability, which, together, determine some measure of usefulness. During the research, we employ various strategies (Maxwell [24]) to mitigate threats to validity (credibility, dependability, reliability). Intensive, on-going involvement, e.g., extended participation and the ability to live in the participants' workplace, provides richer data and data types, less dependence on inference, and opportunity for repeated observations and interviews, all which will help rule out spurious associations and premature theories. The collection and use of rich data (transcribed interviews, thick descriptive note-taking of observations) help provide a more complete and revealing picture of what is going on. Participant checks (obtaining participant and peer feedback on the data collected and conclusions drawn) help rule out possibilities of misinterpretation. Triangulation (collection from a range of participants and settings) reduces the risk of chance associations and systematic biases. Finally, we will be transparent with any discrepant evidence or negative cases. We intend to assess transferability of final results within the context of software product development primarily via reviews of the resulting theory with software product development leaders and, further, to draw comparisons with non-product software development teams to further refine the specificity of transferability claims.

VII. Status of the Research

To-date, we have been working with 5 software companies, 4 of which produce commercial enterprise-class software products (skills management, retail, stem cell therapy, and social media marketing management) and using common Agile approaches. The 5th company develops large-scale aerospace and satellite systems and adopts some Agile philosophies within a large-scale, structured project management methodology. All companies are leaders in their markets. They range in size from 10 to several hundred employees and in maturity from 2 to 50 years old. To-date, 9 product development teams across these companies have participated, resulting in 15 individual semi-structured interviews conducted and 17 team sessions observed. More data gathering is scheduled and more organisations and teams are being recruited.

VIII. Emerging Observations

The first emerging observation is that the organisational model surrounding the cross-functional team significantly impacts the cross-functional team dynamics, individual participation and sense of primary allegiance. Where there is, e.g., a software engineering department, a design department, and a product management department, contributing members to cross-functional product teams, the intra-team dynamics are often strikingly different than when there is no functional organisation surrounding the teams. In the former case, team members are more likely to temper their contributions, identifying more with their functional affiliation than with the product mandate. The analogy we use here is that each are wearing a functional t-shirt (e.g., the software engineering department t-shirt with a small insignia that indicates the person is assigned to a particular product team at the moment). In addition to observing this in team interactions, this also appears in the language, "*I just do my job and they do theirs*", "*I trust them*", "*I think someone else is looking after that*", "*I just do what Product Management (or Design) says*", "*I am on this team -- for now*". A software engineer in this environment is much more likely to care about the how and defer to others on the what and why. In contrast, organisations that do not have a functional structure surrounding the cross-functional product teams tend to have teams with a more complete sense of ownership for their product and richer intra-team interactions. The t-shirt analogy here is that they are all wearing the same product t-shirt with perhaps an insignia that identifies their functional competency. On these teams, sense of *team* is much stronger, thus the language does not refer to 'them'. All team members are more likely to care about what, why, and how because there is a stronger sense of collective ownership for the product, not just their particular contribution to it. We plan to probe this phenomenon further and look at definitions of success and how they may be defined similarly or not across these two models.

The second emerging observation relates to expectation of mobility which appears to be inversely related to an individual's intrinsic connection to the product and, therefore, the product team. We have observed two pressures that inhibit an individual's inclination to be all-in. One pressure is where there is a high degree of staff turnover impacts product development team resourcing. After a certain length of time, people in these environments come to expect they will be reassigned soon and thus have a certain tentativeness to their commitment to the product and the product team. The other pressure is similar, however, more intentional, where there is a Human Resource department policy that encourages a high degree of mobility with respect to team assignment, e.g., 20% of technical staff should change teams every year. This seems to be rooted in a belief that mobility is healthy for the individual and/or adds to corporate robustness. A telling quote from an engineering manager in one of these situations, *"I do not know how a true 'team' can emerge this way."*.

IX. Conclusion and Future Work

Product development is a social process; thus, the organisational dimension is the elephant in the room, a critical factor for success or failure of software product teams. The two observable phenomena surfacing strongly in the analysis to-date both fall into a category of what an organisation may do, consciously or otherwise, to support or inhibit, a cross-functional team to be all it can be. There appears to be a certain blurring of functional boundaries necessary for a team to become a true product team rather than a collection of functional experts assembled around a product.

In the context of requirements engineering, we use the definition of empathy to be *the ability to imaginatively step into another domain, understand the perspectives of those in that domain, and use that understanding to guide decisions* [25]. Stepping into that other domain also involves a certain temporary *blurring of the boundaries* in order to truly understand perspectives in that domain. Thus, further inquiry is needed to determine if this blurring of functional boundaries is a necessary condition for the team to collectively grok the target domain.

Acknowledgment

This work is supported in part by the Institute for Computing, Information and Cognitive Systems (ICICS) at UBC.

References

[1] T. S. Kuhn, The Structure of Scientific Revolutions. 4th ed. University of Chicago Press, 2012.

[2] M. Polanyi, "The Tacit Dimension," Knowledge in Organisations, 1997.

[3] E. Koppen and C. Meinel, "Knowing People: The Empathetic Designer," Design Philosophy Papers, vol. 10, no. 1, pp. 35-51, 2012.

[4] H. Van Rijn, F. S. Visser, P. J. Stappers, and A. D. Özakar, "Achieving empathy with users: the effects of different sources of information," CoDesign, vol. 7, February 2015, pp. 65–77, 2011.

[5] C. Postma, E. Zwartkruis-Pelgrim, E. Daemen, and J. Du, "Challenges of Doing Empathic Design: Experiences from Industry," Int. J. Des. Vol 6, No 1, pp. 59-70, 2012.

[6] A. Woodcock, D. McDonagh, J. Osmond, and W. Scott, "Empathy, Design and Human Factors," Advances in Usability and User Experience, pp. 569-579, 2018.

[7] Y. Dong, H. Dong, and S. Yuan, "Empathy in Design: A Historical and Cross-Disciplinary Perspective," Advances in Neuroergonomics and Cognitive Engineering, pp. 295-304, 2018.

[8] M. Kouprie and F. S. Visser, "A framework for empathy in design: stepping into and out of the user's life," Journal of Engineering Design, vol. 20, no. 5, pp. 437–448, 2009.

[9] J. Kolko, Well-Designed: How to create empathy to create products people love. Harvard Business Review Press, 2014.

[10] R. Wieringa, Design Science Methodology for Information Systems and Software Engineering. Springer, Berlin, 2014.

[11] D. Russell and P. Pirolli, "An Overview of Sensemaking: A View from the Workshop CHI 2009," Sensemaking Work. CHI, pp. 1–2, 2009.

[12] C. F. Kurtz and D. Snowden, "The New Dynamics of Strategy: Sense-making in a Complex-Complicated World," IBM Syst. J., vol. 42, no. 3, pp. 462–483, 2003.

[13] G. Klein, B. Moon, R. Hoffman, and K. Associates, "Making Sense of Sensemaking 2: A Macrocognitive Model," IEEE Intell. Syst., vol. 21, no. 5, pp. 88–92, 2006.

[14] C. Naumer, K. Fisher, and B. Dervin, "Sense-Making: a methodological perspective," CHI2008 Work. SenseMaking Florence, 2008.

[15] J. Kolko, "Sensemaking and Framing: A Theoretical Reflection on Perspective in Design Synthesis," 2010 Des. Res. Soc. Conf., pp. 1–9, 2010.

[16] B. G. Glaser and A. L. Strauss, The discovery of grounded theory: Strategies for qualitative research. Piscataway, NJ: Aldine Transaction, 1967.

[17] K. Charmaz, Constructing grounded theory: a practical guide through qualitative analysis. London: Sage, 2006.

[18] S. Adolph, W. Hall, and P. Kruchten, "Using grounded theory to study the experience of software development," Empirical Software Engineering., vol. 16, no. 4, pp. 487–513, 2011.

[19] B. Dagenais, H. Ossher, R. K. E. Bellamy, M. P. Robillard, and J. P. De Vries, "Moving into a New Software Project Landscape," in ICSE '10 Proceedings of the 32nd ACM/IEEE International Conference on Software Engineering, pp. 275–284, 2010.

[20] G. Coleman and R. O'Connor, "Using grounded theory to understand software process improvement: A study of Irish software product companies," Information Software Technology, vol. 49, no. 6, pp. 654–667, 2007.

[21] A. M. Martin, "The Role of Customers in Extreme Programming Projects," PhD thesis. Victoria University of Wellington, New Zealand, 2009.

[22] R. Hoda, "Self-Organizing Agile Teams : A Grounded Theory," PhD thesis. Victoria University of Wellington, New Zealand, 2011.

[23] E. W. Eisner, The enlightened eye: Qualitative inquiry and the enhancement of educational practice. Upper Saddle River, NJ: Prentice-Hall, 1998.

[24] J. A. Maxwell, Qualitative research design: An interactive approach. Thousand Oaks, Calif.: SAGE Publications, 2012.

[25] R. Krznaric, Empathy: why it matters, and how to get it. New York: Penguin Random House, 2014

User Characteristics Validation for User Scenario Based on Use-Case Models in Requirements Analysis

Saeko Matsuura
Graduate School of Engineering and Science Shibaura Institute of Technology
Saitama, Japan
email: matsuura@se.shibaura-it.ac.jp

***Abstract*—Nonfunctional requirements, such as user characteristics and system architecture, are factors that make it difficult to acquire proper requirements when constructing a system for business improvement by Information and Communication Technology (ICT) for small-scale companies that are behind other medium and large-scale companies. This paper discusses an incremental requirement acquisition and analysis method of a system based on a use-case model in Unified Modeling Language (UML) with the experience of requirements analysis for a small-scale manufacturing company as a joint lesson at our university.**

Keywords*—*Nonfunctional requirements; Use-case analysis; UML; validation.

I. Introduction

It is well known that requirement analysis is a key to success in developing high-quality systems in an efficient manner. Requirements specification must determine not only functional requirements but also nonfunctional requirements. Nonfunctional requirements include the system goal, external interfaces with the user, hardware, software, and communications. Moreover, user characteristics that are general characteristics of the intended users of the product, including educational level, experience, and technical expertise affect not only the system usage but also the service quality.

As the system architecture and users become diverse, the initial model of a system often depends on these features with regard to nonfunctional requirements. These features restrict the specification and need elaboration by considering these features step by step at the early stage of system development, as discussed in the Twin Peaks Model [1]. User characteristics and the system architecture are the factors that make it difficult to acquire proper requirements when constructing a system for business improvement by Information and Communication Technology (ICT) for small-scale companies that are behind other medium and large-scale companies.

On the other hand, functional requirements can be modeled as essential use cases [2] by a semiformal and widely used language such as the Unified Modeling Language (UML) [3] in model-driven development. System usage scenarios can be defined by a combination of these use cases. However, the abovementioned architectural and external factors in nonfunctional requirements strongly affect this combination. Moreover, a change in the need for these use cases may occur. Although this uncertainty of requirements is unavoidable at the early stage of system development, it is important formally to manage the traceability of requirements related to nonfunctional requirements in a system.

We have proposed a method for model-driven requirements analysis [4] [5] using UML. We have also presented an iterative cycle of analysis and verification in which the requirements specification of a system was defined incrementally [6].

If the user does not clearly recognize the effectiveness of ICT, it is more difficult to acquire their requirements for a system to improve their business by ICT. In this case, even if a use-case model is useful to define an expected system, it is difficult to extract and define suitable use cases. The basis of a use case is a normal flow that consists of behaviors and data with preconditions and postconditions. Data has invariant conditions for a system, so it causes exceptional flows in a use case. To acquire user-centric useful requirements, we think the following two things are important points to specify in fundamental use cases at the early stage of the requirement analysis phase:

- Essential data required in executing the domain tasks must be clarified; however, these data often involve the implicit knowledge of the user. Therefore, we must obtain these data via a method, such as ethnography [9] as sufficiently and as far as possible.
- As a system must not obstruct the task process in the actual work site for the users, the requirements should specify the behavioral flows by following a traditional task process.

This paper proposes a method to acquire user-centric useful requirements incrementally at the early stage of system development. Fundamental scenario analysis based on use-case components makes it possible to acquire user-centric useful requirements by clarifying the confirmation points on the models. These points can be used in analysis by requirements elicitation methods such as the ethnography method.

The rest of this paper is organized as follows. Section II describes problems in improving the business of a small-scale company that is behind in introducing ICT technology. Section III explains how to define a UML requirements analysis model and a way to validate user satisfaction using UML models. Section IV explains a case study. Finally,

Section V discusses our results, conclusions, and future research directions.

II. Problems in Improving Business of Small-Scale Companies

A. Barriers to Business Improvement by ICT

It is difficult to introduce a basic management system at work sites, such as small manufacturing industries because of the work environment, a low number of employees, or inexperience in ICT. In such work sites, only responsible people can manage the work process, and they use a whiteboard and paper notes attached to the product parts for process management. As a person's knowledge of process management is their implicit knowledge, this is not the explicit and formal knowledge of the company. Forming implicit knowledge into common specified knowledge is important for business improvement by the utilization of information technology; however, it is difficult to acquire implicit knowledge from the users.

We think that modeling fundamental use cases contributes to formulating implicit knowledge into common specified knowledge that is related to the model elements.

B. Outline of Example Subject

In response to overseas industrial policies such as "Industry 4.0," in Japan, we make efforts to solve solutions using the Internet of Things toward the future innovation of industrial structures. However, in a small-scale manufacturing company, delays in IT conversion are obstacles to such efforts.

This study covers issues in nonmetal products manufacturing companies that are centered on casting technology and are celebrating their centenary in 2018. These companies primarily deal with construction hardware ordered by building material manufacturers, who specialize in small lots of various kinds. As there are fewer than 20 employees, it is a small factory. By using manufacturing technology possessed by each cooperating factory scattered in the area, we provide consistent services from product manufacturing to processing. Cooperation with a factory with a useful and a profit is a strength. However, as many parts move between cooperating factories, leading to various kinds of commercialization, it is difficult to manage these work processes.

While manufacturing a product, it is necessary to request multiple companies to cooperate in order to process many parts to complete the product. Parts that are to be delivered between the parent company and the cooperating companies are placed in returnable boxes that are transported by full-time drivers. The transmission of information about processes and products is carried out by telephones, messages to drivers, and meetings. Although process and product information are the basis of the work, they are implicit knowledge possessed only by the responsible person at the parent company. Sharing such important implicit knowledge is the goal of introducing a system.

C. Difficulties in Requirements Analysis

Ethnography is a qualitative orientation of research that emphasizes the detailed observation of people in naturally occurring settings. It is drawing a considerable amount of attention because it is useful in marketing. The ethnography method is used for observation of work sites and in interviews with the person in the company who is responsible for requirements acquisition; however, it is important that the interviews are carried out by whom which has both domain knowledge and system knowledge. It is important that the project manager or developer is familiar with information technology. However, few people are familiar with both types of knowledge.

We think that modeling fundamental use cases contributes to extracting useful observations and interview questions for the person who use the ethnography method.

III. User Characteristics Validation in User Scenario

A. Use-Case Component

A use-case analysis is an effective method to clarify functional requirements. We propose a method for model-driven requirements analysis using UML. A use-case model is a fundamental component of the requirements defined formally by UML. This method is defined based on a requirements analysis model, as shown in Figure 1.

Figure 1 shows an outline of a requirements analysis model. The relation between the use cases in the specified use-case diagram is expressed by an activity diagram that includes some subactivity nodes corresponding to the use cases. An activity diagram defines each use case. An activity diagram specifies not only normal and exceptional action flows but also data flows that are related to these actions. An action is defined by an action node, and data is defined by an object node that is classified as a member of a class that is defined in a class diagram. Accordingly, these two kinds of diagrams enable us to specify application process flows in connection with the data. The interaction between a user and a system includes requisite flows and data on user input, conditions, and output to execute a use case correctly.

The second feature of this model is an activity diagram that has three types of partitions: user, interaction, and system. These partitions enable ready identification of the following activities: user input, interaction between a user and system caused by the conditions for executing a use case, and the resulting output. Object nodes in the user, interaction, and system partitions represent input data, output data, and entity data, respectively. The requirement analysis model is defined using the modeling tool Astah*[7].

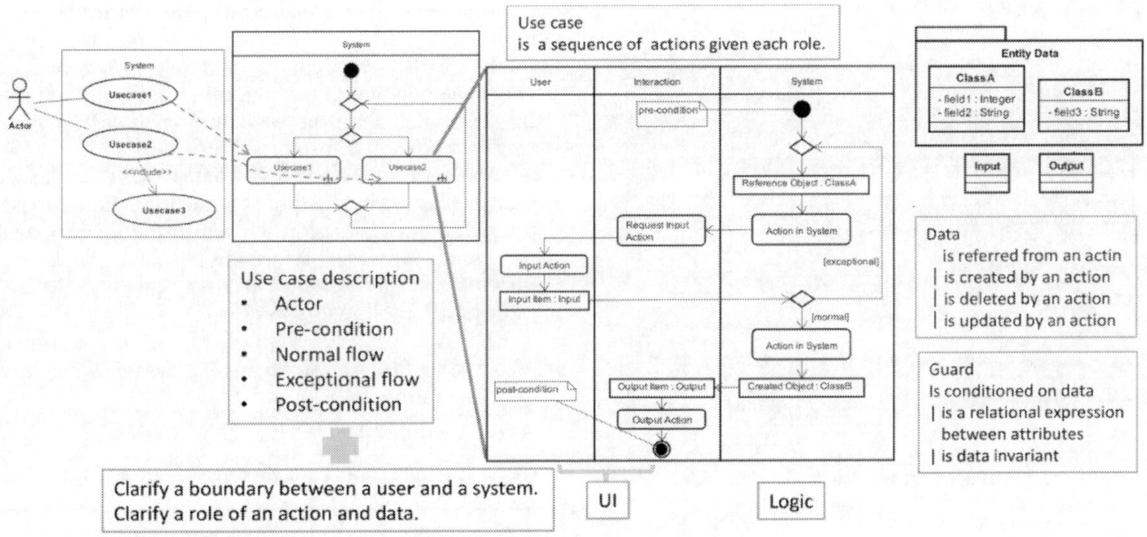

Figure 1. UML requirements analysis model

When user requirements are uncertain owing to users who are unfamiliar with ICT, we must develop a system from the fundamental use case to improve the business. To introduce ICT into the company, it is important that fundamental use cases need to be validated on the benefits. The user scenario consists of these use-case components, and we evaluate whether it satisfies the requirements of each stakeholder by a state machine diagram that represents the state of user recognition.

B. Use-Case Analysis Process

Based on Chapter 4, "Considerations for Producing Good Software Requirements Specifications (SRS)," and Chapter 5, "The Parts of an SRS," in IEEEstd.8300-1998 [8], we focus on the following parts of nonfunctional requirements and propose an iterative requirements analysis process, as shown in Figure 2 [6].

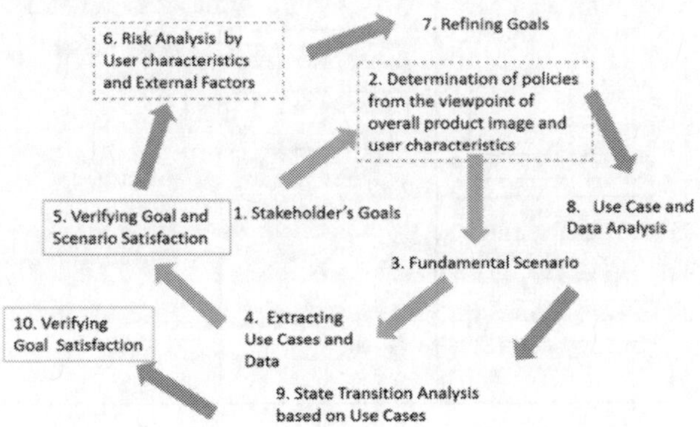

Figure 2. Iterative requirements analysis process

The process indicates that the functional requirements of a system can be specified by fundamental use cases that satisfy "the effective and useful scenarios in the system usage" in order to meet "the goals of the system." We focus on the following internal and external factors of the software:

1) Goals of the stakeholders
2) Overall product image based on the following two external factors:
   a) External interfaces with the user, hardware, software, and communications.
   b) User characteristics that are general characteristics of the intended users of the product, including educational level, experience, and technical expertise, which affect the system usage.

As mentioned in Section II, to solve the problems in a small-scale company, the first factor is often not concrete, and the second factor strongly affects the acceptable system.

In contrast to the standpoint of managers or workers, the goals of stakeholders are significantly different. Furthermore, if there are parent-child relationships between companies, the expected goals of the system are also different. Therefore, first, we set the goals of the manager of the parent company and build a basic scenario. We extract use cases and data models for the fundamental goal, and an activity diagram defines a scenario where all workers operate their tasks using the target system.

C. Definition of Implicit Information

Based on nondigital information on a whiteboard or paper notes attached to the product parts for process management that are given by a responsible person, the actual used information required for process management can be defined by a class diagram, as shown in Figure 3. Figure 3 shows the following things: a product consists of several parts and a process treats one or more target returnable boxes and the factory being in charge and the eight date managed in the process. A task schedule is a sequence of processes.

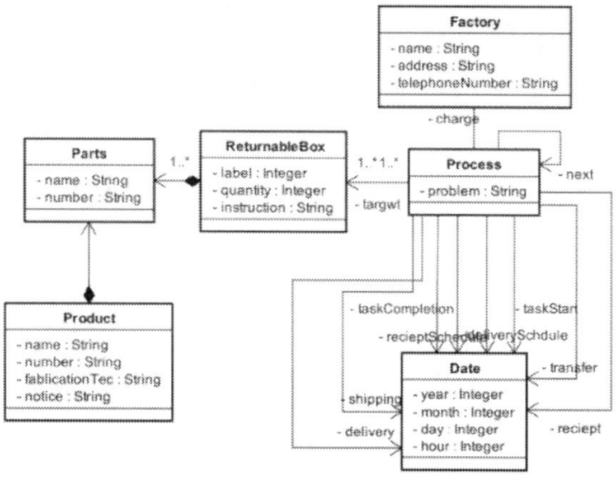

Figure 3. Class diagram

D. Fundamental Scenario

Next, consider a use case that is necessary to satisfy the goal. The basic information for sharing implicit knowledge is the process information and product information, as shown in Figure 3. Based on the fundamental Create, Read, Delete, and Update (CRDU) functions, a use case is extracted, as shown in Figure 4. In this case, there are three actors such as a worker in a parent company and a cooperative company, and a driver.

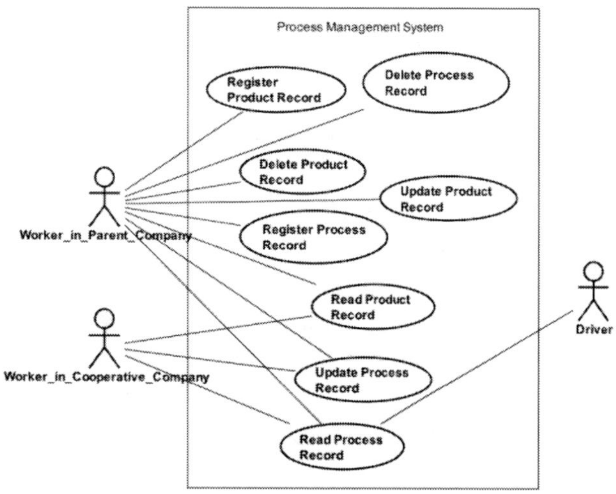

Figure 4. Use-case diagram

Based on these use cases, we defined the workflow of one step of work, as shown in Figure 5. A workflow expresses a scenario where all workers actually operate their tasks in the real world using the developed system. Here, we have not yet assumed the hardware to use. As a premise of the workflow, it is assumed that both the product information and process information as a plan are already registered.

The workflow scenario as shown in Figure 5 is defined under the conditions that the other use cases are completed, for example, that the registration is completed by the "register process information" use case.

The partition represents each worker in this company. That is, the action within the partition limits the action of each worker. The action written in the behavior call action of "read process information" and "update process information" represents a use case. Colored actions represent the following tasks:

- Work done by workers in each partition while using the *Process Management System* with the use case in Figure 4.
- Actual work regardless of the system.

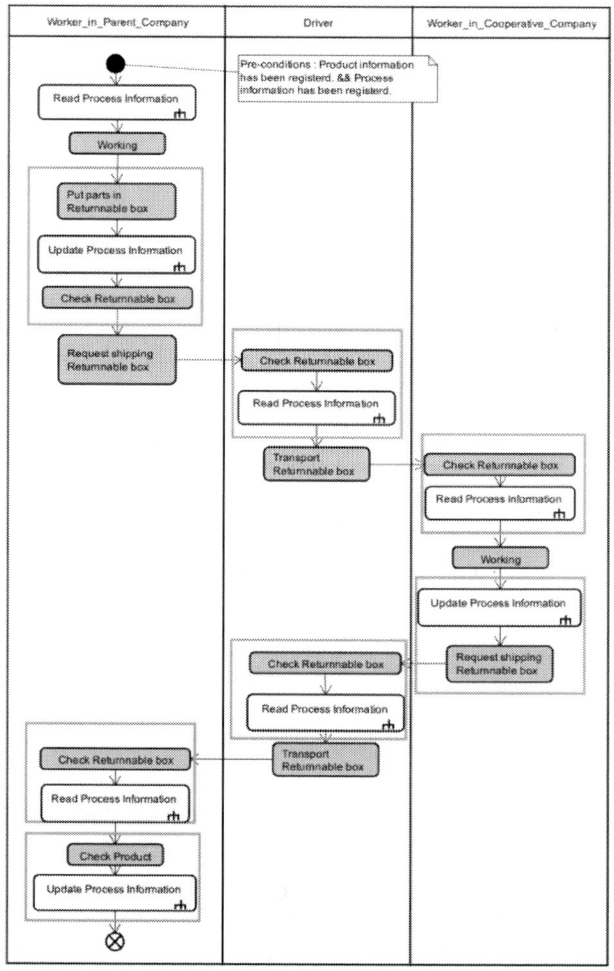

Figure 5. Fundamental scenario

The part surrounded by a rectangle is the work of the former and is necessary to determine the hardware configuration to create merits for the worker by using the system. The merits for workers are their respective goals, but it is important that the introduction of the system itself does not harm their tasks. The user characteristics of the workers need to be sufficiently considered.

Figure 5 shows a workflow in which the process control function, which uses a computer, is introduced into the present work done in the real world. The conditions for satisfying the goals of stakeholders by process control are as follows:

1) Information required for process information (see the class diagram in Figure 3) is valid. This means that the entity in the real world and the information in the system are consistent with each other.
2) It is required to confirm the degree of satisfaction of each goal. For example,
    a) If responsible people can acquire the dates related to a process they want to know as management information, they can "grasp the work situation" by sharing information with other workers.
    b) The efficiency improvement of information transmission can be accomplished by sharing information even without using a telephone so that the next work can be started and the instruction content of the work can be known.
    c) Regarding the driver's goal, the responsible person can confirm with the process chart that the product was delivered to the correct place.

E. Use-Case Scenario Validation

The grasp of the work situation of the abovementioned condition 2) in Section III-D is modeled using a state machine diagram as shown at the upper left of Figure 6.

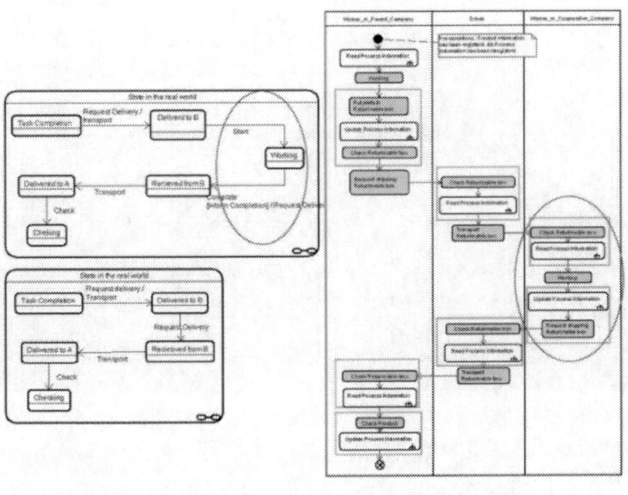

Figure 6. Relationship between work situation and workflow

An activity diagram and a state machine diagram express the behavior of a system from different viewpoints. The former expresses a sequence of actions, and the latter expresses a graph of the system state. Thus, we can see that the column of each state in the real world corresponds to each partition of the workflow.

In the state of the real world at the upper left, we modeled how we can recognize the work performance of each worker in the system by the workflow task of each worker. The part indicated by a red circle represents the state that the worker of the cooperating company can recognize by using the system. Considering the user characteristics, if we do not introduce a system to cooperating companies, they cannot recognize this achievement state, that is, the model in the lower left will be understood in the real world when the parent company uses the system. In the workflow after introducing the system, by associating information that is understandable by the user through the system with the state machine diagram of the actual state arising from the work of the workflow, it is possible to intuitively grasp the merit of introducing the system and to evaluate the value of systemization.

IV. CASE STUDY

We conducted a joint lesson in two master courses of System Engineering & Science and Engineering Management at our university over two years. The students in the Engineering Management course researched the visualization and sharing method of technology and skill succession by extracting tasks from an actual situation based on field observations for small and medium manufacturing companies.

A subject with a realistic problem was given to students in the System Engineering & Science course who had some system development skills with UML. They were given the subject and the research results that were observed in the workplace of a small manufacturing company based on the ethnography method. Then, the students analyzed the system by ICT to contribute to the improvement of the business. The purposes of this lesson were as follows:

- To understand that the analyst has to specify a useful scenario that the user can accomplish by using the system during the actual work. This is because they make the users understand the merit of introducing the system into their work.
- To understand how to check the validity of the requirements defined using the UML requirements analysis method based on the use-case components and the state machine diagrams. This is because it is difficult for the user to confirm whether the assumed scenario has satisfied the goal.
- To understand and organize the viewpoints of various requirements analyses by analyzing the problems of a small-scale metal manufacturing company as an example of a real problem.

V. CONCLUSION

This paper presented a method for the user characteristics validation of a UML requirements analysis model. Regarding this experience in the master course lecture, we discussed the problems in acquiring user-centric requirements considering the user characteristics, as follows:

- If the user cannot master the system convenience, there are often discrepancies between the information within the system and the states in the actual workflow. This causes damage to the effectiveness of the system. Thus, as there are workers unfamiliar with the operation of IT equipment, that a suitable confirmation function should be implemented with the user characteristics is indispensable.
- Although it seemed to some extent that the information the users wanted to manage was gathered through investigation by ethnography, it was not verified whether this is sufficient for developing some functions to improve the current work. This is because, when interviewing or observing, there are times when the observer does not see the points that the analyst wants to clarify from the analyst's point of view.
- As the users may be unfamiliar with the IT environment, they tend to hesitate when introducing a system into their work, and it is necessary to consider the following measures:
  * First, present the initial system where the effects are clear.
  * Consider a system configuration that makes the walls of use as low as possible.
  * Although it is necessary to clarify the actual work process, observation and interview alone are not sufficient. Measures are needed to clarify what the users want to achieve in their work, and we need to develop a prototype that allows the users to check the scenarios directly.

In this case, a requirements analysis model and incremental-model-driven development are useful for generating a prototype efficiently and improving the system gradually at the early stage of development. A fundamental scenario is useful to analyze the system behaviors that are strongly affected by the user characteristics and to present a suitable usage of input and output devices such as sensors. We implemented a prototype system according to a validated UML requirement analysis model, and we are planning to evaluate this prototype system with the users.

REFERENCES

[1] B. Nuseibeh, "Weaving the Software Development Process Between Requirements and Architectures", IEEE Computer, Vol. 34(3), pp. 115–117, 2001.

[2] I. Jacobson, M. Christerson, P. Jonsson, and G. Övergaard, "Object-Oriented Software Engineering: A Usecase Driven Approach", Addison-Wesley Publishing, 1992.

[3] OMG, "Unified Modeling Language", http://www.uml.org/ (access 2018-11-21).

[4] S. Ogata and S. Matsuura, "A UML-based Requirements Analysis with Automatic Prototype System Generation", Communication of SIWN, Vol. 3, pp. 166–172, 2008.

[5] Y. Aoki, S. Ogata, H. Okuda, and S. Matsuura, "Quality Improvement of Requirements Specification Using Model Checking Technique", Proc of ICEIS 2012, Vol. 2, pp. 401–406, 2012.

[6] S. Matsuura, S. Ogata, and Y. Aoki, "Goal-Satisfaction Verification to Combination of Use Case Component", ENASE2018, pp. 343–350, 2018.

[7] ChangeVision, Inc., "Astah professional: Perfect for Software Development," http://astah.net/, (access 2018-11-21).

[8] IEEE Computer Society, "IEEE Recommended Practice for Software Requirements Specifications", IEEE Std 830-1998.

[9] L. Naidoo, "Ethnography: An Introduction to Definition and Method", doi: 10.5772/39248, 2012.

Analysis of Requirements and Technologies to Migrate Software Development to the PaaS Model

Fabiano Rosa
NOVA IMS Information Management School
Nova University Lisbon
Lisbon, Portugal
e-mail: M2016507@novaims.unl.pt

Vitor Santos
NOVA IMS Information Management School
Nova University Lisbon
Lisbon, Portugal
e-mail: vsantos@novaims.unl.pt

***Abstract*—Software development has been evolving during the last years and, more and more, the software architecture to support this development has become increasingly complex to meet the new requirements and new technologies. With the new Cloud Computing architecture and models, Information Technology (IT) departments and Independent Software Vendors (ISVs) are developing new applications and moving the traditional software architecture to the cloud. In this context, the Platform as a Service (PaaS) model can provide software development services and components within a new architecture for building a new generation of software with all benefits of the cloud, like scalability and elasticity. We look at the requirements and technologies for developing software with the PaaS architecture and present a migration model for PaaS, based on the main software architectures and information system types, validated by specialists from software development and Cloud Computing areas. The results show the feasibility of our approach and the possibility to have an initial blueprint for software development in PaaS.**

Keywords-Cloud Computing; PaaS; Software Development; Software Architecture; Migration.

I. INTRODUCTION

Cloud Computing, one of the latest IT innovations, is still taking shape and gaining maturity, and at this stage, different people, from the technology area to the sales area, have divergent views and concepts about it, based on their interests and how to apply and use Cloud Computing in their daily lives [1]. Also, Cloud Computing has been modifying software development and traditional IT and business, introducing new ways to develop software, with more scalability and agility with lower costs, allowing companies, from startups to big corporations, to create new business models or improve existing ones.

Due to the growth of Cloud Computing adoption, Platform as a Service (PaaS) has become an important part of the cloud economy and has been showing the potential of a service model, with a platform that supports the entire lifecycle of an application, from development, testing, deployment and operations, with components, tools and integrated services [2]. Many organizations are planning and migrating their on-premise software to the cloud [3], starting with the Infrastructure as a Service (IaaS) and Software as a Service (SaaS) models. Nonetheless, they are facing some challenges and difficulties, mainly in the PaaS model, related to the complexity in integrating the legacy and internal systems, from their IT area to the new PaaS architecture model and services on the cloud.

The remainder of the paper is structured as follows. In Section 2, we present the background and problem identification. Section 3 presents the details of the PaaS service model. Section 4 presents the details of our proposed migration model. Section 5 discusses existing limitations and future works. Finally, Section 6 summarizes the discussion and conclusions of the paper.

II. BACKGROUND AND PROBLEM IDENTIFICATION

PaaS is a cloud service model that provides capabilities to deploy applications onto the cloud created with languages and tools supported by the provider and uses and integrates application infrastructure services in the application to cloud consumers.

In the PaaS model, the cloud provider manages the foundational infrastructure (network, servers, operating systems, storage, etc.), but the cloud consumer has control over the deployed applications, configurations and lifecycle [4].

PaaS delivers application infrastructure capabilities (middleware) to the software development process, such as runtime and development components, as cloud services like:

- Application Development, Data, Workflow, etc.
- Security Services (Single Sign-On, Authentication, etc.).
- Database Management Systems (DBMSs).
- Directory Services.
- Integration middleware.
- Business process management (BPM) platforms.
- Rules engine.
- Complex-event processing (CEP).
- In-memory computing (IMC) platforms.

Cloud Computing and PaaS model architecture bring new requirements and complexity to the software development process. These contingencies include the new technologies, services and tools available in PaaS, to the adaptation of the traditional software engineering and development process to use new techniques like DevOps, native cloud application models and hybrid cloud deployment (on-premise to cloud integration), until new methodologies, like Agile, used in this new software development scenario to be considered in the traditional software project management practices.

In this hypersonic-growth scenario, the ISVs and IT department of companies need to be able to evaluate the PaaS model and architecture to adapt their software development and architecture, usually complex with countless legacy systems, many integrations and different technologies to this new software development scenario.

III. PaaS Service Model

Considered as the next level of abstraction of the cloud stack, after IaaS, which targets the basic IT infrastructure, PaaS provides the functions from the application stack as services, allowing developers to design and build solutions using platform services for caching, asynchronous messaging, database, and much more. In this way, developers do not need to reinvent the wheel implementing these "commodity" requirements from scratch and can focus on the business logic from the system [5].

However, PaaS is the hardest service model to characterize due to the many ways of building services and the wide range of offerings of PaaS providers. An additional layer of services related to development frameworks, middleware, databases, messaging and queuing is added to PaaS as an integration layer, so the applications can be built to the platform with the supported development languages and tools [6].

Due to the evolution of the Cloud Computing industry and increased cloud customer adoption, new Cloud Computing "as a service" models known as XaaS have emerged, that refer to "anything" or "everything" as a service. These new service models related with the three original cloud service models are being deployed by public cloud providers and into the enterprise private cloud [7].

The PaaS market is growing and becoming segmented with new extended service models for PaaS, as reported by Gartner [8], in 2016 there were 20 specialized PaaS categories from vendors with paying customers, and some new categories will emerge and others will be integrated into new PaaS suites in the next years. This growing market of PaaS solutions reflects the evolution of Cloud Computing and the search for new solutions in the cloud for software development. The main PaaS categories reported by Gartner [8] in 2016 are:

- *Application Platform Services **(aPaaS)**:* a cloud service focused on general-purpose business applications development, deployment, execution, supporting business logic and data handling for back-end services, web, and mobile.

- *Business Analytics Platform Services **(baPaaS)**:* cloud-based business analytics platforms offering capabilities to ingest data from different data sources, prepare data for analysis, visualize and analyze data, develop and publish dashboards or other Business Intelligence (BI) outputs.

- *Business Process Management Services **(bpmPaaS)**:* The delivery of Business Process Management (BPM) capabilities as a cloud service including a graphical business process and rule modeling capabilities, a process registry and repository to handle the modeling metadata, a process execution environment, and rule engine.

- *Business Rule Platform Services **(brPaaS)**:* also referred to as decision management PaaS (dmPaaS), a cloud-based service that aims to support decision making by the business rules management.

- *Communications Platform Services **(cPaaS)***: cloud-based solutions that enable applications to integrate or improve communications functionalities, like telephony calling, SMS, MMS, Speech recognition, Mobile browsing, Video services, and Conferencing.

- *Database Platform Services **(dbPaaS)**:* a cloud service that provides any database management system (DBMS) or data storage engineered as a scalable, elastic and multitenant subscription.

- *Function Platform Services **(fPaaS)**:* cloud-based service that provides a serverless execution environment for small and event-triggered functions, where it is possible to run code without provisioning or managing servers with support to automatically scale processes to support increasing and decreasing load.

- *Enterprise Horizontal Portal Services **(Portal PaaS)**:* cloud-based service that provides an Enterprise Portal with core portal features like security, personalization, integration, content aggregation and presentation, with the ability to run in shared, multitenant environments, including private and public cloud deployments.

- *Integration Platform Services **(iPaaS)**:* provides a platform in the cloud to support application, data and system-to-system integrations, using a mix of cloud services, mobile apps, on-premises systems and Internet of Things (IoT) integrations.

- *Message-Oriented Middleware Services **(momPaaS)**:* cloud-based services focused on provide communication between one part of an application to another or between different applications through the internet, in the case of public cloud momPaaS, and between components in the same LAN with the private cloud model.

IV. MIGRATION MODEL

The proposal and migration model are based on the concepts and fundamentals related to the following assumptions:

- There are different PaaS service models specialized in attending to the different needs of software development and migration to the cloud.
- Although there are several types of software, systems, and applications, the migration model was focused on the main types of information systems that have business content relevance.
- There are a variety of software architectures to use in software development, and each one has specific requirements and characteristics that should be evaluated according to the needs and requirements of the system.
- Although software development for PaaS uses the traditional Software Development Life Cycle (SDLC), it is critical to consider the characteristics of Cloud Computing to adapt software development to PaaS.
- Migration software development to PaaS needs to have a defined roadmap and process to allow the migration in phases, although the migration process may be the same for all software development migration to the cloud.

Design Science Research (DSR) is one of the methodologies that allows producing knowledge in a structured way, focusing on a real problem resolution, ensuring the attainment of scientific results. The authors used DSR as a scientific methodology to produce this academic contribution and the migration model. The approach involved an analysis of current software development processes and PaaS software development requirements. We proposed recommendations based on the study and interviewed specialists validated the recommendations. The authors documented the results and discussions.

The migration model for developing and migrating the software development to the PaaS cloud model, described in Table I, was constructed based on two dimensions: the software architecture style and the type of information system that the software was built or will be built using one or more PaaS specialized categories.

The software architectures used in the model were selected based on the relevance and importance in the software engineering and in the current technologies used in software development. Also, the types of information systems [9] were selected based on the focus on business systems and in most of the legacy software implemented. For a specific software architecture and type of information system relation, one or more PaaS specialized models were recommended based on main PaaS categories and should be evaluated whether it will be necessary to use a PaaS specialized model or more than one combined to use PaaS in software development migration projects.

TABLE I. RECOMMENDATIONS FOR SOFTWARE DEVELOPMENT AND MIGRATION TO PAAS

Software Architectures	**Types of Information Systems**					
			Enterprise Applications			
	Transaction Processing Systems (TPS)	***Business Intelligence (BI)***	***Enterprise Resource Planning (ERP)***	***Supply Chain Management (SCM)***	***Customer Relationship Management (CRM)***	***Knowledge Management Systems (KMS)***
Monolithic	aPaaS *iPaaS* (1)	aPaaS baPaaS *iPaaS* (2)	aPaaS *iPaaS* (1)	aPaaS *iPaaS* (1)	aPaaS *iPaaS* (1)	aPaaS *iPaaS* (1)
Client-Server	dbPaaS *iPaaS* (3)	dbPaaS *iPaaS* (3)	dbPaaS *iPaaS* (3)	dbPaaS *iPaaS* (3)	dbPaaS *iPaaS* (3)	dbPaaS *iPaaS* (3)
N-Tier	aPaaS dbPaaS *iPaaS* (4)	aPaaS dbPaaS *iPaaS* (4)	aPaaS bpmPaaS dbPaaS *iPaaS* (5)	aPaaS dbPaaS Portal PaaS *iPaaS* (6)	aPaaS cPaaS dbPaaS Portal PaaS *iPaaS* (7)	aPaaS dbPaaS Portal PaaS *iPaaS* (6)
Microservices	aPaaS dbPaaS fPaaS *iPaaS* *momPaaS* (8)	aPaaS baPaaS dbPaaS *iPaaS* *momPaaS* (9)	aPaaS bpmPaaS brPaaS dbPaaS *iPaaS* *momPaaS* (10)	aPaaS brPaaS Portal PaaS dbPaaS *iPaaS* *momPaaS* (11)	aPaaS brPaaS cPaaS Portal PaaS dbPaaS *iPaaS* *momPaaS* (12)	aPaaS Portal PaaS dbPaaS *iPaaS* *momPaaS* (13)

The recommendations from the migration model in Table I, resulted from the relation of software architecture style and the type of information system, can be summarized as follows:

- **Monolithic architecture [10] and TPS, ERP, SCM, CRM and KMS information systems [11]:** as a monolithic application is built in a single unit, these types of information systems can use the Application Platform Services (aPaaS) model to implement and deploy the system in the cloud, using an embedded database and one or more programming language runtimes to implement the application (UI, business logic and data access layer) *(Recommendation 1)*.

- **Monolithic architecture [10] and BI information system [11]:** To implement BI information systems in the cloud as a monolithic application, Application Platform Services (aPaaS) can be used to build an application with BI capabilities from scratch or the Business Analytics Platform Services (baPaaS) model can be used to prepare data for analysis, visualize and analyze data, develop and publish dashboards or other Business Intelligence (BI) outputs *(Recommendation 2)*.

- **Client-server architecture [10] and TPS, BI, ERP, SCM, CRM and KMS information systems [11]:** Database Platform Services (dbPaaS) can be used to host the server logic and data for client-server applications and the respective information systems types, but as the application logic is implemented with database stored procedures and database triggers, the dbPaaS vendors and products offer needs to be analyzed and evaluated, before any implementation or migration, to attend these requirements *(Recommendation 3)*.

- **N-tier architecture [10] and TPS/BI information systems [11]:** Application Platform Services (aPaaS) and Database Platform Services (dbPaaS) can be used to implement an n-tier application for TPS and BI information systems, where the data layer can be hosted in dbPaaS and the presentation and business logic layer (and other layers if needed) can be implemented and deployed in an aPaaS as separated applications/modules *(Recommendation 4)*.

- **N-tier architecture [10] and ERP information system [11]:** Like recommendation 4, Application Platform Services (aPaaS) and Database Platform Services (dbPaaS) can be used to implement an ERP information system. Additionally, Business Process Management Services (bpmPaaS) can be used to model and execute the business process related with the functional areas in ERP, such as manufacturing and production, finance and accounting, sales and marketing, and human resources *(Recommendation 5)*.

- **N-tier architecture [10] and SCM/KMS information systems [11]:** Like recommendation 4, Application Platform Services (aPaaS) and Database Platform Services (dbPaaS) can be used to implement an SCM and KMS information systems. Also, an Enterprise Horizontal Portal Services (Portal PaaS) can be used to provide a corporate portal with the enterprise knowledge base for KMS systems and a Business-to-Business (B2B) portal for the interaction between the company and the suppliers, purchasing firms, distributors and logistics companies *(Recommendation 6)*.

- **N-tier architecture [10] and CRM information system [11]:** Like recommendation 6, Application Platform Services (aPaaS), Database Platform Services (dbPaaS) and Enterprise Horizontal Portal Services (Portal PaaS) can be used to implement a CRM information system. Besides, a Communications Platform Services (cPaaS) can be used to provide communications functionalities to enhance the communication and interaction with customers *(Recommendation 7)*.

- **Microservices architecture [12]-[14] and TPS information system [11]:** In the case of a TPS information system, it can be implemented in microservices architecture using: Application Platform Services (aPaaS) to implement each microservice application, Database Platform Services (dbPaaS) to be used by each microservice and encapsulate the business data domain, and Function Platform Services (fPaaS) to implement small functions and procedures to be executed as a microservice by the system *(Recommendation 8)*.

- **Microservices architecture [12]-[14] and BI information system [11]:** Application Platform Services (aPaaS) and Database Platform Services (dbPaaS) can be used to implement each microservice of BI information systems and a Business Analytics Platform Services (baPaaS) can be used together with the microservices to provide analytical reports and dashboards *(Recommendation 9)*.

- **Microservices architecture [12]-[14] and ERP information system [11]:** Application Platform Services (aPaaS) and Database Platform Services (dbPaaS) can be used to implement each ERP information system microservice, and can additionally use a Business Process Management Services (bpmPaaS) for modeling and executing the business process and Business Rule Platform Services (brPaaS) to encapsulate some business rules to be executed by the microservices in the system *(Recommendation 10)*.

- **Microservices [12]-[14] architecture and SCM information system [11]:** Application Platform Services (aPaaS) and Database Platform Services (dbPaaS) can be used to implement each SCM information system microservice and Business Rule Platform Services (brPaaS) to encapsulate the business rules that can be consumed by the microservices. Additionally, Enterprise Horizontal Portal Services (Portal PaaS) can be used to provide a B2B portal that is integrated with the microservices layer *(Recommendation 11)*.

- **Microservices architecture [12]-[14] and CRM information system [11]:** Like recommendation 11, a CRM information system can be implemented in microservices architecture using Application Platform Services (aPaaS), Database Platform Services (dbPaaS), Business Rule Platform Services (brPaaS) and Enterprise Horizontal Portal Services (Portal PaaS). Also, Communications Platform Services (cPaaS) can be used by the microservices to provide communications functionalities to customers *(Recommendation 12)*.

- **Microservices architecture [12]-[14] and KMS information system [11]:** KMS Information system types can be implemented in a microservice architecture using Application Platform Services (aPaaS) and Database Platform Services (dbPaaS) to build each system microservice, and Enterprise Horizontal Portal Services (Portal PaaS) can be used to provide a knowledge base portal that is integrated with the microservices layer *(Recommendation 13)*.

For all the recommended scenarios in the migration model (Table I), Integration Platform Services (iPaaS) was recommended for situations when the integration and exchange of information between cloud applications and on-premise and legacy applications are required.

In the recommendations related to Microservices Architecture (8, 9, 10, 11, 12 and 13), a Message-Oriented Middleware Services (momPaaS) was proposed to support the communication and integration between the different microservices implemented in the respective system, thus supporting the message exchange with different protocols.

The proposed migration model and respective recommendations were validated through interviews, where the objective of the interviews was to validate the migration model with specialists in Cloud Computing and Software Development from academic institutions and IT companies.

The following three questions and the identification of each interviewee were considered fundamental in the interview step and aim to validate the study, validate and improve the model and the work.

1. Does it make sense to propose a model that systematizes the different specializations of PaaS for software development?

2. Do you agree with the strategy followed in the presented migration model (Software Architecture/Information System Type/Recommendations)?

3. Do you have suggestions to improve the migration model proposed?

Based on the interview answers collected from the specialists, it was possible to verify that the migration model proposed in this work is valid and the recommendations presented in the model can be applied in software development scenarios with PaaS, according to what has been proposed in the migration model.

Regarding question 1, which aimed to validate if it makes sense to propose the model presented, all interviewees agreed that the proposed model makes sense and the importance of having precise definitions of PaaS specialized models was highlighted, thus avoiding overlaps of concepts.

The strategy followed in the model was agreed by all interviewees, according to the answers from question 2, and it was suggested that some examples of the application of recommendations to enrich the work should be described.

In question 3 answers, the interviewees collaborated with interesting suggestions for improvements in the model, but there did not agree on how to evolve the model, since one interviewee suggested keeping it as simple as possible and not include new types of information systems and new software architectures, while another interviewee suggested exactly the opposite, evolving the model to consider new types of information systems and new software architectures.

Thus, analyzing the results of the validation of the proposed model by the specialists through interviews, it was clear that it can add value to the software development process for PaaS and thus support decision makers, managers and technical specialists in trying to choose the most appropriate PaaS models for the needs and requirements of their projects.

V. Limitations and Future Work

Although Cloud Computing is not a recent technology, Platform as a Service has been gaining attention in the IT market in the last years, and consequently, the platform has been evolving. Even though the migration model presented tries to address the main aspects of PaaS, there are still open challenges remaining which can be worked on in future projects and studies.

An exhaustive investigation was necessary in different sources of information, like research and advisory companies in IT, academic papers and theses, books related with Cloud Computing and software development, producing this scientific contribution with more impartiality and objectivity and contributing to the scientific community. Gathering experts in the Cloud Computing area and getting an agenda for the interviews was difficult too, so the focus was on selecting at least one specialist from the university, one from a software consulting company and one from a software technology company, thus allowing to validate the migration model with different perspectives and experiences.

Currently, we can notice that Cloud Computing has been revolutionizing the IT market and the way we build applications and solutions, and if we analyze the conclusions of this study, it is evident that there is a need to study and explore the PaaS cloud model and its specializations further, also the changes and adaptations required in the software development arising from this "new way" to build software.

VI. Discussion and Conclusions

Every day, agility and innovation have become key factors for organizations to continue to grow and be competitive in the local and globalized market. Cloud Computing is increasingly playing a key role to support IT departments and ISV to drive organizations to achieve these goals, supporting new software and hardware technologies, and new software development methodologies and software architectures. More and more users are deploying strategical business applications in IaaS, PaaS, and SaaS, thus making platform capabilities the center of the cloud innovation. PaaS has been evolving and specializing in specific platforms to attend the different software development needs and the IT market trends, like Big Data, Internet of Things, Mobility, Cloud Native and others.

However, with continuous PaaS specialization and new software development technologies that come up every day, migrating legacy systems or developing new systems in the cloud becomes complex and challenging in some situations. The migration model presented originated because of the previously mentioned scenarios and built based on the study of the concepts and technologies related to PaaS. We tried to give recommendations and solutions, to help IT departments and ISV to start entering in PaaS software development with an initial blueprint. We validated our proposal with a model mediating to specialists in Cloud Computing and Software Development from academic institutions and IT companies.

References

[1] N. B. Ruparelia, *Cloud Computing*, First Edit. MIT Press, 2016.

[2] D. Beimborn, T. Miletzki, and S. Wenzel, "Platform as a Service (PaaS)," *Bus. Inf. Syst. Eng.*, vol. 3, no. 6, pp. 381–384, 2011.

[3] C. Pahl and H. Xiong, "Migration to PaaS clouds - Migration process and architectural concerns," in *2013 IEEE 7th International Symposium on the Maintenance and Evolution of Service-Oriented and Cloud-Based Systems*, 2013, pp. 86–91.

[4] P. Mell and T. Grance, "The NIST Definition of Cloud Computing Recommendations of the National Institute of Standards and Technology," *Nist Spec. Publ.*, vol. 145, p. 7, 2011.

[5] M. J. Kavis, *Architecting the Cloud: Design Decisions for Cloud Computing Service Models (SaaS, PaaS, and IaaS)*. Wiley; 1 edition (January 28, 2014), 2014.

[6] R. Mogull *et al.*, "The Security Guidance for Critical Areas of Focus in Cloud Computing v4.0 ('Guidance v4.0')," *Cloud Secur. Alliance*, vol. 4.0, p. 152, 2017.

[7] J. Bond, *The Enterprise Cloud*, First Edit. O'Reilly Media, 2015.

[8] Y. V. Natis *et al.*, "Platform as a Service: Definition, Taxonomy and Vendor Landscape, 2016," *Gartner*, 2016. [Online]. Available: https://www.gartner.com/doc/3334517/platform-service-definition-taxonomy-vendor. [retrieved: Feb, 2018].

[9] J. O'Brien and G. Marakas, *Management Information Systems*, 10th Editi. McGraw-Hill Education, 2010.

[10] J. Ingeno, *Software Architect's Handbook Become a Successful Software Architect by Implementing Effective Architecture Concepts*. Packt Publishing Ltd, 2018.

[11] K. C. Laudon and J. P. Laudon, *Management information systems: Managing The Digital Firm*, 15th Editi. Pearson Education Limited, 2018.

[12] B. Burns, *Designing Distributed Systems - Patterns and Paradigms for Scalable, Reliable Services*. 2018.

[13] C. Posta, *Microservices for Java Developers*, First Edit. O'Reilly Media, Inc., 2016.

[14] Microsoft, "Cloud Application Architecture Guide," Microsoft Press, 2017.

Methodology for Splitting Business Capabilities into a Microservice Architecture: Design and Maintenance Using a Domain-Driven Approach

Benjamin Hippchen, Michael Schneider, Iris Landerer, Pascal Giessler
Sebastian Abeck

Cooperation & Management (C&M), Institute for Telematics
Karlsruhe Institute of Technology
Karlsruhe, Germany
{benjamin.hippchen, michael.schneider, iris.landerer9, pascal.giessler, abeck}@kit.edu

Abstract—**The ongoing digital transformation is forcing organizations to rethink not only their business domains but also their (often monolithic) application landscapes. A more flexible architecture is needed: microservice architecture. Migrating, developing and operating such a flexible architecture requires predetermined architectural decisions. Because splitting the business domain into a more distributed software architecture is challenging, a methodology must be created that supports software architects by designing and systematically maintaining this kind of architecture. During our research, we discovered that there are only a few publications in this field that ignore the business domain and omit the maintenance of the architecture. Therefore, we provide a methodology for splitting business capabilities into a microservice architecture based on concepts of domain-driven design, which was proved over a longer time and continuously incorporated with new results. Our results indicate that we established a systematic and comprehensible creation process for microservice architecture, which also has a verifiable positive effect on the organization's application landscape.**

Keywords–Microservice; Microservice Architecture; Domain-Driven Design; Context Map; Bounded Context.

I. Introduction

The digital transformation is in progress and organizations must participate; otherwise, they will be left behind. Existing business models need to be rethought and new ones created. Tightly coupled to the business model is the organization's application landscape. Thus, this landscape also has to be reimagined. Meanwhile, microservice architectures have established themselves as an important architectural style and can be considered enablers of the digital transformation [1]. Therefore, one major step towards a digital organization is the migration of legacy applications into a microservice architecture. Afterwards, the architecture must be maintained to provide long-lived software systems. However, neither the migration, design and development of a microservice architecture nor its maintenance are easy to achieve.

The structure of the new microservice-based application seems straightforward for the development team. Some microservices communicate with each other and deliver business-related functionalities over web application interfaces (web APIs). However, at this point, the corresponding development team must ask itself decisive questions: How many microservices do we need? In which microservice do we put which functionality? Do we interact with third party applications? Domain-driven design (DDD) by Evans [2] can provides important concepts which help answering this questions. As a software engineering approach, DDD focuses on the customer's domain and wants to reflect this structure into the intended application. The business and its business objects are the focus of each developing activity. Technical details, like the deployment environment or technology decisions, are omitted and do not appear in design artifacts. Domain-driven design emphasizes the use of a domain model as a main development artifact: all relevant information about the domain, or business, is stored in it.

For microservice architecture, DDD helps structuring the application along business boundaries. Likely, these boundaries match the customer's domain boundaries. In his book *Domain-Driven Design: Tackling Complexity in the Heart of Software*, Evans introduces the "context map" diagram. This diagram's main purpose is to explore the customer's domain and state it as visual elements. The context map focuses on the macro structure of the domain, sub domains, departments and so on instead of micro elements like business objects. A further essential DDD element and pattern is the "bounded context," which represents a container for domain information. This container is filled with the mentioned domain's micro structure, creating a domain model. The name bounded context is derived from its explicit boundary. Through this boundary, the container's content is only valid inside of the bounded context. From the strategic point of view, a bounded context is a candidate for a microservice. Thus, the context map could display the organisation's microservice architecture.

Like most DDD concepts, creating a context map is challenging and the tasks are not straightforward. The vague definitions and lack of process description create problems. The following example illustrates the problem. A development team wants to establish a microservice architecture at Karlsruhe Institute of Technology (KIT) for the administration of students. Typically, for this purpose, universities introduce Student Information Systems (SIS) to support the business process execution for their employees. There are several problems with those SIS: (1) in the hands of software companies, (2) little to no understanding of the university's domain, (3) primarily monolithic architecture, and, (4) little to no insights for third parties. Because the development team has no affect on the SIS and its architecture, the goal is to advance the SIS with social media aspects to support interaction between students. A microservice architecture is planned for the new functionality. Starting with the development and using DDD, the team must gather information about the domain and create a domain model and a context map. The first uncertainty is the artifacts creation order. Both artifacts rely on information from each other. While creating the domain model, the development team needs to know where to look for specific domain information, which is stated in the context map. When creating the context map, several bounded contexts are needed, which contain a domain model. In addition to this problem, the content of a context map is not precisely defined. The literature states that the context map contains bounded contexts and relationships but does not state how to elicit them or even what they represent in the real world. This lack of real-world representation is especially a problem for development teams, who need to interact with an existing application. On the one hand, it is necessary to provide the third party application in the context map, because the context map can capture the information transferred between the third-party and the university. On the other hand, it is unclear how to represent the third-party application in the context map. A bounded context needs a domain model, and there is no domain model in this case. These are only two problems with the application of the context map, but they illustrate how import it is to enhance usability. In the following sections, we discuss these and other problems in more detail.

In this paper, we provide the following contributions to enhance the application of the context map and support the design and maintenance of a microservice-based application:

- **Context Map Foundations**: One major problem of DDD is the lack of integration and placement in existing software development processes. It is unclear in which phases the context map must be created and in which phases it supports the development. Therefore, in Section III, we provide the first integration and placement of this map. In addition, we discuss the foundations of the context map and define the elements in this section.
- **Context Choreography**: While applying DDD for the development of microservice-based applications, we realized the existing artifacts did not capture all relevant information. Thus, in Section II and Section III, we introduce a new type of diagram, the "context choreography". This diagram's purpose is to display the choreography between multiple microservices for the application.
- **Artifact Creating Order**: As mentioned, it is unclear in which order the DDD artifacts must be created. Therefore, in Section III, we also provide a detailed order with an emphasis on the context map. The application of the order is presented in our case study in Section IV.

II. Placement and Integration of the Context Map

One main problem of DDD is its lack of placement in the field of software development. Neither its models nor its patterns, including the context map, are placed in common software development processes. For our placement, we focus on the context of microservices. Because the context map has some weakness in development, a new diagram is introduced to close the gap.

A. Placement

As mentioned in Section I, the use of the context map is not straightforward. The development team must analyze the domain, create a domain model, and develop a context map. On the one hand, the context map has a great benefit for microservice architectures. On the other hand, applying the map correctly is difficult.

Each DDD practice should be performed with the focus on an intended application [2]. This ensures the "perfect fit" of the gathered information, called "domain knowledge," for the application. Domain knowledge is captured in domain models. At this point, the pattern "bounded context" becomes important. An application consists of multiple bounded contexts, which all have their own domain models. With respect to the complexity of the domain knowledge, it makes sense to split the domain knowledge into multiple domain models. The validity of each domain model is limited through the bounded context. Furthermore, each bounded context has its own "ubiquitous language," which is based on the domain knowledge and acts as a contract for communication between project members and stakeholders. For the development of microservice-based applications especially, the multiple bounded contexts support the idea of a microservice architecture. Through connections between the bounded contexts, the domain knowledge is joined together in the application. The arising relationships are application-specific and differ from application to application. There are several types of relationships [3]. Modeling the bounded contexts and their relationships is the purpose of a context map.

Considering a microservice architecture, the purpose of a context map is not only to elicit domain knowledge. Organizations that introduce microsevices need to manage their application landscape to maintain the microservice architecture. Without the knowledge about which microservices are available and who is in charge of them, the microservice architecture loses its advantages. Existing microservices are simply not used, even the domain knowledge they provide is required, due to the fact that other development teams could not find it, oversee it or forgot about it. The required domain knowledge is redeveloped in new microservices and the existing microservices become legacy. Sustaining the advantages of a microservice architecture is therefore important for organizations and the context map is one tool which helps to achieve this. In addition, the aspect that DDD focus its development artifacts on the customer's domain, supports the maintenance of the microservice architecture. Aligning the context map to the customer's domain leads to a natural-looking architecture [4]. Conway's Law [5] also supports the idea behind a natural-looking microservice architecture. The organizational structure is adapted in the microservice architecture and vice versa. Looking at concepts like Martin Fowler's "HumaneRegistry" [6] or API management products like "apigee" [7], the idea and approach of the context map is required and furthermore it supports such concepts and products.

Using the context map as a tool for maintaining the microservice architecture is contrary to one DDD aspect: focus always on an application. The mentioned maintenance does not require any kind of application-specific information. A microservice is firstly an application-independent software building block [8] and needs to be treated as such while maintaining the microservice architecture. Even if the development of a microservice is motivated through the development of an application. Thus, we see the context map as an application-independent diagram.

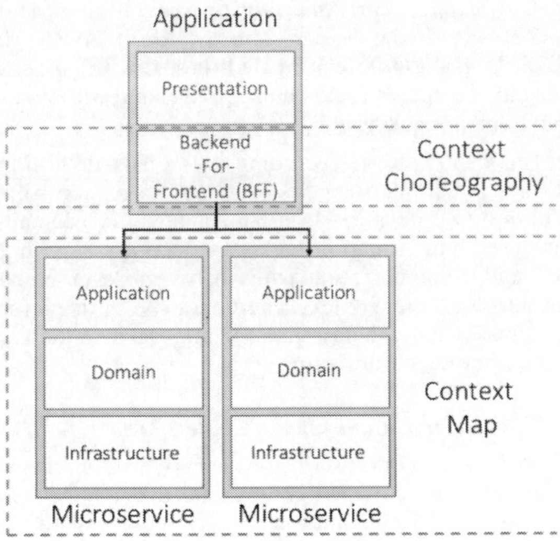

Figure 1. Placement of context mapping artifacts regarding the software building blocks from [8]

According to [8], for microservice-based applications, microservices are choreographed in applications through a backend-for-frontend (BFF) pattern. This is where application-specific information comes into play. Fig. 1 depicts the software architecture, including the application's BFF. To capture the choreography in the BFF, a new type of diagram is needed. The "context choreography" provides a view of the bounded context necessary for the application. Furthermore, the context choreography indicates which domain knowledge the bounded context transfers.

The context map can also be placed into software development activities. In [8], the first steps to place DDD into the software development activities from Brügge et al. [9] were taken. However, the context map itself was omitted. We built on these results for our placement of the context map. Domain-driven design introduces two types of "design activities" [2]. The first is the "strategic design," with tasks in modeling and structuring the domain's macroarchitecture (e.g., departments are used to define boundaries). This macroarchitecture is captured in the context map. Secondly, the "tactical design" further refines the macroarchitecture and enriches the bounded contexts with domain knowledge. This activity represents the microarchitecture of the domain and therefore of the microservice. Both activities rely on creating diagrams. Considering the software development activities from Brügge et al., Evans' designation as strategic and tactical "design" is misleading. Those focus more on the analysis than on the design phase. Many DDD practices and principles, such as "knowledge crunching," aim to analyze the domain. The development team explores the customer's domain and should simultaneously create the context map and domain model. Thus, the strategic and tactical designs are completed out, which is why the context map must be integrated at this point.

As mentioned, the content of the context map depends on its purpose. This is even the case for the relationships between the bounded contexts. Developing a monolithic application requires a different viewpoint on these relationships than a microservice-based application requires. A microservice architecture has many different microservices, which are managed by different development teams. By choreographing microservices in applications, development teams are automatically interdependent. This dependency is illustrated in the relationships in the context map. They could also be seen as communication paths between those development teams.

Our placement indicates that the context map has several possibilities to support the development of microservice architectures and microservice-based applications. We distinguish between a microservice architecture and the development of a microservice-based application. With regard to the microservice architecture style, the context map provides an overview of all in the application landscape existing microservices and further the dependencies of the responsible development teams—which are also necessary information for maintaining the microservice architecture. Due to the application-independence of these information, the context map is an application-independent diagram. Additionally, we saw a lack of the context map while specifying microservice-based applications. Information transferred between microservices was missing a specification, which is necessary for choreographing the BFF of the application. Thus, we introduced the context choreography, which displays the application-specific dependencies between the microservices and their transferred domain knowledge. With this placement, we make a first step in advancing the use of the context map.

III. Foundations and Artifact Order

In addition to the placement, we see a high need for clear definitions and guidance in creating the context choreography and context map. Therefore, this section provides definitions for terms regarding both artifacts. Afterward, we explain how the artifacts could be created.

A. Foundations

We found that, in addition to the development process, terminology around the context map is not clearly defined. This also leads to difficult application. Therefore, we want to provide some basics.

1) Bounded Context: The bounded context is the main element for the context map and is an explicit boundary for limiting the validity of domain knowledge [2]. Thus, within this context, there is a domain model and its ubiquitous language. A bounded context does not represent an application. This is based on the layered architecture of DDD, which consists of four layers: (1) presentation, (2) application, (3) domain, and (4) infrastructure. Domain-driven design and its artifacts focus only on the domain layer and omit the others. Therefore, without any application logic in a domain model, a bounded context cannot represent an application. This definition is necessary, when creating a context map. An intended application is usually integrated into an existing application landscape.

When developing a microservice-based application, a bounded context initially only represents a candidate for a microservice [4]. Thus, a bounded context is either large enough that two or more microservices are necessary or small enough that they are included in one microservice. The best practice, however, should be the one-to-one relationship. This relationship eases the maintenance of the architecture through a clearer mapping between bounded contexts, microservices, and the responsible development teams. Reconsidering the size of the bounded context helps achieve this mapping. Therefore, we have collected several indicators, or more precisely possible influence factors, for the size of bounded contexts from our experiences in research and practice. This list should not be considered complete or verified with an empirical study but should rather be seen as an aid. A bounded context (1) has a high cohesion and low coupling, (2) can be managed by one development team, (3) has ideally a high autonomy to reduce the communication/coordination effort between development teams, (4) has a unique language that is not (necessarily) shared, and (5) represents a meaningful excerpt of the domain.

2) Context choreography: As mentioned (see Section II), the specification of a microservice-based application was lacking some information. Thus, we introduced the context choreography as a new diagram.

For microservice-based application development, it is important to state the other needed microservices—and thus the bounded context also. Furthermore, the exchanged data between those microservices are important information. As a microservice-based application is developed, existing microservices could still be used, while new ones are developed. In both cases, the context choreography is supportive. Regarding the application itself, the context choreography states all necessary microservices and the transferred domain knowledge between them, literally displaying the choreography of the microservices to achieve the application functionality. According to the software architecture provided by [8], the application's BFF is specified. Independent from the application, the context choreography states the microservice interfaces. Both the consumed and the provided interfaces of the microservice are provided. Thus, while developing the application, the first hints of the API can be derived. With regard to the subsequent maintenance of the microservice, development teams are able to identify the microservices that rely on them and vice versa.

3) Context Map: The DDD's original purpose for the context map differs from the one provided in this paper. In the context of microservice architecture, the context map is a useful diagram for maintaining the architecture and supporting application development.

One major advantage is the comprehensive overview of existing microservices. According to the best practice from Section III-A1, each bounded context in the context map represents a microservice. Further, in software architecture, social and organization aspects have to be considered [10]. Therefore, dependencies between microservices, and thus development teams, are stated. When development teams want to evolve their microservices, it is important to ask who depends on these microservices. At this point, the dependencies on other teams must be considered because any change could affect the stability of the other microservices. Thus, changes have to be communicated.

Also, for the development of a microservice-based application, the context map is advantageous. Regarding the context choreography, existing microservices are used to compose functionality for the intended application. Using existing microservices is only possible if they are traceable in the microservice architecture. This is where the context map comes into play. After developing a microservice, it is placed as a bounded context into the model. While the application is in development, the development team can use the context map as a tool to locate the needed microservices.

4) Domain Experts and other Target Groups: The interaction between domain experts and developers is one principle of DDD [2]. Each artifact is created for and with domain experts. Thus, the artifacts should be understandable without a software development background.

The context map according to DDD's definition is also relevant for domain experts [11]. However, according to our definition, we do not see any advantages for domain experts since the context map provides an overview of bounded contexts and communication paths between development teams. Furthermore, the context choreography is irrelevant. Only the subdomains, which represent the organization's structure, contain helpful information.

B. Process for Establishing a Context Map

To develop a microservice-based application, it is necessary to establish the bounded contexts needed for the application. The developed application also may reuse existing microservices, which should be integrated into the application landscape. To obtain an overview of the microservice landscape, the context map is useful. In this section, we focus on the establishment of the bounded contexts, the context choreography, and the context map. For developing an application, we build on a development process based on behavior-driven development (BDD) [12] and DDD [2] introduced in [8]. We omit the steps in [8] and focus on the creation of context choreography and a context map. Therefore, this section describes how the context map is established and enhanced within the development process.

1) Forming the Initial Domain Model: Forming the initial domain model occurs in the analysis and design phases. Before developing an application, the requirements are specified with BDD in the form of features. As Fig. 2 illustrates, a tactical diagram is derived from the features (e.g., the domain objects and their relationships). If a domain model already exists (e.g., from an existing microservice), this should be taken into account. The resulting diagram represents the initial domain model, which contains the application's business logic. Thus, the domain model provides the semantic foundation for all the specified features. The resulting diagram is comparable to a Unified Modeling Language (UML) class diagram and displays the structural aspects of the domain objects. If the domain structure is still vague when the number of features is satisfied, more features are considered until the domain model appears to be meaningful. Afterward, as presented in Fig. 2, this initial domain model is examined and structured into several bounded contexts.

2) Forming the Bounded Contexts: The model is strategical analyzed and separated based on the business and its functionality. This step depends on the domain knowledge and the structure of the business. Therefore, knowledge crunching from DDD [2] is applied to gather that knowledge. Often, a business's domain knowledge is scattered through the whole business. Therefore, analyzing the business is important to

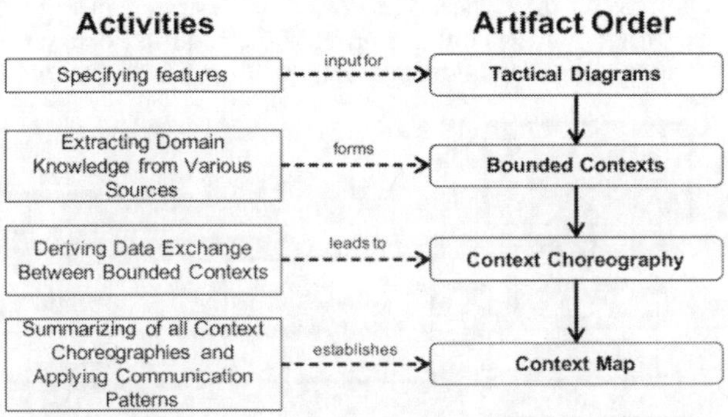

Figure 2. Creating order for artifacts their and impacting activities

TABLE I. Overview of communication patterns and their impact

Comm. pattern	Description	Effort
Partnership	Cooperation between bounded contexts to avoid failure	Very high
Shared Kernel	Explicit shared functionality between different development teams	Medium to high
Customer/ Supplier	Supplier provides required functionality for the customer. The customer has influence on the supplier's design decisions	High to very high
Conformist	Similar to customer/supplier but with no influence on design decisions.	Low to medium
Separate Ways	No cooperation between development teams	Low
Anticorruption Layer	Additional layer that transforms one context into another	Low
Open Host Service	Uniform interface for accessing the bounded context	Low
Published Language	Information exchange is achieved using the ubiquitous language of the bounded context	Low

understand the business processes and the interaction of different departments. By default, each department knows its tasks the best. To extract the domain knowledge, various sources should be considered. These sources include domain experts who are part of a department, as well as documents and organizational aspects. This domain knowledge provides hints for structuring the domain and has to be considered while forming the bounded contexts. Considering the application analysis and the business analysis from [8] leads to the bounded contexts, as illustrated in Figure 2. If a context map has been established, then the context map is searched for the required domain knowledge of the application. If a bounded context representing the domain knowledge already exists, then this bounded context is taken into account. A new bounded context is established if the context map does not contain the required domain knowledge. For example, we integrated a profile context into an existing context map of the campus management domain.

3) Toward the Context Choreography: Forming the bounded contexts is only the first step towards a working application. Each previously established bounded context is considered a microservice and requires or offers a unique interface for communication that can be based on REST or other architectural styles. Without interfaces, a microservice-based application would not work. The microservices are choreographed with the BFF. To allow choreography, the data exchange between the bounded contexts is considered next. The required data exchange is modeled in the context choreography. For each bounded context, a context choreography diagram is modeled. Domain objects that need to be shared or consumed from other bounded contexts are modeled as shared entities. The considered bounded context can either share the domain object itself or consume the domain object. This model also provides hints for the API of a bounded context if the bounded context shares entities.

4) Toward the Context Map: In microservice architectures, each established bounded context represents a microservice and is implemented by autonomous development teams. Thus, for relating bounded contexts, teams may need to communicate with each other. Therefore, the communication effort between the teams should be considered. The communication effort indicates how much communication between the teams is required. Clear communication paths are necessary, because a team needs to know which other team is responsible for relating bounded contexts. Therefore, dependencies and communication channels between teams are defined. Depending on the teams and the possible communication effort, a communication pattern is chosen based on [2] [3] (see Table I). The last three communication patterns listed in Table I are special patterns designed to reduce the communication between different teams, as well as the impact on interface changes. Other benefits and drawbacks of particular patterns exist but they are out of the scope for the current discussion. The context map illustrates the determined communication path between the bounded contexts. For example, when the communication between teams is not possible, such as when foreign services are adopted, DDD patterns need to be applied. For foreign services, the ACL pattern should be applied. In the last step, as depicted in Figure 2, the relationships (including the pattern) and the bounded contexts are added to the context map diagram.

Adding those bounded contexts and communication relationships is an essential part of the context map. This concludes the first cycle of the analysis and design phases.

5) Adjustments of the models: After the design phase, the implementation phase follows. In this phase, the models are implemented and tested. Afterward, specific parts of the application are developed. Following the iterative process, new features are implemented into the next cycle. These features need to be analyzed and may change the domain model. In addition, this may lead to the establishment of new bounded contexts. Thus, the models, including the tactical diagrams, the context choreography, and the context map, are refined according to the features and the knowledge crunching process in the previous steps.

IV. Case Study: Campus Management

In our case study, we illustrate our approach of establishing a new bounded context and integrating it into an existing context map. The case study orientates itself on the process as described in Section III. Over three semesters, we expanded the campus management system of KIT with microservice-based applications. The case study represents our recent project in this field and adds a social media component to the campus management system.

A. Project Scope

Our vision is to simply and efficiently support the exchange of information and facilitate cooperation between students. For this purpose, we wanted to introduce a profile service in the campus management system. This profile service should allow students to create custom profiles to display information about their studies, like currently visited lectures and future exams. The purpose of this service is to assist students with their studies and their search for learning partners. For example, students can find learning partners with the help of the profile service when other students share the lectures they attend.

B. Requirement Elicitation

In our process, we began by eliciting the requirements with BDD and formulating them as features. Fig. 3 presents one of the main features that enables students to edit their profile.

1. **Feature**: Providing student profiles
2. As a student
3. I can provide relevant information about myself
4. So that others can see my interests and study information

5. **Scenario**: Publish profile
6. **Given** I was never logged in to the ProfileService
7. **When** I log in to the ProfileService for the first time
8. **Then** my study account is linked to the ProfileService
9. **And** I choose which profile information I want to publish

Figure 3. Example of a BDD feature for publishing an user profile

C. Initial Domain Model

Analyzing the features leads to the initial domain model by deriving domain objects and their relationships. In our previously defined feature (see Section IV-B), we identified, the terms "Profile," "Examination," and "Student" and added them to the initial domain model. By repeating this procedure with all features, the domain model is enriched with the business logic. The result of the initial tactical diagram is presented in Fig. 4.

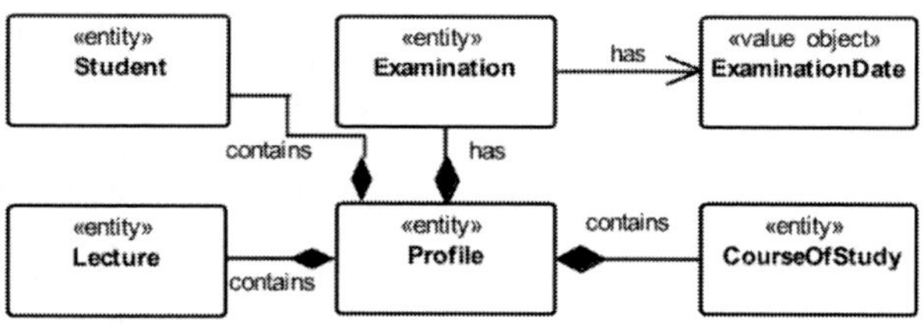

Figure 4. Initial domain model derived from BDD features and other sources

D. Bounded Contexts and Context Choreography

While we analyzed the domain, we also considered the existing context map of the campus management domain. We noticed that the bounded contexts "StudentManagement," "ExaminationManagement," "ModuleManagement," and "CourseMapping" already offered the required functionality. Only "ProfileManagement" had to be established as a new bounded context. Therefore, we considered the data exchange between the bounded contexts and created the context choreography on that basis. The result is illustrated in Fig. 5. The existing bounded contexts provide the required data as shared entities. The new bounded context "Profiles" adapts the shared

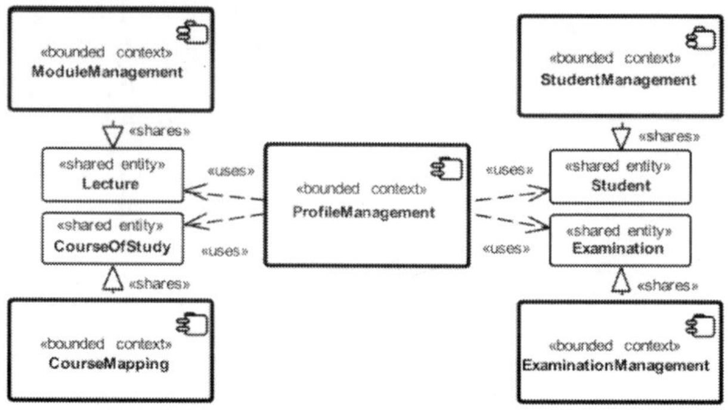

Figure 5. New bounded context "ProfileManagement" in a context choreography

entities and delivers the data required from the profile service. Last, the microservices are choreographed in the BFF of the intended application, to achieve the required application logic.

E. Integrating in Context Map

After we had established the bounded contexts and the context choreography, we needed to add the profile management context to the context map. Therefore, we determined the dependencies and communication channels between bounded contexts based on the context choreography. We found our development team did not influence any other bounded context. Thus, we applied the conformist as communication pattern. As a result, the context map depicted in Figure 6 was enhanced with the "Profiles" context. Afterward, we started the first

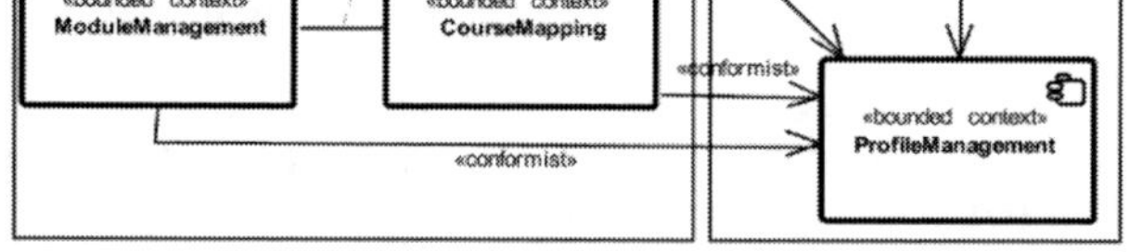

Figure 6. "ProfileManagement" context integrated into context map

implementation cycle.

F. Context Map as Template for a Deployment Map

The resulting context map provides an overview of the microservices that need to be deployed. Assuming that each bounded context represents one microservice, we can enhance the context map with technical information that is needed for the deployment in a secure manner. For instance, we can define which ports listen for incoming or are allowed for outgoing requests. By following such an approach each microservice is initially considered in isolation. We enforce this by defining default policies on the execution environment that need to be taken into account during deployment. The enhancement with technical information is transferred into a new diagram called a deployment map. For the modeling, we use a UML deployment diagram. In addition to a general overview of the deployment, it can also be used for an upfront security audit. We are planning to present the derivation rules in an upcoming publication.

For testing purpose, we have used a hosted Kubernetes [13] cluster on a cloud provider. Kubernetes is an open source system for provisioning and management of container-based applications and aroused from the collected experience behind Omega and Borg. First of all, we have defined policies to deny all ingress and egress traffic to all running Pods by default. A Pod groups one or more container and can be seen as the central brick of Kubernetes when deploying applications. Each bounded context will be represented by a microservice running in a container (Docker or rkt). Depending on their relation to each other (see TABLE I), we put them in corresponding Pods. Next, we have used the ports for incoming and outgoing traffic to derive the network policies. Finally, we have defined the services that wrap the Pods and offer a central access point for interaction. The application shows us that the underlying context map can be used as a basic scaffolding for deriving the deployment map but need to be enhanced with technical information as well as information from the development teams that realize the microservices. For instance, a persistent storage is missing in a context map due to its domain orientation but is needed for the deployment map.

V. Related Work

During our research, we searched for works comparable to the context map and its purpose. We encountered several inspiring works regarding different aspects of the context map. Especially, the focus on the microservice architecture is an important part of this paper.

A. Microservice Architecture

A microservice should concentrate on the fulfilment of one task and should be small, so a team of five to seven developers can be responsible for the microservice's implementation [4]. A microservice itself is not an application, but rather a software building block [8]. In microservice architecture, applications are realized through choreography of these building blocks. A central aspect of microservice architecture is the autonomy of the single microservices [14]. Each microservice is developed and released independently to achieve continuous integration.

B. Approaches for Designing a Microservice Architecture

The objective of microservice architectures is to subdivide large components into smaller ones to reduce complexity and create more clarity in the single elements of the system [14]. In this paper, we described our approach of designing microservice architecture with a context map from DDD. However, there are further strategies to identify microservices, which we considered in this paper.

One possible approach is event storming, as introduced by Alberto Brandolini in the context of DDD [15]. Event storming is a workshop-based group technique to quickly determine the domain of a software program. The group starts with the workshop by "storming out" all domain events. A domain event covers every topic of interest to a domain expert. Afterward, the group adds the commands that cause these events. Then, the group detects aggregates, which accept commands and accomplish events, and begins to cluster them together into bounded contexts. Finally, the relationships between bounded contexts are considered to create a context map. Like our approach, this strategy is based on DDD and results in a context map displaying the bounded contexts. Instead of a workshop for exploring the domain and defining domain events, we develop our bounded contexts through an iterative analysis and design phase. Furthermore, we enhanced the context map with maintenance aspect for microservice discovery and dependencies between development teams. The purpose of the resulting context map from [15] is comparable to the context choreography. Both focusing on the interactions between bounded context and identify the transferred domain knowledge.

Another method for approaching a microservice architecture is described in [16]. First, required system operations and state variables are identified based on use case specifications of software requirements. System operations define public operations, which comprise the system's API, and state variables contain information that system operations read or write. The relationships between these systems operations and state variables are detected and then are visualized as a graph. The visualization enables developers to build clusters of dense relationships, which are weakly connected to other clusters. Each cluster is considered a candidate for a microservice. This bears a resemblance to our approach because we also begin by focusing on the software requirements and take visualization for better understanding the domain.

A further widely used illustration of partitioning monolithic applications is a scaling cube, which uses a three-dimensional approach as described in [17]. Here, Y-axis scaling is important because it splits a monolithic application into a set of services. Each service implements a set of related functionalities. There are different ways to decompose the application which differ from our domain-driven approach. One approach is to use verb-based decomposition and define services that implement a single use case. The other possibility is to partition the application by nouns and establish services liable for all operations related to a specific entity. An application might use a combination of verb-based and noun-based decomposition. X-axis and Z-axis regards the operation of the microservices. The X-axis describes the horizontal scaling which means cloning and load balancing the same microservice into multiple instances. Meanwhile, the Z-axis denotes the degree of data separation. Both axis are important for microservice architectures and currently omitted in our context map approach.

C. Software Development Approaches

The development process we apply is based on BDD and DDD. As a method of agile software development, BDD should specify a software system by referencing its behavior. The basic artifact of BDD is the feature, which describes a functionality of the application. The use of natural language

and predefined keywords allows the developer to create features directly with the customer [18]. During our analysis phase, we used BDD for requirement elicitation.
In our design phase, we applied DDD based on the features we defined with BDD. DDD's main focus is the domain and the domain's functionality, rather than technical aspects [11]. The central design artifact is the domain model, which represents the target domain. In his book *Domain Driven Design - Tackling Complexity in the Heart of Software*, Eric Evans describes patterns, principles, and activities that support the process of software development [2]. Although DDD is not tied to a specific software development process, it is orientated toward agile software development. In particular, DDD requires iterative software development and a close collaboration between developers and domain experts.

D. Application of the Context Map

The goal of a context map, which Evans describes as one main activity of DDD, is to structure the target domain [2]. For this purpose, the domain is classified into subdomains, and in those subdomains, the boarders and interfaces of possible bounded contexts are defined. A bounded context is a candidate for a microservice, and one team is responsible for its development and operations [4]. Moreover, the relationships between bounded contexts are defined in a context map. Both the technical relationships and the organizational dependencies between different teams are considered.
A further aspect of the context map involves the maintenance of the miscroservice architecture. Without managing the application (or service) landscape, existing microservices are not used, even if they provide needed domain knowledge. The usage of a context map helps concepts like humane registry or API management products which tries to achieve maintenance goals. Martin Fowler introduced humane registry as a place, where both developers and users can record information about a particular service in a wiki [6]. In addition, some information can be collected automatically, e.g., by evaluating data from source code control and issue tracking systems. API management products like "apigee" [7] reach maintenance by pre-defining API guidelines such as key validation, quota management, transformation, authorization, and access control.

VI. Limitations and Conclusion

The concepts we provide in this in paper have some limitations. These are addressed in the next section. Afterward, we provide a short conclusion discussing our results.

A. Limitations

Domain-driven design has no special application or architectural style in mind. The concepts should be applied to DDD's layered architecture but could be applied to different architectural styles. For a better fit while developing microservice-based applications, we always had the microservice architecture in mind. Therefore, our provided concepts are only valid when developing a microservice-based application.

The concepts provided by this paper are built from our experiences which we gathered in various projects. Most of our projects were in the academic branch, but we also worked with industrial partners. For the context map, we developed and proved our concepts over a longer time. The case study describes our last project. Project members and partners gave us useful feedback about the concepts when they applied them. In addition, the feedback also included points we had not yet addressed, like a modeling language for context mapping. Nevertheless, evidence of our concepts in large microservice architectures, such as 50 or more microservices, still lacks. Our goal is to obtain prove for large microservice architectures in such projects.

Another limitation to our concepts is we only applied them in "clean" microservice architectures. However, in the real world, there are also legacy applications in the application landscapes of organizations. Typically, a legacy application is not a microservice-based one; often, it is a monolithic architecture. In future work, we must determine how to integrate legacy applications into the context choreography and context map.

B. Conclusion

During our research, we found many different studies that consider model-driven approaches for developing microservices. Using these approaches for microservices is common. In domain-driven design, especially, the approaches focus on the development itself but omit the design and maintenance phases. Therefore, we wanted to provide details on the design and maintenance of a microservice architecture using DDD's context map.

The context map has great potential to aid in developing and maintaining applications and is more useful when considering a microservice architecture. However, the context map shares a problem with most DDD concepts: its lacking placement in software engineering, foundations and concrete guidelines. Therefore, we first provided placement for the context map. Next, we clarified its foundations with a focus on the bounded context, the main concept of the context map. After the foundations were clear, we could develop a systematic approach for creating the context map. This approach began in the analysis phase with an initial domain model, separating the domain knowledge into bounded contexts, stating relationships between them, and putting the bounded contexts into a context map. The separation of bounded contexts and their relationships are stated in our new diagram, the "context choreography." This diagram's purpose is to illustrate necessary bounded contexts for microservice-based applications.

This paper's contributions are the first step in making the use of the context map, and now the context choreography, more efficient. Nevertheless, we see more opportunities for research, like a modeling language for the context map. Such a modeling language could be UML.

Acknowledgment

We want to give special thanks to Chris Irrgang and Tobias Hülsken for always providing their opinions and useful feedback on our concepts. Furthermore, we would like to thank the following development team, which provided the results in our case study: Alessa Radkohl, Nico Peter, and Stefan Throner.

References

[1] M. Gebhart, P. Giessler, and S. Abeck, "Challenges of the Digital Transformation in Software Engineering," *ICSEA 2016*, p. 149, 2016.

[2] E. Evans, *Domain-Driven Design: Tackling Complexity in the Heart of Software*. Addison-Wesley Professional, 2004.

[3] V. Vernon, Ed., *Implementing Domain-Driven Design.* Addison-Wesley, 2013.

[4] S. Newman, *Building Microservices: Designing Fine-grained Systems.* " O'Reilly Media, Inc.", 2015.

[5] M. E. Conway, "How do Committees Invent," *Datamation*, vol. 14, no. 4, pp. 28–31, 1968.

[6] M. Fowler, "HumaneRegistry," URL: https://martinfowler.com/bliki/HumaneRegistry.html [retrieved: 02, 2019].

[7] Google, "apigee, API management," https://apigee.com/api-management/ [retrieved: 02, 2019].

[8] B. Hippchen, P. Giessler, R. Steinegger, M. Schneider, and S. Abeck, "Designing Microservice-Based Applications by Using a Domain-Driven Design Approach," in *International Journal on Advances in Software, Vol. 10, No. 3&4, pp. 432–445*, 2017.

[9] B. Bruegge and A. H. Dutoit, *Object-Oriented Software Engineering Using UML, Patterns and Java-(Required).* Prentice Hall, 2004.

[10] O. Vogel, I. Arnold, A. Chughtai, and T. Kehrer, *Software Architecture: A Comprehensive Framework and Guide for Practitioners.* Springer Science & Business Media, 2011.

[11] S. Millett, *Patterns, Principles and Practices of Domain-Driven Design.* John Wiley & Sons, 2015.

[12] J. F. Smart, *BDD in Action: Behavior-Driven Development for the Whole Software Lifecycle.* Manning, 2015.

[13] K. Hightower, B. Burns, and J. Beda, *Kubernetes: Up and Running: Dive Into the Future of Infrastructure.* O'Reilly Media, 2017.

[14] I. Nadareishvili, R. Mitra, M. McLarty, and M. Amundsen, *Microservice Architecture: Aligning Principles, Practices, and Culture.* " O'Reilly Media, Inc.", 2016.

[15] A. Brandolini, "Introducing Event Storming," *blog, Ziobrando's Lair*, vol. 18, 2013, URL: http://ziobrando.blogspot.com/2013/11/introducing-event-storming.html [retrieved: 02, 2019].

[16] S. Tyszberowicz, R. Heinrich, B. Liu, and Z. Liu, "Identifying Microservices Using Functional Decomposition," pp. 50–65, 2018.

[17] N. Dmitry and S.-S. Manfred, "On Micro-Services Architecture," *International Journal of Open Information Technologies*, vol. 2, no. 9, 2014.

[18] M. Wynne, A. Hellesoy, and S. Tooke, *The Cucumber Book: Behaviour-Driven Development for Testers and Developers.* Pragmatic Bookshelf, 2017.

Improving Code Smell Predictions in Continuous Integration by Differentiating Organic from Cumulative Measures

Md Abdullah Al Mamun, Miroslaw Staron
Christian Berger, Regina Hebig
Department of Computer Science and Engineering
Chalmers | University of Gothenburg, Sweden
Email: abdullah.mamun@chalmers.se,
[miroslaw.staron, christian.berger,
regina.hebig]@cse.gu.se

Jörgen Hansson
School of Informatics
University of Skövde
Skövde, Sweden
Email: jorgen.hansson@his.se

Abstract—**Continuous integration and deployment are enablers of quick innovation cycles of software and systems through incremental releases of a product within short periods of time. If software qualities can be predicted for the next release, quality managers can plan ahead with resource allocation for concerning issues. Cumulative metrics are observed to have much higher correlation coefficients compared to non-cumulative metrics. Given the difference in correlation coefficients of cumulative and non-cumulative metrics, this study investigates the difference between metrics of these two categories concerning the correctness of predicting code smell which is internal software quality. This study considers 12 metrics from each measurement category, and 35 code smells collected from 36,217 software revisions (commits) of 242 open source Java projects. We build 8,190 predictive models and evaluate them to determine how measurement categories of predictors and targets affect model accuracies predicting code smells. To further validate our approach, we compared our results with Principal Component Analysis (PCA), a statistical procedure for dimensionality reduction. Results of the study show that within the context of continuous integration, non-cumulative metrics as predictors build better predictive models with respect to model accuracy compared to cumulative metrics. When the results are compared with models built from extracted PCA components, we found better results using our approach.**

Keywords–Software metrics; code smells; effects of measurement types; cumulative metrics; organic metrics; random forest; training-test-split cross-validation; time-series cross-validation; principal component analysis; interactions.

I. Introduction

Continuous integration and deployment shorten the release cycles and speed up the innovation cycles [1]. Fortunately, Agile software development can support continuous integration and deployment through sprints, time-boxes of one to four weeks, during which a releasable product increment is created [2]. As the release cycles are becoming shorter, it would be helpful for quality managers if they can predict internal and external software quality within a short span of time. For example, if quality managers have tools to predict the maintainability of code base at the end of the current sprint, they can already start allocating hours on the maintainability issue or plan for the next sprint. With the introduction of modern version control systems, we can address the problem of *how to predict internal quality changes between different revisions of software code base?* A version control system stores every revision or commit of a project; such commit-level data are much fine-grained with the possibility to reflect actual software development within a short span of time. Now we ask the question: can such refined-level data explain or predict software qualities at a short time span better compared to the traditionally counted cumulative way of measures?

Software metrics can be measured in various ways, or they have different measurement types. By organic or non-cumulative metrics, we refer to delta measures or code churn measures. If we take the example of Lines Of Code (LOC), the organic measure of LOC for a software revision or commit is the actual number of LOC written since the previous commit. On the other hand, cumulative measurement is the most commonly used technique in software engineering. The cumulative-way of measuring LOC for a commit would be to sum the organic measure of LOC for a specific commit with the cumulative measure of LOC from the previous commit. Therefore, cumulative measures develop as a moving sum. If ten new LOC are added for a commit, the organic measure of LOC for that specific commit would be ten, reflecting the actual change of LOC. However, when measured cumulatively, the value of LOC should be ten plus the total LOC from the previous commit. For each cumulative metric, a corresponding organic metric can be constructed. These measurement types are explained in Section II. A recent study [3] exclusively targeting cumulative and organic measures confirms that correlations of cumulative metrics are much higher than their corresponding organic metrics. Since that study [3] is still in the final minor review round, we are reporting the relevant part of the results in Table I. In addition, in a previous study [4], we had indications that correlations between cumulative metrics are higher than their corresponding organic metrics.

High correlation coefficients between metrics imply high collinearity between them. If the correlation coefficient is as high as 0.9, it can be considered as very strong [5]. Thus, corresponding metrics can be considered collinear meaning they are redundant. Non-collinearity is mentioned as a validation criterion for software metrics [6]. However, some methods for predictive analyses, such as multiple linear regression, rely on the assumption that input features are non-collinear. Thus, it is to be expected that combinations of cumulative metrics (which have higher collinearity) are less fit to be used in predictive models compared to their corresponding organic metrics. However, to our knowledge, to this day no studies have investigated whether organic metrics can lead to better predictions of aspects, such as code smells or bugs compared to their corresponding cumulative metrics. Therefore, we want

Day	Day-wise changed Lines of Code (Organic Measure)	Written so far Lines of Code (Cumulative Measure)
1	10	10
2	15	25
3	30	55
4	0	55
5	50	105
6	5	110
7	10	120
8	8	128
9	75	203
10	47	250
11	39	289
12	61	350
13	34	384
14	7	391
15	0	391
16	0	391
17	12	403
18	35	438
19	23	461
20	20	481

(a) Textual Representation

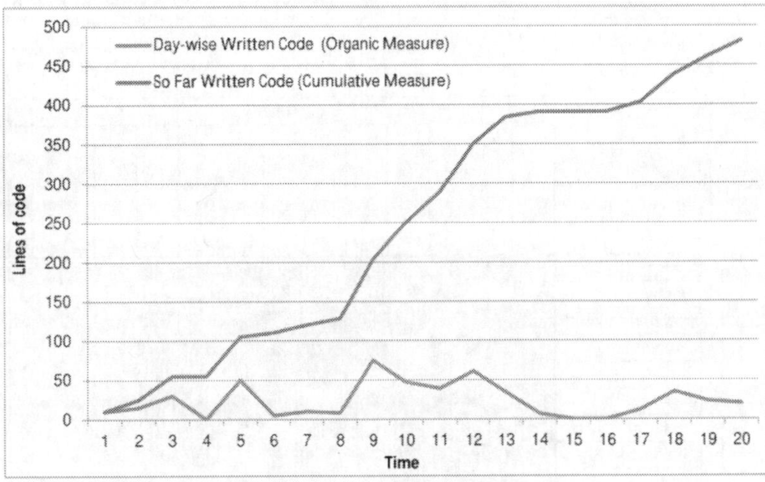

(b) Equivalent Graphical Representation

Figure 1. Organic and Cumulative Measures.

to investigate this. Code smells are internal software qualities that are associated with code maintainability [7] [8] and using code smells has significantly less internal validity threat in the context of this research because unlike the bugs, we can precisely determine which code smells are originated from which revisions. Thus, code smell is a good candidate as a target for this study. Note that we are using code smell as an interesting example to validate whether there is any difference between the two measurement categories, our objective is not to build the best predictive model for code smells. This study has the following research question:

- RQ: What is the difference between organic and cumulative measures with respect to the correctness of predicting code smells within the context of continuous integration?

In this paper, we analyzed 36,217 revisions of 242 open source Java projects to mine various measures and code smells. Our results show that measurement types of metrics have a significant impact on model accuracies. The findings will help to build predictive models specifically targeted to predict software artifacts within a short period of time. Our findings are also significant to clearly understand the difference between cumulative and organic measures of software artifacts.

Section II of this paper describes the ideas of cumulative and organic measures, followed by related work in Section. III. The design of this study including project selection (IV-A), data collection (IV-B), analysis procedure (IV-C) and threats to validity (IV-D) are discussed in Section IV.

II. Cumulative and Organic Measures

In this section, we explain cumulative and organic measures with a simple example, as illustrated in Fig. 1. The figure illustrates the change of the measure lines of code of a fictional example system developed over 20 days with daily commits. Considering LOC as a measure, the actual changes in values of LOC from each day compared to the day before reflects the organic measurement of LOC. However, if we calculate the total LOC written up to a day by summing up the changes of LOC from day one up to that day, we get the cumulative measurement of LOC. In this example, we have considered "daily commits" or "day" as a unit of time, but it can also be week, sprint, or release.

Correlation of various size and complexity metrics of type cumulative result in high coefficients, which is observed by many studies [9]–[13]. Correlations between organic metrics are significantly lower than their corresponding cumulative metrics. We have observed this phenomenon in earlier research [4] and in a recent study (in submission) specific to this topic, the result of which is presented in Table I. The reported correlation coefficients (τ_b) in Table I are mean values of Kendall τ_b from 11,874 software revisions of 21 open source Java projects. In Table I, if a τ_b value is greater than or equal to 0.9 (i.e., with very strong correlation coefficient), we can consider the corresponding two metrics of the τ_b as collinear, meaning they are redundant and either of them can represent the other. Because their r^2 (coefficient of determination) becomes minimum 0.81, meaning one metric can at minimum explain 81% variability in the other. Based on this, eight metrics out of 12 metrics in the cumulative category in Table I become redundant. On the other hand, from the corresponding organic metrics, we do not see a single pair of metrics for which the correlation coefficient is greater than 0.9. Thus, we can expect that combinations of organic metrics can bring added value to predict code smells. This observation is one of the key motivations for this study where we want to see how these two groups of measures, i.e., cumulative and organic, perform predicting code smells.

III. Related Work

After Fowler et al. [15] first introduced the term bad code smells, there have been many studies investigating this subject. Zhang et al. [16] report on a systematic literature review on code smells and find that most of the studies in this area are focused on the identification or detection of code smells. Automated detection of code smells has become an

TABLE I. KENDALL'S τ [14] CORRELATION COEFFICIENTS (τ_b) FOR CUMULATIVE AND ORGANIC METRICS.
The whole range of τ_b ($-0.1 \leqslant \tau_b \leqslant +1.0$) is labeled into four levels according to strength. Three gray-scale cell colors indicate three levels of τ_b (Very Strong: $0.9 \leqslant abs(\tau_b) \leqslant +1.0$, Strong: $0.7 \leqslant abs(\tau_b) < 0.9$, and Moderate: $0.4 \leqslant abs(\tau_b) < 0.7$). Weak τ_b ($0 \leqslant abs(\tau_b) < 0.9$) is indicated with red font color. A dot (.) in a cell indicates zero value. All cells in the diagonal represent correlation of a metric with itself (always having τ_b = 1) are left blank.

		Cumulative													Organic												
		ncloc	functions	statements	complexity	classes	files	public_api	pub_undoc_api	comment_ln	directories	dup_lines	dup_blocks	dup_files	_ncloc	_functions	_statements	_complexity	_classes	_files	_public_api	_pub_undoc_api	_comment_ln	_directories	_dup_lines	_dup_blocks	_dup_files
Cumulative	ncloc		.97	.98	.97	.93	.93	.94	.87	.86	.71	.63	.64	.64	.03	.	.01	.01	.	.	.01	.02	.01	.	.02	.02	.01
	functions	.97		.96	.98	.93	.92	.94	.88	.86	.71	.64	.65	.65	.03	.01	.02	.01	.01	.	.01	.02	.01	.	.02	.02	.01
	statements	.98	.96		.97	.92	.91	.94	.87	.86	.7	.63	.65	.64	.03	.	.02	.01	.	.	.01	.02	.02	.	.02	.02	.01
	complexity	.97	.98	.97		.92	.91	.93	.87	.86	.71	.63	.65	.65	.03	.	.02	.01	.	.	.01	.02	.01	.	.02	.02	.01
	classes	.93	.93	.92	.92		.98	.92	.86	.84	.73	.63	.63	.64	.03	.	.02	.01	.01	.01	.02	.02	.01	.	.02	.02	.01
	files	.93	.92	.91	.91	.98		.91	.85	.84	.73	.62	.63	.63	.03	.	.02	.02	.01	.01	.03	.03	.01	.	.02	.02	.01
	public_api	.94	.94	.94	.93	.92	.91		.91	.85	.7	.64	.64	.64	.01	.01	.01	.01	.	.	.03	.02	.02	.	.02	.01	.01
	pub_undoc_api	.87	.88	.87	.87	.86	.85	.91		.77	.66	.62	.61	.62	.01	.	.	.01	-.01	.	.02	.02	.	.01	.	.01	.
	comment_ln	.86	.86	.86	.86	.84	.84	.85	.77		.71	.55	.56	.59	.01	.	.01	.01	.	.	.02	.01	.02	.	.02	.02	.02
	directories	.71	.71	.7	.71	.73	.73	.7	.66	.71		.57	.59	.62	.01	-.01	.01	.01	-.01	.01	.	.01	.	.01	.02	.02	.02
	dup_lines	.63	.64	.63	.63	.63	.62	.64	.62	.55	.57		.86	.84	.02	.01	.02	.02	-.01	.	.01	.01	.02	.01	.03	.03	.02
	dup_blocks	.64	.65	.65	.65	.63	.63	.64	.61	.56	.59	.86		.85	.02	.01	.02	.02	.	.	.01	.01	.02	.	.03	.03	.02
	dup_files	.64	.65	.64	.65	.64	.63	.64	.62	.59	.62	.84	.85		.02	.	.02	.03	.	.01	.02	.01	.02	.01	.03	.03	.04
Organic	_ncloc	.03	.03	.03	.03	.03	.03	.01	.01	.01	.01	.02	.02	.02		.75	.89	.82	.55	.52	.68	.64	.49	.24	.25	.25	.26
	_functions	.	.01	.	.	.	.	.01	.	.	-.01	.01	.01	.	.75		.75	.81	.65	.59	.82	.76	.54	.26	.26	.28	.28
	_statements	.01	.02	.02	.02	.02	.02	.01	.	.01	.01	.02	.02	.02	.89	.75		.85	.54	.51	.69	.65	.49	.23	.26	.27	.27
	_complexity	.01	.01	.01	.01	.01	.02	.01	.01	.01	.01	.02	.02	.03	.82	.81	.85		.56	.53	.7	.66	.52	.23	.25	.26	.27
	_classes	.	.01	.	.	.01	.01	.	-.01	.	-.01	-.01	.	.	.55	.65	.54	.56		.88	.67	.64	.46	.4	.25	.27	.29
	_files	.	.	.	.	.01	.01	.	.	.	.01	.	.	.01	.52	.59	.51	.53	.88		.65	.6	.45	.44	.26	.29	.32
	_public_api	.01	.01	.01	.01	.02	.03	.03	.02	.02	.	.01	.01	.02	.68	.82	.69	.7	.67	.65		.89	.51	.31	.24	.26	.26
	_pub_undoc_api	.02	.02	.02	.02	.02	.03	.02	.02	.01	.01	.01	.01	.01	.64	.76	.65	.66	.64	.6	.89		.4	.29	.24	.27	.26
	_comment_ln	.01	.01	.02	.01	.01	.01	.02	.	.02	.	.02	.02	.02	.49	.54	.49	.52	.46	.45	.51	.4		.25	.23	.22	.23
	_directories	.	.	.	.	.	.	.	.01	.	.01	.01	.	.01	.24	.26	.23	.23	.4	.44	.31	.29	.25		.14	.15	.17
	_dup_lines	.02	.02	.02	.02	.02	.02	.02	.	.02	.02	.03	.03	.03	.25	.26	.26	.25	.25	.26	.24	.24	.23	.14		.84	.75
	_dup_blocks	.02	.02	.02	.02	.02	.02	.01	.01	.02	.02	.03	.03	.03	.25	.28	.27	.26	.27	.29	.26	.27	.22	.15	.84		.81
	_dup_files	.01	.01	.01	.01	.01	.01	.01	.	.02	.02	.02	.02	.04	.26	.28	.27	.27	.29	.32	.26	.26	.23	.17	.75	.81	

integral part of many static analysis tools, e.g., SonarQube [17], SpotBugs [18], Jtest [19], JArchitect [20], PMD [21], etc. In a proposed method to identify two code smells (lazy class and temporary field), Munro [22] used five code metrics (LOC, number of methods, weighted methods per class, coupling, and depth of inheritance tree). He used a programmatic approach, meaning studying the characteristics of the code smells he devised rules using the metrics to identify the code smells. Fontana et al. [23] performed an empirical investigation to code smells detection and how frequent certain code smells are in various application domains. They also investigated the Spearman ranks correlations between software metrics and code smells. In an extensive study, Fontana et al. [24] experimented with 16 machine learning algorithms to detect four code smells. They worked on 74 software systems with 1986 validated code smells and found Random Forest and J48 as the best performing algorithms. While some of these studies have used code metrics to detect code smells, we are using code metrics to predict code smells in the future software revisions.

Few studies have focused on the impact of code smells. Monden et al. [7] performed a quantitative study on a legacy system to assess the impact of duplicated code smells on software reliability and maintainability. Yamashita and Moonen [25] identified various factors that affect software maintainability and investigated to what extent code smells reflect those factors. Kapser and Godfrey [26] also studied duplication on software quality. Other studies [27], [28] attempted to reveal relations between code smells and software faults. Another study [29] investigated whether source code files with code smells are more prone to change and found that classes with code smells are more change-prone.

Maneerat and Muenchaisri [30] possibly made the first attempt to predict code smells. They used seven machine learning algorithms to predict seven code smells. However, they used K-folds cross-validation, which is inappropriate for time-series data. According to our experience, the high accuracy of their predictive models is due to the wrong choice of cross-validation technique. When we evaluated our models using K-folds, we get model accuracies greater than 90%. However, we have avoided it as K-folds is methodologically wrong to validate time-series data. A recent study by Gupta et al. [31] build entropy based statistical model to predict six code smells on different versions of Apache Abdera project. Among the three selected entropies, Shannon performed best with a r^2 value 0.567. This study differs from their research in different ways. First, we have taken a machine learning based approach. Seconds, we are focusing on code smells prediction in the continuous integration environment where the release cycle is very short. Their measure of code smells is cumulative whereas we focus on only new code smells that might be added to the future revisions. Moreover, we have a focus on the difference between cumulative and organic predictors, and our study is based on a large number of randomly selected projects.

IV. METHODOLOGY

This empirical study is designed as a case study. We follow the compiled guideline of software engineering case studies by Runeson and Höst [32]. Research design related terminologies used in this study is also adopted from the same guideline [32]. This case study is "explanatory" according to the classification of Robson [33] which Runeson and Höst interpreted as similar to the type "confirmatory" by Easterbrook et al. [34]. Collected data of this case study is quantitative, and the design of the study is more fixed than flexible, meaning we have a defined set of measurement categories, independent and dependent measures, machine learning algorithm, and cross-validation techniques that we are particularly interested in answering the research question. Triangulation is essential because it increases the precision of empirical research. For studies with quantitative data, triangulation is important as it can compensate for measurement or modeling errors [32]. For triangulation, we have considered data source triangulation [35], meaning, more than one data source or project is used in this case study. Runeson and Höst mentioned three major research methods that are related to case studies and experiment is one of them. Since this study is involved with quantitative data, it has some overlap with experiments, e.g., we have identified independent and dependent variables, and have carefully worked with the instrumentation. Runeson and Höst [32] have also mentioned that quasi-experiments have many characteristics that are common with case studies. Quasi-experiments and controlled experiments are similar except that in quasi-experiment subjects are not randomly assigned to treatments. However, since we have randomly selected the projects and exhaustively created all possible models, like a full factorial design, this study is more of a controlled experiment than a quasi-experiment.

A. Project Selection

Open source software projects on GitHub serve as the data source for this study. There are millions of Java projects on GitHub. GitHub provides REST API for users through which meta-data about projects can be collected. However, it is very limited considering the massive number of projects. Therefore, we have used the GHTorrent [36], a project that gathers meta-data of publicly hosted projects on GitHub. We downloaded GHTorrent's database dumps of size about 300GB and extracted on a local MySQL database because, GHTorrent's free online database queries have limitations.

We initially selected 2,188,033 candidate GitHub Java projects from GHTorrent's database. We selected them in such a way that there are no forked projects to avoid partial duplications. We also exclude projects that are marked as deleted by GHTorrent. Fig. 2 shows the distribution of the 145,980 projects from the 2.2 million candidate projects between 50-500 commits. Since the actual distribution consisting all the projects is exponential, projects with commits less than 50 are not shown for better visual presentation. About 1.3 million of the 2.2 million projects have 5 or fewer commits.

We have randomly selected 1000 projects from the 2.2 million candidate projects. Among them, we found 232 projects that have zero or one commit. In case a project has multiple commits from the same day, we consider the latest commit and ignore others, meaning one commit from a day. We have ignored any project that results in less than 10 commits. Because when computing correlations between metrics using Kendall's τ, the minimum sample size should be 10, which still has some bias and for an unbiased result the sample size should be 50 [37]. We also found some projects that were no more publicly accessible or lack the GIT master branch, which we ignored. Finally, we have 242 projects that are considered for this study.

B. Data Collection

Software revisions in the Git version control system is a form of archival data, which Lethbridge et al. [39] described as a third-degree technique for data collection. In our case, the source of data is of third-degree. However, we have used the SonarQube [17] tool to process the archival data and generate measures of our interest. For data collection, we have considered the entire commits or revision history in the master branch of a project's Git repository. However, if there are multiple commits from a single day, we analyzed the latest commit of a day using SonarQube. Therefore, for a project, we have collected data from everyday that has at least a single commit.

Table II shows metrics used for this study. Descriptions of these metrics are taken from the SonarQube's database and metric definition page [40]. Of them, cumulative metrics are measured by the SonarQube tool, and the organic metrics are calculated from the difference of two consecutive values of the cumulative metrics. In this paper, we refer to an organic version of a cumulative metric, by adding an underscore sign _ at the start of the metric name, e.g., the organic form of the cumulative metric *statements* is *_statements*.

SonarQube's Java plugin has more than 300 code smells classified into different categories. We have skipped all code smells from minor and info categories because these code smells are less severe and the probability of worst things

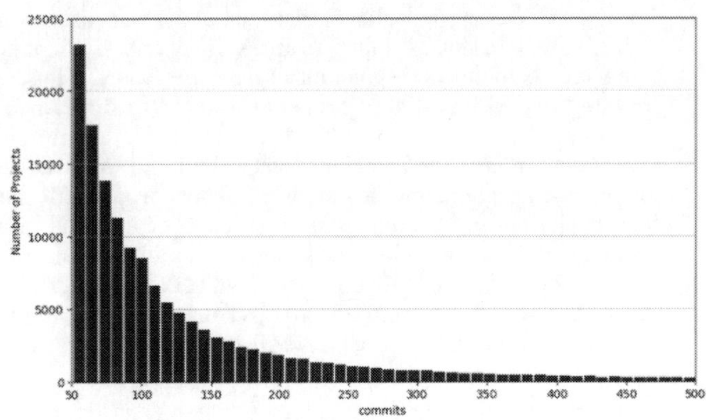

Figure 2. Histogram of candidate GitHub projects from 50 to 500 commits.

TABLE II. COLLECTED CODE METRICS. ALL THE 12 METRICS IN THE INDEPENDENT SECTION ARE CUMULATIVE. WE ALSO HAVE CORRESPONDING ORGANIC METRICS OF THESE 12 CUMULATIVE METRICS. THIS PAPER INDICATES AN ORGANIC METRIC WITH A _ SIGN AT THE BEGINNING OF THE METRIC NAME. INTEGER IS THE DATA TYPE OF ALL THESE METRICS.

Variable Type	Metric Name	Description	Short Name
Independent	ncloc	Number of physical lines of code that are not comments (line only containing space, tab, and carriage return are ignored)	ncloc
	classes	Number of classes (including nested classes, interfaces, enums, and annotations)	cls
	files	Number of files	fil
	directories	Number of directories	dir
	functions	Number of methods	func
	statements	Number of statements according to Java language specifications	stmt
	comment_lines	Number of lines containing either comment or commented-out code (Empty comment lines and comment lines containing only special characters are ignored)	com_ln
	cognitive_complexity	A complexity measure of understandability of code [38]	cgn_cmplx
	complexity	Cyclomatic complexity (else, default, and finally keywords are ignored)	cmplx
	duplicated_lines	Number of duplicated lines	dp_ln
	duplicated_blocks	Number of duplicated blocks. To count a block, at least 10 successive duplicated statements are needed. Indentation & string literals are ignored	dp_blk
	duplicated_files	Number of duplicated files	dp_fil
Dependant	_code_smells	Organic measure of identified code smells (named new_code_smells by SonarQube) (Total count of code smells identified for the first time since the last analyzed commit)	_cs

happening due to such code smells is low. We have also ignored code smells that seem to have an obvious linear relation with the single predictors, e.g., a code smell reporting cases when the complexity of a class or method reaches a certain limit, has a high linear relation with the complexity measures. We reviewed the rest of the code smells and selected 35 code smells from the "blocker" and "critical" categories, as listed in Table V in the Appendix.

SonarQube calculates the metric *new_code_smells* (which we have denoted as *_code_smells*) and saves the measure into the database but automatically deletes measures from the earlier runs, if there is any. We have instrumented the database with triggers to automatically retrieve this metric when deleted. Among all metrics, *_code_smells* is used as the dependent variable and rest of the metrics in Table II are used as independent variables or predictors.

C. Analysis Procedure

In Section II, we have discussed the idea, cumulative measures have high collinearity among themselves. Therefore, there is a reason to believe that cumulative measures are collectively weaker as input features for predictive models compared to their corresponding organic measures. Thus, we are interested in investigating whether it makes a difference to use organic measures instead of their cumulative counterparts to predict *_code_smells*. Thus, when building our models, we do not combine predictors or measures from both categories. Therefore, we can denote predictors of a model either cumulative or organic since they always come from the same category because we will not mix them. On the other hand, our target variables *_code_smells* is from the measurement category organic. Therefore, we will denote *_code_smells* as organic.

For prediction, we use random forest regression for this study. Random forest is an ensemble algorithm. It consists of multiple decision trees making a forest where the accuracy of a model is calculated by averaging the accuracies of every single tree in the forest. While a decision tree algorithm generally suffers from overfitting, a random forest prevents overfitting by design. The random forest algorithm is suitable in our case as it can better handle non-normal data compared to many machine-learning algorithms. Moreover, the random forest is known for its quick training time given its effectiveness.

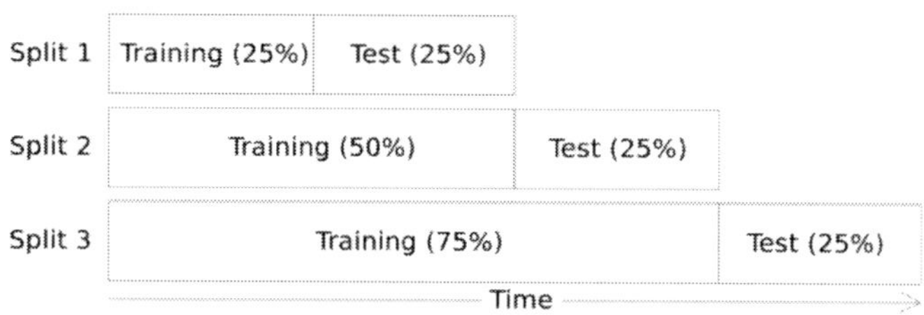

Figure 3. Split of a single dataset in different iterations in a `TimeSeriesSplit` cross-validation technique.

For validation of models, we like to use cross-validation techniques from the popular `Scikit-Learn` Python library. Since, the collected data from the revision history is time-bound, `TimeSeriesSplit` cross-validation from the `Scikit-Learn` library is appropriate in our case. We use the default number of splits (`n_splits = 3`) for our data. In `TimeSeriesSplit` cross-validation, the order of data is important, and unlike general cross-validation, randomization is avoided because, if data is randomized, the training datasets shall have a rough idea about the trend of the future already based on the random data assigned from the later parts of the projects. In our case, we are interested in predicting the future based on the available data (and there is no point in predicting the past). In `TimeSeriesSplit` cross-validation, data is split without disordering time, as shown in Fig. 3.

TABLE III. PCA COMPONENTS. HERE, WE USED SHORT NAMES FOR METRICS, AS MENTIONED IN TABLE. II.

	Cumulative Metrics											
	ncloc	func	stmt	cmplx	cgn_cmplx	cls	fil	com_ln	dir	dp_ln	dp_blk	dp_fil
PC_1	.79	.09	.32	.14	.08	.01	.01	.32	.00	.36	.01	.00
PC_2	-.38	.02	-.29	-.04	-.09	-.01	.00	.40	.00	.77	.01	.00
PC_3	-.21	-.04	.19	.02	.04	-.02	-.01	.84	.00	-.46	-.01	.00
PC_4	.41	.02	-.82	-.16	-.21	.06	.04	.18	.01	-.23	-.01	.00
PC_5	-.05	.14	-.31	.49	.79	-.01	-.02	.00	-.01	-.03	.09	.00
PC_6	.09	-.76	-.01	-.48	.43	-.03	-.03	.02	.01	.07	-.01	.01
PC_7	.00	-.30	-.04	.40	-.11	-.05	.10	-.01	.02	.01	-.85	-.02
PC_8	.02	-.52	-.05	.54	-.33	-.24	-.08	-.01	-.04	-.01	.49	.12
PC_9	-.04	-.16	.04	.13	-.03	.78	.55	.01	.14	.01	.14	.03
PC_10	.00	.08	.00	-.09	.05	-.56	.75	.00	.28	.00	.04	.16
PC_11	.00	.04	.00	-.01	.01	.10	-.30	.00	.58	.00	-.06	.74
PC_12	.00	-.04	.00	.05	-.03	-.03	-.16	.00	.75	.00	.06	-.64

	Organic Metrics											
	_ncloc	_func	_stmt	_cmplx	_cgn_cmplx	_cls	_fil	_com_ln	_dir	_dp_ln	_dp_blk	_dp_fil
PC_1	-.89	-.14	-.31	-.16	-.07	-.02	-.02	-.24	.00	-.09	.00	.00
PC_2	-.20	.08	-.01	.01	-.09	-.01	.01	.42	.01	.88	.02	.01
PC_3	-.24	.25	.04	.14	-.07	-.01	.01	.80	.00	-.47	-.01	.00
PC_4	.33	-.02	-.85	-.25	-.27	.09	.03	.15	.00	-.03	-.01	.00
PC_5	.04	-.67	-.11	-.09	.65	-.09	-.12	.29	-.05	-.01	-.02	-.02
PC_6	.04	-.40	.40	-.63	-.50	.02	-.01	.15	.03	-.06	-.01	.00
PC_7	.05	-.26	-.06	.40	-.38	-.57	-.47	-.01	-.17	-.01	.22	.00
PC_8	.01	.42	.01	-.51	.29	-.32	-.25	-.01	-.04	.00	.55	-.02
PC_9	-.02	-.25	.00	.23	-.09	.34	.33	.02	.10	-.02	.80	.03
PC_10	.02	-.03	-.03	-.02	.01	-.66	.70	.00	.26	.00	-.04	.09
PC_11	.00	.01	.02	-.04	-.01	-.04	.34	.00	-.90	.00	.01	-.27
PC_12	.00	-.01	.00	.03	-.02	-.03	-.01	.00	.28	.01	.01	-.96

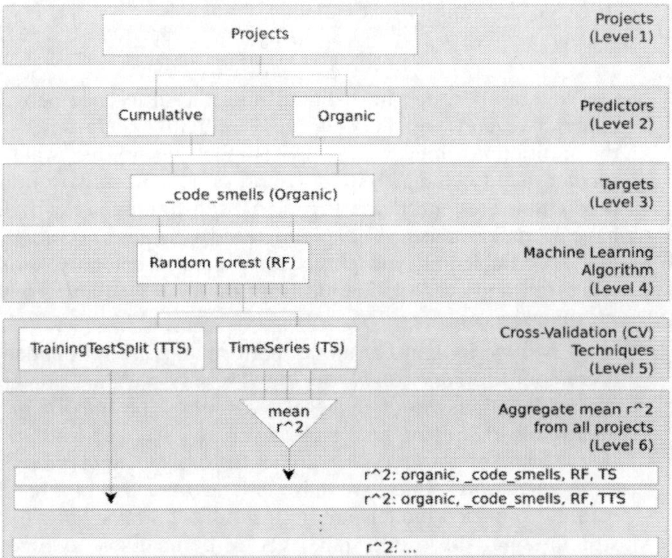

Figure 4. The overall process of model evaluation. At least one sub-level process is expanded from each horizontally highlighted level (i.e., projects, predictors, targets, etc.) Unexpanded sub-processes are indicated with open-ended vertical lines or connectors (e.g., the small vertical lines connected to `Random Forest (RF)` at `Level 4`). Any unexpanded or open-ended vertical connector contains the same expanded sub-process tree from the same level.

A simpler cross-validation technique compared to `TimeSeriesSplit` is `training_test_split`, where the dataset is split only once. For `training_test_split` cross-validation for time-series data, if we avoid randomization when splitting the training and the test sets, we get a coarse-level cross-validation compared to `TimeSeriesSplit`, which is still valid. For `training_test_split`, we will use 70% data for training set and 30% data for test set. K-folds is another popular cross-validation technique, which is similar to time-series cross-validation. However, the k-folds technique has no strict ordering of time, meaning older data corresponding to the earlier commits can be in the test sets and newer data corresponding to the recent commits can appear in the training set. Due to this, it is methodologically wrong to evaluate time-series data with k-folds cross-validation. Therefore, we have avoided it.

The overall process of model evaluation is pictured in Fig. 4. This figure shows how the selected machine learning regressor with two cross-validation methods are used to process the data from the selected projects and calculate the accuracies of regression models. Since, this study has a strong focus to understand the impact of using multiple features from different measurement categories (i.e., cumulative and organic) when predicting the target measures, we want to exhaustively check all possible combinations of the predictors while building machine learning models to predict the target measures. In `Level 2` of Fig. 4, we can select one or multiple predictors to predict the metric in `Level 3`. Then, in `Level 4`, machine learning models are built based on the selections from the prior two levels. Table IV shows all possible number of models that can be generated based on the process shown in Fig. 4, considering all possible lengths of predictors and all possible number of evaluations of such a number of total possible models.

TABLE IV. NUMBER OF MODELS AND EVALUATIONS BASED ON THE STUDY DESIGN.

'Combination length' of predictors (k)	No. of prediction models (nopm)	No. of r^2 values	No. of aggregated r^2 values
1	24	168	48
2	132	924	264
3	440	3,080	880
4	990	6,930	1,980
5	1,584	11,088	3,168
6	1,848	12,936	3,696
7	1,584	11,088	3,168
8	990	6,930	1,980
9	440	3,080	880
10	132	924	264
11	24	168	48
12	2	14	4
Total	8,190	57,330	16,380

Accuracies of the predictive models are calculated as r^2, which is also known as the coefficient of determination. It expresses the proportion of the variance in the dependent measure or target, predictable from the independent measures or predictors. The maximum value of r^2 is $+1$, which implies 100% variability of the target measure has been accounted. It can also be negative suggesting the model has even a worse fit than a horizontal line on the x-axis.

Within the context of this study, 'no. of predictor' (n) = 12, 'no. of category of predictors' (pc) = 2, 'no. of target' (t) = 1, 'no. of regressor' (r) = 1, and 'no. of cross-validation' (cv) = 2. This study has considered generating all possible models and all possible evaluations of the models, as shown in Table IV. Therefore, we build in total 8,190 predictive models and this numerical figure is calculated as $total\_nopm = \sum_{k=1}^{12}(\binom{n}{k} \times pc \times t \times r)$. Then, we evaluate these models 57,330 times and generate the same number of r^2 values by $total\_norv = \sum_{k=1}^{12}(\binom{n}{k} \times pc \times t \times r \times 4)$. In this equation, the numerical term four comes as we have one r^2 value from `training_test_split` and three r^2 values from `TimeSeriesSplit` cross-validations. Then, aggregating r^2 values for `TimeSeriesSplit`, we have the total 16,380 r^2 values calculated by $total\_noarv = \sum_{k=1}^{12}(\binom{n}{k} \times pc \times t \times r \times cv)$ that will be used for results of this study. All evaluations are based on test data sets while models are built with training data sets. The whole model training and evaluation process is automated using Python scripts and MySQL database. When reporting the results, we select the best r^2 value (which means the associated predictive model is best) for each combination length of predictors (k).

To validate our model building and prediction approach, we have performed PCA on both sets of metrics and extracted the maximum possible components, i.e., the total number of metrics in each category, which is 12. The details of the extracted components are shown in Table III. For cumulative metrics, the first two components explain about 98.3% and for cumulative metrics 97.6% variability. Therefore, it would be enough to consider these two components to build models. However, as we have exhaustively built models in the first approach, we want to develop models using PCA by using all the components. For each measurement category, we will build 12 prediction models where the first model would only use the first PCA component and the last model would use all 12 components.

D. Threats to Validity

A general weakness of case study research is generalizability due to the reason that samples are not randomly selected from the population. However, this study has randomly selected the projects from the population.

According to GitHub's statistics for 2017 [41], 6.7 million new users joined the platform, of them 48% are students, 45% are entirely new to programming, and 4.1 million people created their first repository. This means, there are a lot of classroom projects or projects that have little or no code base. Here, we have a trade-off, we want to be inclusive by equally letting all projects the same chance to appear as subjects. But we do not want to include meaningless projects. As we have disregarded all projects that result in less than 10 commits, a lot of such unwanted projects was removed.

Programming languages have different constructs. Therefore, measures of code metrics may vary due to programming languages. To minimize the effects of programming languages, we have selected projects that are mainly labeled as Java projects.

We have selected 35 code smells for this study. This could be seen as a threat as not all code smells are equally severe and we have not tracked which code smells are more present than the others. To minimize this threat, we selected code smells from the top two severity-levels ("blocker" and "critical"). We have removed code smells that are subjective to projects (e.g., code smells related to coding conventions) and that seem to have obvious correlations with the input feature metrics. Since we have collectively predicted the code smells, it would not be possible to differentiate which code smells are more predictable than others. From our results, we have an overall understanding of predictability of the selected code smells as a whole. Therefore, it was important that the severity of the selected code smells do not vary much. From another point of view, since our research question is specific to the context of prediction accuracies between organic and cumulative measures, our approach of not differentiating between the selected code smells do not pose any significant threat to the validity of this study.

V. Results and Discussions

We are interested in distinguishing the difference between cumulative and organic measures predicting code smells in the continuous integration environment where we want to predict quality change within a short period. Results from our predictions are reported in Fig. 5. All sub-figures in this figure have 12 data points each depicting the best found r^2 value for that specific length and choice of predictor category, target, regressor, and cross-validation from the total available 16,380 r^2 values.

When we look at the model performance from cumulative predictors to *_code_smells* in Fig. 5b, all r^2 values for both cross-validations result in negative values. The maximum r^2 values of -0.25 (for `training_test_split`) and -0.88 (for `TimeSeriesSplit`) come from the single predictor *duplicated_files*. Since we have all negative r^2 in Fig. 5b, results from such models are not useful in practice but we can still interpret the results relatively in comparison to Fig. 5a to understand how prediction accuracies vary when predictor types are different.

For organic metrics predicting *_code_smells*, we see positive prediction accuracies in Fig. 5a. Here, both cross-validation methods yield positive results ($r^2 \geq 0$). It is clear from this sub-figure that the model accuracy increases as the number of predictor increases. In Fig. 5a for `training_test_split`, we see that the maximum r^2 value is 0.25 for a combination of six predictors; then the model accuracy gradually decreases as the number of predictor increases. The six predictors are *_ncloc*, *_statements*, *_classes*, *_comment_lines*, *_duplicated_lines*, and *_duplicated_blocks*. For `training_test_split` cross-validation, the maximum model accuracy r^2 = 0.18 is found for four predictors, which are *_ncloc*, *_directories*, *_duplicated_lines*, and *_duplicated_blocks*.

We see that `TimeSeriesSplit` cross-validation results in lower model performance compared to `training_test_split`. This is most likely because the r^2 value of `TimeSeriesSplit` comes from three r^2 values or three models where the first model is trained with only 25% of the data to evaluate 25% of the data, which is 'Split 1' in Fig. 3. Models corresponding to 'Split 1' not only

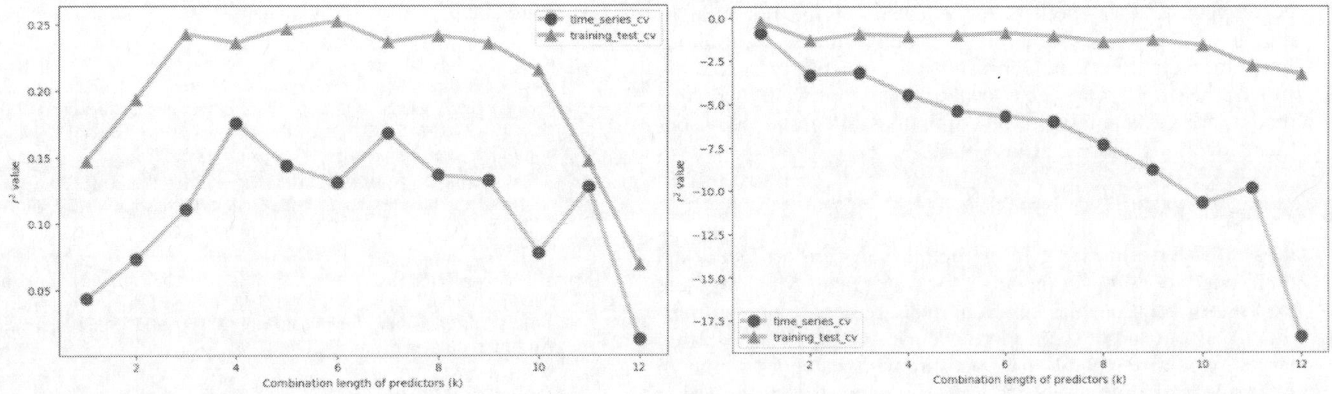

(a) Predictor: Organic metrics, Target: *_code_smells*

(b) Predictor: Cumulative metrics, Target: *_code_smells*

Figure 5. Prediction Accuracies using Random Forest Regressor.

have less portion of training data but also the split between training and test is equal. Still, the r^2 graphs corresponding to both cross-validation techniques in two sub-figures in Fig. 5 roughly follow a similar trend concerning shape or slope.

The interactions among predictors are more visible in the `TimeSeriesSplit` graphs than `training_test_split` in both sub-figures in Fig. 5. For example, in Fig. 5a, if we carefully look at the `TimeSeriesSplit` graph, we see that combination lengths 5 and 6 yield lower accuracies than combination lengths 4 and 7. Similar observations are seen for `training_test_split`, e.g., model accuracy for combination length 4 is lower than accuracies for combination lengths 3 and 5. Such observations could most likely be due to the interactions among the predictors. Interactions among predictors are interesting. However, we have not investigated them further, as it falls beyond the scope of this study.

Results from the 24 prediction models where features are extracted through PCA, are presented in Fig. 6. Since we evaluated these models only using `training_test_split` cross-validation technique, we would compare these results with `training_test_split` graphs in Fig. 5a and 5b. We see that our approach outperformed PCA in both cases. For organic metrics predicting *_code_smells*, we get the best r^2 value 0.10 when eight components are used together. However, if we had used maximum two components, we could have achieved 0.05 as the maximum accuracy which is half of 0.10. For cumulative metrics predicting *_code_smells*, all r^2 values are negative. However, the best r^2 is -1.96 compared to -0.25 in Fig. 5b. Interestingly, for PCA, we have similar observations as seen for Random Forest in Fig. 5, i.e., when we use more organic metrics to build predictive models the model accuracy increases. Six metrics for Random Forest in Fig. 5a and 8 components for PCA in Fig. 6 produce the best results.

Based on the observations, we can answer the RQ as organic metrics can better predict *_code_smells* compared to cumulative metrics. Furthermore, as more organic measures are combined to form sets of predictors, the accuracies of the models increase as seen in Fig. 5a. Compared to this, cumulative measures do not contribute to the model accuracies as observed in Fig. 5b. This could be an indication that organic

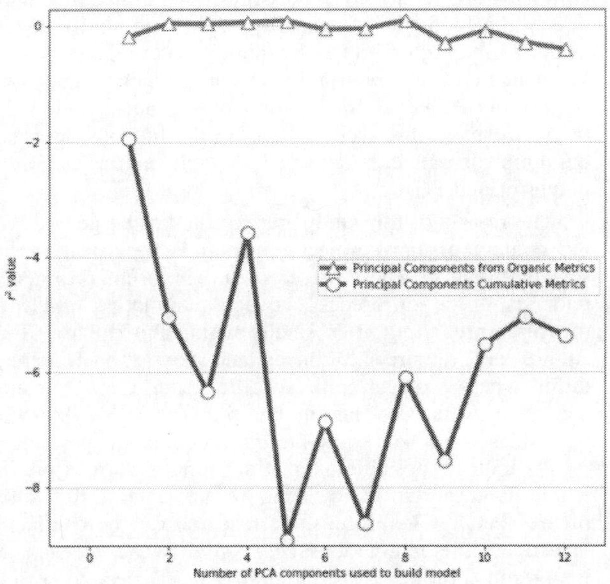

Figure 6. Prediction accuracies of Random Forest Regressors evaluated with `training_test_split` where features are extracted through PCA.

measures collectively contribute more to the predictive models than their corresponding cumulative measures. This could potentially be due to the multicollinearity of the cumulative metrics.

Among the 12 organic metrics used in this study, a combination of six metrics gives the best prediction accuracy (r^2 = 0.25) concerning `training_test_split` as seen in Fig. 5a. Concerning `TimeSeriesSplit` in the same figure, a set of four metrics gives the best prediction accuracy (r^2 = 0.18). The model accuracies are not that high and it can be noted that finding the best predictive model was not an objective of this study. Nevertheless, organic metrics better predict code smells in the continuous integration environment compared to their corresponding cumulative metrics which is the main focus of this study.

Results of this study would help the practitioners, tool developers, and researchers to be aware of the potential of organic metrics to predict code smells in the continuous integration environment. Our results are particularly interesting for the researchers to focus on building improved predictive models for code smells in the continuous integration environment involving more metrics.

VI. Conclusions and Outlook

This empirical study set out to investigate whether organic measures perform better in predicting software artifacts than their corresponding cumulative measures and whether there exists any relationship between measurement types of predictors and a target. Considering code smells as the desired target, we have found that measurement categories play a vital role regarding the accuracies of random forest regression models. Organic measures are found to be much better predicting organic code smells than their corresponding cumulative predictors. Furthermore, organic measures exhibit increased model accuracies when more than one organic measures are combined to form the set of predictors compared to their corresponding cumulative measures. We think, this happens due to the high multicollinearity of the cumulative measures or due to the high correlation among the cumulative measures. We validated our model building and prediction approach by performing PCA to extract components to build models. Using PCA, we have observed similar results but our approach to build models with cumulative and organic metrics as predictors outperformed PCA.

The results of this study are expected to be general within the context of Java projects since it is based on randomly selected projects. Therefore, this study is essential to generally understand the difference between cumulative and organic measures predicting code smells within this context. Further studies are required to understand how model accuracies differ when projects with specific criteria are considered, e.g., size (small vs. large), duration (short vs. long-lived), type (classroom vs. real), programming languages, etc. Our results indicate possible interactions among various predictors which is important knowledge to understand the software metrics better. Therefore, more research can be conducted to investigate the interactions between software metrics. More importantly, further research should be carried out primarily focusing on building improved models to predict code smells in the continuous integration environment using more metrics.

Acknowledgment

The authors would like to thank Dr. Miroslaw Ochodek, Dr. Bartosz Walter, and Dr. Cigdem Gencel for their feedback.

References

[1] J. Bosch, "Speed, Data, and Ecosystems: The Future of Software Engineering," IEEE Software, vol. 33, no. 1, Jan. 2016, pp. 82–88.

[2] L. Rising and N. S. Janoff, "The scrum software development process for small teams," IEEE Software, vol. 17, no. 4, Jul 2000, pp. 26–32.

[3] M. A. A. Mamun, C. Berger, and J. Hansson, "Effects of measurements on correlations of software code metrics," Empirical Software Engineering, 2019.

[4] ——, "Correlations of software code metrics: An empirical study," in Proceedings of the 27th International Workshop on Software Measurement and 12th International Conference on Software Process and Product Measurement, ser. IWSM Mensura '17. New York, NY, USA: ACM, 2017, pp. 255–266, [retrieved: Feb, 2019]. [Online]. Available: http://doi.acm.org/10.1145/3143434.3143445

[5] R. Taylor, "Interpretation of the correlation coefficient: a basic review," Journal of diagnostic medical sonography, vol. 6, no. 1, 1990, pp. 35–39.

[6] K. El Emam and N. F. Schneidewind, "Methodology for Validating Software Product Metrics," National Research Council of Canada, Ottawa, Ontario, Canada, Technical Report NCR/ERC-1076, 2000, [retrieved: Feb, 2019]. [Online]. Available: http://nick.adjective.com/work/ElEmam2000.pdf

[7] A. Monden, D. Nakae, T. Kamiya, S. Sato, and K. Matsumoto, "Software quality analysis by code clones in industrial legacy software," in Proceedings Eighth IEEE Symposium on Software Metrics, 2002, pp. 87–94.

[8] M. A. A. Mamun, C. Berger, and J. Hansson, "Explicating, understanding, and managing technical debt from self-driving miniature car projects," in Managing Technical Debt (MTD), 2014 Sixth International Workshop on. IEEE, 2014, pp. 11–18.

[9] S. Henry, D. Kafura, and K. Harris, "On the Relationships Among Three Software Metrics," in Proceedings of the 1981 ACM Workshop/Symposium on Measurement and Evaluation of Software Quality. New York, NY, USA: ACM, 1981, pp. 81–88. [Online]. Available: http://doi.acm.org/10.1145/800003.807911

[10] Y. Tashtoush, M. Al-Maolegi, and B. Arkok, "The Correlation among Software Complexity Metrics with Case Study," arXiv:1408.4523 [cs], Aug. 2014, arXiv: 1408.4523. [Online]. Available: http://arxiv.org/abs/1408.4523

[11] S. Saini, S. Sharma, and R. Singh, "Better utilization of correlation between metrics using Principal Component Analysis (PCA)," in 2015 Annual IEEE India Conference (INDICON), Dec. 2015, pp. 1–6.

[12] G. Jay, J. E. Hale, R. K. Smith, D. Hale, N. A. Kraft, and C. Ward, "Cyclomatic Complexity and Lines of Code: Empirical Evidence of a Stable Linear Relationship," Journal of Software Engineering and Applications, vol. 02, no. 03, Oct. 2009, p. 137.

[13] M. J. P. v. d. Meulen and M. A. Revilla, "Correlations between Internal Software Metrics and Software Dependability in a Large Population of Small C/C++ Programs," in The 18th IEEE International Symposium on Software Reliability (ISSRE '07), Nov. 2007, pp. 203–208.

[14] M. G. Kendall, "A new measure of rank correlation," Biometrika, vol. 30, no. 1/2, 1938, pp. 81–93. [Online]. Available: http://www.jstor.org/stable/2332226

[15] M. Fowler, K. Beck, J. Brant, W. Opdyke, and D. Roberts, Refactoring: improving the design of existing code. Addison-Wesley Professional, 1999.

[16] M. Zhang, T. Hall, and N. Baddoo, "Code Bad Smells: a review of current knowledge," Journal of Software Maintenance and Evolution: Research and Practice, vol. 23, no. 3, 2010, pp. 179–202. [Online]. Available: https://onlinelibrary.wiley.com/doi/abs/10.1002/smr.521

[17] "SonarQube | Continuous Inspection," [retrieved: Feb, 2019]. [Online]. Available: https://www.sonarqube.org/

[18] "SpotBugs | Find bugs in Java Programs," [retrieved: Mar, 2019]. [Online]. Available: https://spotbugs.github.io/

[19] "Jtest | Java Development Testing for the Enterprise | Parasoft," [retrieved: Mar, 2019]. [Online]. Available: https://www.parasoft.com/products/jtest

[20] "JArchitect :: Achieve Higher Java code quality," [retrieved: Mar, 2019]. [Online]. Available: https://www.jarchitect.com

[21] "PMD | Source Code Analyzer," [retrieved: Mar, 2019]. [Online]. Available: https://pmd.github.io/

[22] M. J. Munro, "Product metrics for automatic identification of "bad smell" design problems in java source-code," in 11th IEEE International Software Metrics Symposium (METRICS'05), Sept 2005, p. 15.

[23] F. A. Fontana, V. Ferme, A. Marino, B. Walter, and P. Martenka, "Investigating the Impact of Code Smells on System's Quality: An Empirical Study on Systems of Different Application Domains," in 2013 IEEE International Conference on Software Maintenance, Sep. 2013, pp. 260–269.

[24] F. Arcelli Fontana, M. V. Mntyl, M. Zanoni, and A. Marino, "Comparing and experimenting machine learning techniques for code smell detection," Empirical Software Engineering, vol. 21, no. 3, Jun. 2016, pp. 1143–1191. [Online]. Available: https://doi.org/10.1007/s10664-015-9378-4

[25] A. Yamashita and L. Moonen, "Do code smells reflect important maintainability aspects?" in 2012 28th IEEE International Conference on Software Maintenance (ICSM), Sep. 2012, pp. 306–315.

[26] C. J. Kapser and M. W. Godfrey, ""cloning considered harmful" considered harmful: patterns of cloning in software," Empirical Software Engineering, vol. 13, no. 6, Jul 2008, p. 645. [Online]. Available: https://doi.org/10.1007/s10664-008-9076-6

[27] R. Shatnawi and W. Li, "An Investigation of Bad Smells in Object-Oriented Design," in Third International Conference on Information Technology: New Generations (ITNG'06), Apr. 2006, pp. 161–165.

[28] W. Li and R. Shatnawi, "An empirical study of the bad smells and class error probability in the post-release object-oriented system evolution," Journal of Systems and Software, vol. 80, no. 7, Jul. 2007, pp. 1120–1128. [Online]. Available: http://www.sciencedirect.com/science/article/pii/ S0164121206002780

[29] F. Khomh, M. D. Penta, and Y. G. Gueheneuc, "An Exploratory Study of the Impact of Code Smells on Software Change-proneness," in 2009 16th Working Conference on Reverse Engineering, Oct. 2009, pp. 75–84.

[30] N. Maneerat and P. Muenchaisri, "Bad-smell prediction from software design model using machine learning techniques," in 2011 Eighth International Joint Conference on Computer Science and Software Engineering (JCSSE), May 2011, pp. 331–336.

[31] A. Gupta, B. Suri, V. Kumar, S. Misra, T. Blaauskas, and R. Damaeviius, "Software Code Smell Prediction Model Using Shannon, Rnyi and Tsallis Entropies," Entropy, vol. 20, no. 5, May 2018, p. 372. [Online]. Available: https://www.mdpi.com/1099-4300/20/5/372

[32] P. Runeson and M. Höst, "Guidelines for Conducting and Reporting Case Study Research in Software Engineering," Empirical Software Engineering, vol. 14, no. 2, Dec. 2008, pp. 131–164. [Online]. Available: http://link.springer.com/10.1007/s10664-008-9102-8

[33] C. Robson, "Real world research. 2nd," Edition. Blackwell Publishing, Malden, 2002.

[34] S. Easterbrook, J. Singer, M.-A. Storey, and D. Damian, Selecting Empirical Methods for Software Engineering Research. London: Springer London, 2008, pp. 285–311. [Online]. Available: https://doi.org/10.1007/978-1-84800-044-5_11

[35] R. E. Stake, The Art of Case Study Research. California, USA: SAGE Publications, Apr. 1995, google-Books-ID: ApGdBx76b9kC.

[36] G. Gousios and D. Spinellis, "GHTorrent: GitHub's data from a firehose," in MSR '12: Proceedings of the 9th Working Conference on Mining Software Repositories, M. W. Godfrey and J. Whitehead, Eds. IEEE, Jun. 2012, pp. 12–21. [Online]. Available: /pub/ghtorrent-githubs-data-from-a-firehose.pdf

[37] J. D. Long and N. Cliff, "Confidence intervals for Kendall's tau," British Journal of Mathematical and Statistical Psychology, vol. 50, no. 1, May 1997, pp. 31–41. [Online]. Available: https://onlinelibrary.wiley.com/doi/abs/10.1111/j.2044-8317.1997.tb01100.x

[38] G. A. Campbell, "Cognitive complexity: An overview and evaluation," in Proceedings of the 2018 International Conference on Technical Debt, ser. TechDebt '18. New York, NY, USA: ACM, 2018, pp. 57–58. [Online]. Available: http://doi.acm.org/10.1145/3194164.3194186

[39] T. C. Lethbridge, S. E. Sim, and J. Singer, "Studying software engineers: Data collection techniques for software field studies," Empirical Software Engineering, vol. 10, no. 3, Jul 2005, pp. 311–341. [Online]. Available: https://doi.org/10.1007/s10664-005-1290-x

[40] "SonarQube Metric Definitions," [retrieved: Feb, 2019]. [Online]. Available: https://docs.sonarqube.org/latest/user-guide/metric-definitions/

[41] "GitHub Octoverse 2017 | Highlights from the last twelve months," [retrieved: Feb, 2019]. [Online]. Available: https://web.archive.org/web/20180602170102/ https://octoverse.github.com/

APPENDIX

TABLE V. LIST OF CODE SMELLS USED IN THIS STUDY.

"main" should not "throw" anything
Class names should not shadow interfaces or superclasses
Short-circuit logic should be used in boolean contexts
Future keywords should not be used as names
String literals should not be duplicated
Modulus results should not be checked for direct equality
"readResolve" methods should be inheritable
Methods & field names should not be the same or differ only by capitalization
Switch cases should end with an unconditional "break" statement
"if ... else if" constructs should end with "else" clauses
"switch" statements should not be nested
Fields in a "Serializable" class should either be transient or serializable
The Object.finalize() method should not be overriden
Execution of the Garbage Collector should be triggered only by the JVM
Constructors should only call non-overridable methods
Methods returns should not be invariant
"switch" statements should not contain non-case labels
"clone" should not be overridden
Assertions should be complete
"for" loop increment clauses should modify the loops' counters
Method overrides should not change contracts
Exceptions should not be thrown in finally blocks
Classes should not access their own subclasses during initialization
"Object.wait()" and "Condition.await()" should be called inside a "while" loop
"Cloneables" should implement "clone"
"Object.finalize()" should remain protected (versus public) when overriding
Child class fields should not shadow parent class fields
Factory method injection should be used in "@Configuration" classes
Threads should not be started in constructors
"indexOf" checks should not be for positive numbers
Instance methods should not write to "static" fields
Tests should include assertions
Null should not be returned from a "Boolean" method
Lazy initialization of "static" fields should be "synchronized"
IllegalMonitorStateException should not be caught

Using SPICE Models for Flexible and Scalable Assessments

Tomas Schweigert
SQS Software Quality Systems AG Köln
Köln, Germany
Email: Tomas.schweigert@sqs.com

Gizem Kemaneci
Kemaneci Consultancy
Ankara, Turkey
Email: gizem@kemaneci.com

***Abstract*— System and software development and testing have become more and more complex on the one hand and cost and time sensitive on the other. The capability to execute processes in an organized manner, as well as to be flexible and customer responsive, is key to business success. One challenge for those who want to manage the capabilities of their processes is that lots of capability and maturity models are in the market. This makes it hard to understand their business value and the impacts of improvement campaigns. This paper describes an approach how to deal with this problem.**

Keywords-Measurement Framework; Automotive SPICE; TestSPICE; SPI Manifesto; ISO/IEC 33020;ISO/IEC 33003; Process Capability; Capability Model; Process Improvement; Process Integration; ISO/IEC 15504 Part 5; ISO/IEC 15504 Part 6.

I. Introduction

Software Process Improvement and Capability dEtermination (SPICE) has been an Information Technology (IT) topic for over 20 Years. With the exception of Automotive SPICE [1] in the automotive domain and ISO/IEC (International Organization for Standardization/ International Electrotechnical Commission) 15504 Part 6 in the Dutch infrastructure industry [2], it does not seem like ISO/IEC 15504 / ISO/IEC 330## (SPICE) and Capability Maturity Model Integration (CMMI) have a lot of visible impact in modern system, software and testing businesses. One observable key point is that, by focusing on formal points and capability levels, the original message got lost. Process improvement drives business success. The influence might be direct, e.g., change of effort structure by reducing budgets and capacity for error correction and expanding the budget and capability to deliver new features. Or the influence may be indirect, by reducing business risks rising from poor quality of deliverables or delay of the delivery itself.

As the benefits are so clear, why are SPICE Assessments not as common as it could be expected? The answer is that, often, process knowledge is concentrated in so called Software Process Engineering Groups (SEPG), which have an observable tendency to create an ivory tower. These ivory towers have the tendency to create complete, cumbersome process models which are frustrating practitioners and are not maintainable or adaptable at all. These models were always criticized [3].

Another challenge is the cost consuming approach of capability analysis. As there are lots of models on the market, an organization might try to extract the building blocks of the relevant models and recombine them to define the individual analysis and improvement approach [4], but this approach might create a constant research program that will never pay back on individual organization level. Or, an organization might run lots of uncoordinated assessment and improvement campaigns which might create misalignments and disorganization at working and management level.

One of the drivers behind this challenge is that lots of SPICE Models like ISO/IEC 15504 Part 6, Automotive SPICE and TestSPICE [5] are very focused on a defined topic. As a consequence, an organization might have to pay for many assessments which have overlapping topics and overlapping findings.

One of the proposed benefits of every capability measurement framework is that the capability of processes will be measured in a comparable way, allowing organizations to define targets for process capability that support business benefits.

By using the original ideas of the SPICE model, to abstract process content from capability measurement, an approach can be created that combines the business relevant processes of all models and brings them into one complete model. To safe cost and to focus on the real important points, the approach also contains scalability features.

The rest of the paper si structured as follows.

II. Setting the Context

In 2010, the SPI Manifesto [6] was launched. It shows the modern thinking of Process Improvement (PI) describing core values and principles, as indicated in Figure 1.

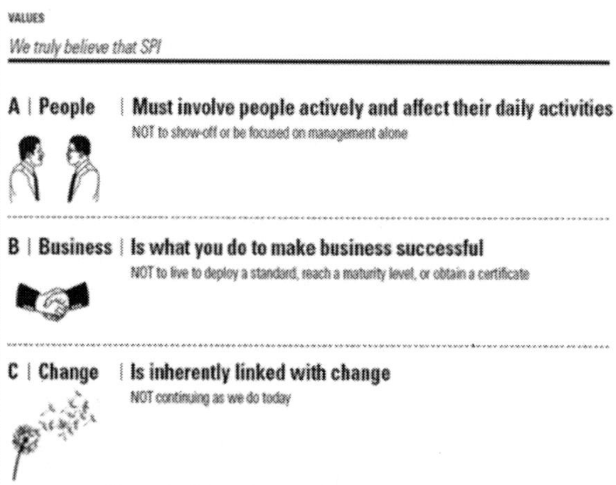

Figure 1. The values of the SPI Manifesto

These values are explained by a set of principles (see Figure 2.) that give guidance to improve the achievement of these values. Each principle is explained in detail in a later section of the SPI Manifesto.

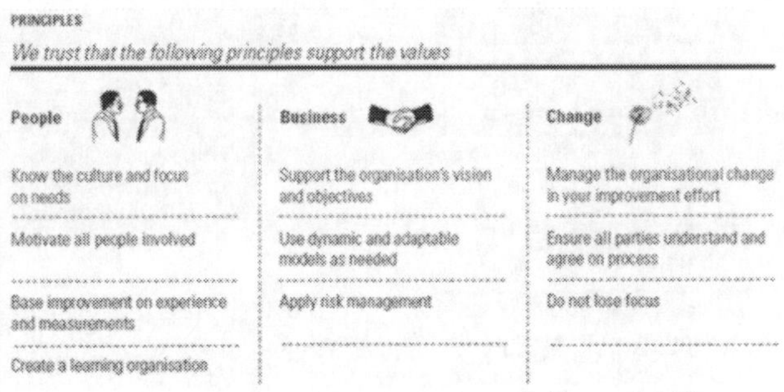

Figure 2. SPI Manifesto Principles

The presented approach is based mostly on the principle "use dynamic and adaptable models as needed". By doing this, the approach also contributes to the principle "support the organisations vision and objectives".

III. Taking the Sources of the Approach: Incorporated Models and Capability Frameworks

The presented approach incorporates the following models as a source:

1) ISO/IEC 15504 Part 5 [7]
2) ISO/IEC 15504 Part 6
3) Automotive SPICE 3.1
4) TestSPICE 4.0

It also incorporates ISO/IEC 33020 [8] as capability measurement framework

A. ISO/IEC 15504 Part 6

ISO/IEC 15504 Part 6 (Systems Engineering) was developed with a strong view on the organisations capacity to deliver large scale projects. Therefore, this model always had a strong focus on the business environment. The assessment model is based on ISO/IEC 15288 [9] as process reference model and incorporates the ISO/IEC 15504 Part 2 [10] as measurement framework. Due to the architecture of the whole SPICE approach, this can be easily replaced by ISO/IEC 33020.

The model shows the typical structure of process groups and processes. This structure makes it easier to understand the model and to set the right scope for process assessments.

The model contains the following process groups:

- Organisational Project Enabling Processes
- Agreement processes
- Project Processes
- Technical Processes
- Tailoring Processes

The whole model is presented in Figure 3.

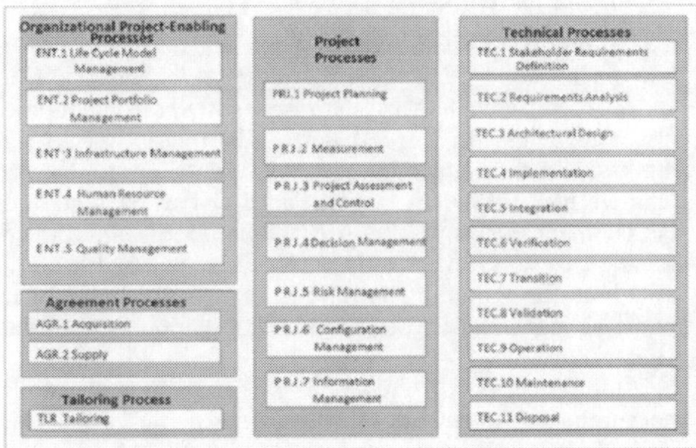

Figure 3. The process model of ISO/IEC 15504 Part 6

Reviewing modern literature about business agility, portfolio management is reported as one cornerstone of success [11].

B. ISO/IEC 15504 Part 5

ISO/IEC 15504 Part 5 (Software Engineering) was developed with a strong view on the capacity to deliver software projects of all types. Therefore, this model always had a strong focus on the software development lifecycle. The assessment model is based on ISO/IEC 12207 as process reference model and incorporates the ISO/IEC 15504 Part 2 as measurement framework. Due to the architecture of the whole SPICE approach, this can be easily replaced by ISO/IEC 33020.

The model has the highest level of completeness regarding systems and software development.

The whole model is presented in Figure 4.

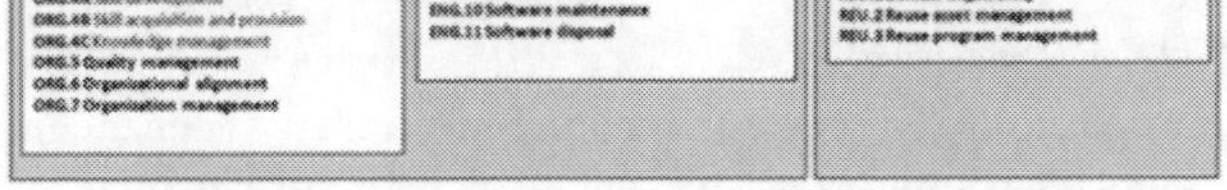

Figure 4. The process model of ISO/IEC 15504 Part 5

The model is -as ISO/IEC 15504 Part 6- Departed in Process groups and processes.

The following process groups are included:

- Agreement Processes
- Organizational Project Enabling Processes
- Project Processes
- Technical Processes

- Software Implementation Process
- Software Support Process
- Software Reuse Process.

C. *Automotive SPICE (3.1)*

Automotive SPICE (newest version 3.1) is the process assessment model of the German automotive industry. While having incorporated the system and software development processes of ISO/IEC 15504 Part 6, the model has a strong emphasis on the acquisition processes. They are much more detailed than in ISO/IEC 15504 Part 5 or Part 6. In addition, the German Verband der Automobilindustrie, Qualitäts Management Center (VDA QMC) developed a rating guideline for Automotive SPICE which highlights many interdependencies between the process components of each level.

Automotive SPICE uses the ISO/IEC 33020 as capability measurement framework. Earlier versions used ISO/IEC 15504 Part 2.

The whole model is presented in Figure 5.

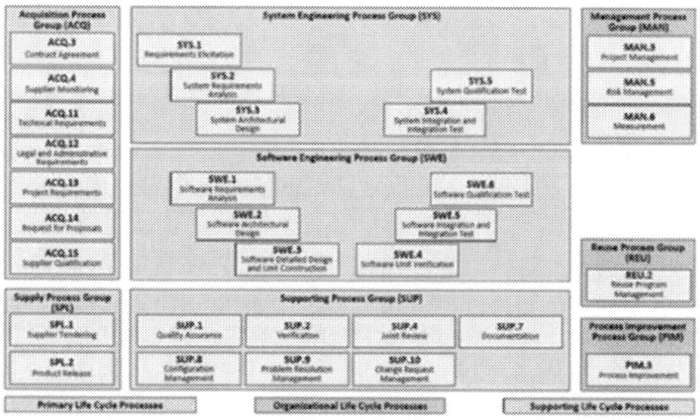

Figure 5. The process model of Automotive SPICE 3.1

The structure of the model consists of processes and process groups. The following process groups are defined:

- Acquisition Process Group
- Supply Process Group
- System Engineering Process Group
- Software Engineering Process Group
- Supporting Process Group
- Management Process Group
- Reuse Process Group
- Process Improvement Process Group.

D. *TestSPICE (4.0)*

TestSPICE (newest version 4.0) is an independently developed process assessment model for testing processes, based on the ISTQB Syllabus and the ISO/IEC 29119 process model.

TestSPICE is completely focused on the testing processes, designed to plug in to other SPICE based process assessment models.

TestSPICE incorporates the ISO/IEC 15504 Part 2 as measurement framework. Due to the architecture of the whole SPICE approach, this can be easily replaced by ISO/IEC 33020.

TestSPICE also includes an agile extension to support the assessment of agile capabilities.

The whole model is presented Figure 6.

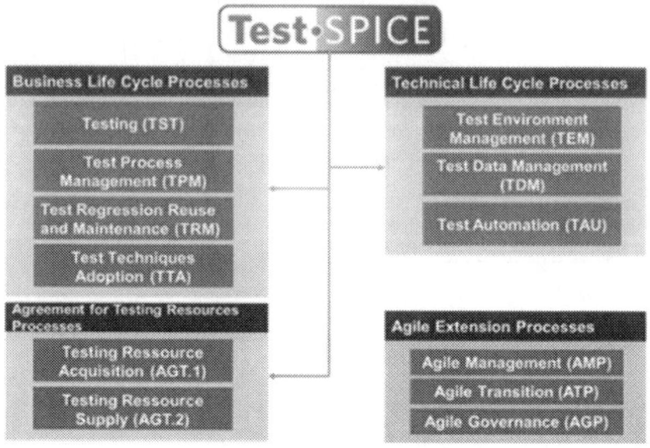

Figure 6. The process model of TestSPICE 4.0

E. *The capability measurement framework ISO/IEC 33020*

The capability measurement framework of ISO/IEC 33020 consists of 6 Levels divided in 9 process attributes.

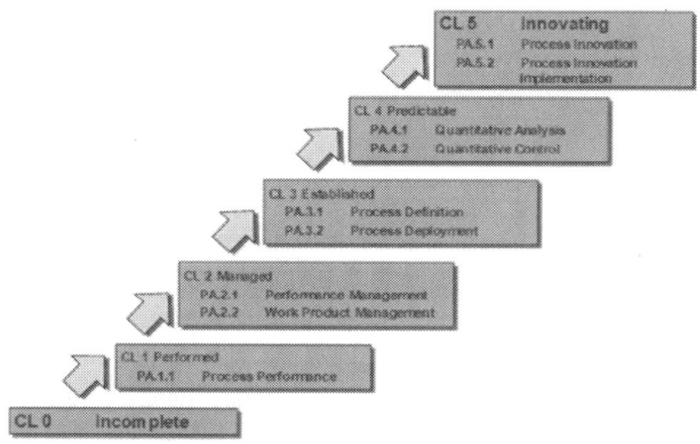

Figure 7. Capability levels and process attributes of ISO/IEC 33020

IV. Common Components of SPICE Process Assessment Models

To create a combined approach of several SPICE models, a set of common building blocks is needed that supports adaptability and scalability.

The following components are common in all SPICE models:

- 1 Process Assessment Model
  - o 1 Process Reference Model
    - □ 1-n process groups
      - 1-n processes (Specific / Overarching)

o 1 purpose
o 1-n outcomes
o 1-n process related indicators
 Base practices
 Input/Output Workproducts
o 1-n levels
 0-n Process Attributes
• 1 Indicator set
o 1-n generic practices
o 1-n generic work products
o 1-n generic resources

ISO/IEC 15504 Part 5 or TestSPICE 4.0 use overarching processes. An overarching process summarizes a complete process group by using the processes of the group as base practices (or an equivalent mapping). As an example, there is an acquisition process, and there are sub-processes that are linked to the overarching process by name (AGR.1 BP.3 "Select Supplier" to AGR.1C Supplier selection) or by content base practices of the overarching process map to base practices of the sub-processes, but sub-processes provide more details.

V. Using Common Components to Align Assessment Models with Business Needs

These common set of components allows several levels of adoption combined into one approach:

1) Combine processes of several models (e.g. acquisition processes of automotive SPICE and organisational management of ISO/IEC 15504 Part 6) to have the right set of processes at hand.

2) Define the target capabilities of the selected processes in order to achieve the necessary or expected business support (a standardized process supports fast acting teams and allows to quickly reconfigure teams, but its development might require some budget and its deployment might restrict creative ad hoc solutions).

3) Define if overarching or detailed processes will be assessed.

4) Define the in depth of process assessments. It makes a huge difference in cost and effort if an assessment team just checks if the process purpose is met and quickly gathers strengths and weaknesses, or if the team has to deliver an in-depth report reflecting purpose, outcomes and all types of indicators.

This approach supports the way of process improvement as described in ISO/IEC 15504 Part 4 or ISO/IEC 33014. Both standards recommend to 1st check influences on the business as given from the business ecosystem or from technological innovations, and next define a target profile. The profile can be expressed in capability levels, as described in ISO/IEC 33020.

Having the targets set, an assessment team will analyse to what degree the targets are met and if gaps create immediate business impact or business-related risks.

VI. Conclusion

Using SPICE Assessments in an inflexible and bureaucratic manner was on potential cause of decrease of usage of assessments. Consequently, binding SPI to business success and using a very flexible way to plan and execute assessments might be the first steps for a comeback.

References

[1] VDA QMC Working Group 13 / Automotive SIG Automotive SPICE Process Assessment / Reference Model, Version 3.1, 2017-11-01

[2] D. T. Schweigert and P. Hendriks, Using SPICE in the Real World: A Large Infrastructural Project Example, Software Quality Professional, Volume Twenty, Issue two, March 2018, p 27 ff.

[3] I. Jacobsen, P. Wei Ng and I. Spence, Enough of Processes – Let's do Practices, Journal of Object Technology, vol. 6, no. 6, July-August 2007.

[4] S. Jeners, H. Lichter: Smart Integration of Process Improvement Reference Models Based on an Automated Comparison Approach.in F. McCaffery, R. V. O'Connor, R. Messnarz (Eds.) Proceedings of the 20th Europea Conference EuroSPI 2013, Heidelberg, New York, Dordrecht, London (Springer), 2013 ISBN 978-3-642-39178-1; PP143-154

[5] K. Dussa-Zieger, M. Ekssir-Monfared, T. Schweigert, M. Philipp, and M. Blaschke: The Current Status of the TestSPICE® Project, in J. Stolfa, S. Stolfa, R. V. O'Connor, R. Messnarz (Eds.) Proceedings of the 24th Europea Conference EuroSPI 2017, Heidelberg, New York, Dordrecht, London (Springer), 2013 ISBN 978-3-319-64287-8; PP 589-598

[6] J. Pries-Heje and J. Johansen, eds. MANIFESTO Software Process Improvement eurospi.net, Alcala, Spain, 1010, http://www.iscn.com/Images/SPI_Manifesto_A.1.2.2010.pdf

[7] ISO/IEC 15504 Part 5:2012 Information technology - Process assessment - Part 5: An exemplar software life cycle process assessment model

[8] ISO/IEC 33020: 2014 - Information technology - Process assessment - Process measurement framework for assessment of process capability

[9] ISO/IEC 15288: 2008 - Systems and software engineering — System life cycle processes

[10] ISO/IEC 15504 Part 2 - Software engineering — Process assessment — Part 2: Performing an assessment

[11] K. Leopold, Agilität neu denken, Wien 1918, ISBN 978-3-903205-50-5

International Academy, Research,
and Industry Association (IARIA)
412 Derby Way
Wilmington, DE 19810

ISBN 978-1-5108-8374-1

CURRAN ASSOCIATES INC.
proceedings.com